The Fair Garden
and
the Swarm of Beasts

Margaret Alexander Edwards
October 1902–April 1988

MARGARET A. EDWARDS

The Fair Garden and the Swarm of Beasts

The Library and the Young Adult

With a Foreword by
Betty Carter
for the Young Adult
Library Services Association
with the support of the
Margaret Alexander Edwards Trust

CENTENNIAL EDITION

American Library Association

Chicago   2002

The paper used in this publication meets the minimum requirements of American National Standard for Information Sciences—Permanence of Paper for Printed Library Materials, ANSI Z39.48-1992. ∞

Frontispiece of Margaret Edwards by Bradford Bachrach. Used with permission of the Margaret Alexander Edwards Trust

Originally published by Hawthorn Books, Inc., in 1969 and reprinted in 1974. Reprint edition published by American Library Association in 1994.

Library of Congress Cataloging-in-Publication Data

Edwards, Margaret A.
    The fair garden and the swarm of beasts : the library and the young
adult / Margaret A. Edwards.— Centennial ed. / with a foreword by Betty
Carter for the Young Adult Library Services Association.
        p. cm.
    Includes bibliographical references and index.
    ISBN 0-8389-3533-8
    1. Young adults' libraries—United States—Administration.
    2. Teenagers—Books and reading—United States. I. Title
    Z718.5.E36 2002
    025.1'97626—dc21   2002033276

Printed in the United States of America

06 05 04 03 02   5 4 3 2 1

Dedicated to the past and present members of the Margaret Alexander Edwards Trust, Anna Curry, Ray Fry, Julian Lapides, Linda Lapides, and Sara Siebert, who, through both their professional service and monetary funding for this publication, have brought Margaret Edwards's philosophy to a new generation of librarians who serve young adults

Contents

Foreword

by Betty Carter

Margaret Alexander Edwards knew how to put on a show. From planned exhibitions such as orchestrated book fairs in the Baltimore Public Schools or a conspicuous horse-drawn carriage weaving through the city streets loaded with books to an ill-fated, impromptu encounter with a supervisor on the steps of a Towson, Maryland, high school, Edwards, known as "Alex" by her friends, was always a presence to be reckoned with. Her greatest role, though, played out on the stage of the Enoch Pratt Free Library, was that of young adult librarian, a woman who believed absolutely in the power of books to influence lives and the ability of adults to get those books into the hands of teenagers.

Apart from her ancestry of strong pioneer stock, there is little indication in Edwards's childhood that she would become the professional force she did. She was a protected youngster raised in Childress, Texas, at the turn of the century, with little reading matter available at home except for the Bible, "Dickens and Sir Walter Scott, *Paradise Lost* with Doré illustrations, a set of 'complete masterpieces,' and various other titles" (Edwards 1994, 3). Yet she grew to become a champion of wide reading among young adults and the librarians who served them, exhorting the latter to read about four books a week in order to better serve their teenage patrons. During her childhood Edwards found books in the town library, "an empty room in one of the business houses" (Edwards 1994, 6) stocked with donations. As a young child she devoured series books (the sole offerings for children in the small Childress library) and discovered that while reading might not be rewarding in an aesthetic sense, at least it was fun. Although Edwards always saw young adult reading as pleasurable, she never settled for accepting it as diversionary, as had been her experience.

A few incidents, however, do provide glimpses into her life's work. Edwards believed in the power of a well-trained adult to make books come alive to teenagers and in the equal power of an ill-trained adult to thwart reading interest. In her own experiences teachers embodied both of these roles. While she was in high school, one remarkable educator brought *Silas Marner* to life for Edwards while another dichotomous, but equally remarkable, teacher squelched the wonder of Shakespeare.

In some of her reading as a child, Edwards found ideas and conventions completely alien to the strict religious beliefs stressed at home. For example, Louise Mülbach's *Henry VIII and His Court* introduced her to previously unknown life styles of broken marriages and adultery. This book began a love affair with historical fiction that remained with Edwards for life, although its frank discussions of Henry's "unrestrained amours" (Edwards 1994, 8) failed to encourage her to try and duplicate the court's personal and political machinations. Looking back over her reading history, Edwards surmised that one book will not alter an individual's personal values, or, as she once put it: "One swallow doesn't make a summer and one book will neither destroy nor save a reader" (Edwards 1994, 57). In later years she discovered that contemporary psychiatrists had also reached the same conclusion, thus allowing her additional ammunition to fight efforts of adults wanting to censor young adult reading material. That this naive child grew up to become a champion of intellectual freedom and of the rights of young adults to read books that, despite their frankness or subject matter, will "widen the boundaries of adolescents' thinking, that enrich their life, and help them fulfill their recreational and emotional needs" (Edwards 1994, 138) is not so surprising when put in context with her encounters with *Henry VIII*.

One other recalled memory that mirrors Edwards's professional passions concerns her grandmother, a religious zealot who believed "In season and out of season—serving the Lord" (Edwards 1994, 4). Edwards carried that fervor with her in working with young adults; there was no season that precluded wide reading by the assistants and no season that allowed service to teenagers to lie fallow.

The Development of Library Service to Young Adults

When Margaret Edwards began work in the Pratt Library in 1932, young adult services were practically as new and unformed as she. Library services directed toward children in the nineteenth century often focused on youth between the ages of twelve and sixteen (Fenwick 1976, 348), a portion of the population today defined as young adults. By the turn of the century, however, youth services began targeting younger and younger children. Children's reading rooms flourished in public libraries. The growth of literature directed toward this new audience of young children, ranging in quality from *Elsie Dinsmore* (Farley 1897) to *Chicken World* (Smith 1910), called for reading guidance, which in turn led to the creation of various recommended reading lists, such as *Books for Boys and Girls: A Selection List Compiled by Caroline M. Hewins* (Hewins 1897), first developed by Caroline M. Hewins in 1883 (Vandergrift 1996, 691). These two activities, coupled with a dedication to storytelling (initially aimed at older children), became the foundation for early library services to children. And while children's rooms, with their small chairs and scaled-down tables, invited a wider and wider audience into the library, they nonetheless crowded out teenagers, too large for the furniture and too mature for the collections.

As the public library grew from a collection of books for a few to a perceived social institution for the many, its services also needed to expand to include all segments of the population. As Fenwick (1976) notes, "The continuing concept of the public library as the pinnacle of the educational pyramid of ongoing education was breaking down because of the failure of the library to provide the bridge between the children's room and the wide and open ranges of the adult department" (Fenwick 1976, 348). Clearly, young adults needed a room of their own that housed a collection of books and, at best, a trained and at least sympathetic person to administer it.

In her retrospective reading autobiography, one woman succinctly describes the situation: "My problem in adolescent reading was finding something to read. After I had read all the young girl teen stories, I wanted something of the same type on a more adult level. However, I didn't know any titles and didn't know where to go. When I was younger, the children's librarian had been very helpful, but when I graduated to the adult department, the librarians seemed too formidable or else too busy to ask for help" (Carlsen and Sherrill 1988, 116).

By the 1920s these needs became realities as young adult reading rooms were being established across the United States, with the Stevenson Room located in the Cleveland Public Library being the most celebrated example. Primarily designed to keep teenagers out of the adult part of the library, the Stevenson Room nonetheless represented a real breakthrough in young adult services. Under the direction of Jane Roos, the Stevenson Room provided "special service for the fourteen- to twenty-one-year-old by having a trained staff and a collection of adult books selected with the interests of young readers in mind" (Atkinson 1986, 35).

About this time, young adults readers' advisory borrowed a page from children's services, and in 1929, under the direction of Mabel Williams, the New York Public Library published the prototype of *Books for the Teen Age*, an annual book list intended primarily for recreational reading. Books appearing on this list represented volumes read and enjoyed by teenagers, a stark contrast to required school reading, which at that time consisted most often of classics or selections from required textbooks. More than anecdotal evidence exists as to the unsuitability of these selections; a 1928 educational study reveals that only "one fourth of the students understood the average classic that was required reading in high school" (Monseau 1991, 76).

A year after the birth of *Books for the Teen Age*, a committee within the American Library Association (under the auspices of the School Libraries Section) compiled its own list of recommended reading, "Books for Young People, 1930." How the list was compiled remains a mystery, but its purpose and field of selection are clear: the committee focused on recreational reading and considered both juvenile and adult titles (Madden 1967, 3). The thirty recommended books vary from Will James's autobiographical classic *Lone Cowboy* to Edna Ferber's popular adult release *Cimarron*. Like *Books for the Teen Age*, "Books for Young People, 1930" remains alive today although the contemporary name for this list is "Best Books for Young Adults."

Edwards's Vision of Library Service to Young Adults

According to Fannette Thomas, youth services librarianship is defined by meeting these five conditions: "(1) specialized collections, (2) specialized space, (3) specialized personnel, and (4) specialized programs/services designed for youth, (5) all existing within a network of other youth services organizations and agencies" (cited in Jenkins

2000, 104). When Margaret Edwards completed her library training and begin working with young adults at Enoch Pratt, at best she enjoyed three out of five. The "specialized space" for young adults was in reality a small corner located behind the popular reading section for adults. The "specialized collection" entailed a few books haphazardly chosen for young adult recreational reading. The "specialized personnel" consisted solely of Margaret Edwards, working in the small corner only three hours a day.

Edwards's first victories in developing young adult librarianship came from that triumvirate of personal skills most often cited as prerequisites for success in working with adolescents: respect for the individual, a sense of humor, and an open and friendly attitude. While young adults responded to her personality, and she was able to serve as an "amateur readers' advisor" (Edwards 1994, 11), Edwards realized that her suggestions were running thin and that many of her teenager readers knew books better than she. Her solution? "I read with desperate determination. I took armloads of books home, piling them on one side of my chair to read and then stacking them, as finished, on the other. I read in streetcars, on buses, in my dentist's waiting room, and on lunch hours" (Edwards 1994, 11).

This total immersion in reading for adolescents was not unique to Edwards, although I suspect she didn't know it at the time. With progressive education's emphasis on the individual (in much the same way Edwards centered her library service on the individual), a few teachers abdicated their role as suppliers of the classics and instead embraced the concept of paying attention to adolescent psychology and the personal needs of teenagers when suggesting reading material to them. By 1930 Dora V. Smith, teaching at the University of Minnesota, had organized the first formal class in adolescent literature. Her method of teaching others was remarkably similar to Edwards's autodidactism. "Stanley Kegler, a former student of Smith's, described how she would come into the Saturday morning class with her assistant behind her, each lugging a huge cart full of books to be used in her lectures and as part of her hands-on instruction. 'There would be a hundred people in this room. [They] would be clamoring for books. Then at the end of the hour people were expected to take some of the books home, read them, and bring them back the following week. And they did. They were all willing. She left with an empty cart, usually'" (cited in Monseau 1991, 78).

During her tenure at Enoch Pratt, Margaret Edwards never saw her area next to the popular reading section grow into a full-fledged young adult room such as the one in Cleveland, which not only physically isolated teenagers, but was also an architectural necessity. "The Cleveland Library building is all broken up into separate rooms anyway on account of big Brett Hall right in the middle of everything, like a sore thumb that everybody has to run around" (Braverman 1979, 179–180). Dr. Joseph Wheeler, director of the Enoch Pratt Free Library, believed (and Margaret Edwards concurred) that the young adult area at Enoch Pratt was a far preferable configuration to those that separated young adults from other patrons. Edwards also "considered young adults to be adults and she wished to be associated with the adult collection rather than be segregated in a separate room or associated with the children's collection" (Lapides 2002b, 1). This plan for young adult space became a model for small- and medium-sized public libraries unable, or unwilling, to build a separate young adult area (Hannigan 1996, 863).

Other changes came steadily, each leading to Thomas's definition of full-fledged youth services librarianship. Margaret Edwards refined the young adult collection at the central library. Although this collection may seem small, particularly when compared to senior high school libraries of today, in reality it was most probably the size of many contemporary young adult collections in public libraries that are still frequently limited and precisely defined. Edwards's own wide reading and the responses of teenagers to her recommendations provided the major shape of the collection. Sources such as *Books for the Teen Age* and ALA's annual "Books for Young People" were available. In 1929 H. W. Wilson published its *Standard Catalog for High School Libraries*, known after 1967 as *Senior High School Library Catalog*. But other familiar selection aids of today were nonexistent. *The Horn Book Magazine* had begun its tenure, although book recommendations at that time appear to address children and young adolescents rather than the high school crowd Edwards courted. There was no *School Library Journal*, not even its predecessor *Junior Libraries*, and no *Voice of Youth Advocates (VOYA)*. *Booklist* gave a nod to young adult reading by publishing the annual ALA lists and annotated recommended books for children, a few of which appealed to younger adolescents, but the "Books for Young People" section (a precursor to the young adult reviews) was several years away from making an appearance, and there were no repeat notes or recommendations of adult books that would appeal to young adults. Still, do it she did, and after a couple of years she had enough confidence in the validity of these choices (as well as a strong clientele who voted on the books and whose endorsements she followed) to expand the collections to the branches. And then Margaret Edwards hit a snag.

Library staff at the branches did not automatically adopt Edwards's philosophy about developing individual young adult readers to their fullest potential. Although enthusiastic and full of energy, Edwards simply could not continue her responsibilities at the main library and service the branches as well. Gradually she hired assistants and converted support staff at the branches, demanding that each undergo a rigorous training program in order to offer reading guidance to the growing numbers of teenage patrons. In just thirteen years from the date of her initial hiring at Enoch Pratt, Edwards had placed a staff member responsible for working with young adults in each of the branches (Lapides 2002a, 48).

At the same time Edwards began moving toward achieving the fourth ("specialized programs/services designed for youth") and fifth ("all existing within a network of other youth services organizations and agencies") criteria Thomas cites as fundamental for establishing library service to youth (Jenkins 2000, 104). Some programming (such as booktalking in the schools) and a horse-drawn bookmobile encouraged reading, while other activities did not. Edwards encouraged the former and abandoned the latter. She exhorted teenage patrons to write book reviews and began publishing them in 1948 in a pamphlet entitled *You're the Critic,* concluding that "a book-reviewing publication is good promotion for reading, since the recommendations teenagers make to each other are often more effective than those the librarian makes" (Edwards 1994, 38). She sponsored book discussion groups for a while but found the demands overwhelming and the rewards meager. Edwards abandoned such programming and discouraged it among the assistants.

Another seemingly good programming idea that never took off was that of a Book Week party to be held at Enoch Pratt in celebration of Children's Book Week. Although these parties were innovative because both black and white teenagers were invited in the then racially segregated Baltimore, and even though they featured prominent young adult authors (Maureen Daly and John Tunis), the ever-present goal of encouraging reading did not appear to be enhanced by such social affairs. Two years after their inception Edwards discontinued them. But other programming services grew. For example, Edwards produced scores of recommended book lists just to acquaint young adults with the Pratt offerings and to entice them to visit. Such book lists continued throughout her career.

In meeting the fifth condition for young adult services, Edwards went to school. Or, to be more exact, she went to *the* schools. After all, she reasoned, libraries don't exist just to provide books to young adults that answer specific questions or solve immediate problems. Edwards saw these kinds of collections as the province of the school library. She envisioned the public library not only as a social institution, but also as a civilizing one. Librarians, according to Edwards, had a mission of introducing adolescents to books that could change their lives. She writes, young adults "walk our streets by the thousands, unchallenged by the culture in books. When half the country's high school graduates do not read a single book a year, the library is not fulfilling its mission" (Edwards 1997, 53).

The best way she saw to fulfill that charge was to bring more young adult patrons into the Enoch Pratt library environment. And the best way to contact great numbers of young adults was to go to the place where they were: the schools. At first these forays into Baltimore's high schools were sporadic and dependent upon individual contacts, for the superintendent frowned on anyone coming into the buildings and hawking wares, even books, like a "broom salesman" (Edwards 1994, 31). By 1945, however, she and Joseph Wheeler convinced the superintendent to relax his policy and allow Edwards and her staff wide access to Baltimore's students. Edwards turned that access into untold opportunities to visit classrooms, deliver booktalks, and generally interest young people in books and reading. Several years later (1951) Edwards expanded her presence by directing book fairs for every senior in the Baltimore Public Schools. She worked with other youth-serving agencies, such as the Boy and Girl Scouts and the United Nations, but never saw those partnerships encourage reading to the extent that school visits did.

Margaret Edwards not only established youth services librarianship at Enoch Pratt, but she also gave that service unity. She believed unequivocally that young adult librarians "should attempt through books to take each individual, whatever his reading level, and develop him to his full potential as a reader, widening his interests and deepening his understanding until he came to know that he was a member of one race—the human race—and a citizen of one planet—the earth" (Edwards 1994, 68). She created spaces for young adults so they would have a recognizable place to come to and make contact with a trained librarian able to offer readers' advisory services. She created collections for young adults (although never limited them to those particular books) as a kind of ready reference for the kinds of materials they most often requested. She trained young adult assistants so they could offer the kind of reading guidance that encouraged teenagers to move beyond simple diversionary reading and into increasingly complex themes and issues. She developed programming, and continued only those activities that encouraged young people to come to the library and to read widely. And she worked within the framework of other youth-serving agencies, giving particular attention to those organizations that best encouraged teenagers to read.

These were the contributions cited when she received the American

Library Association's Grolier Award in 1957: "the enrichment she has given to the lives of young people [and] her contagious enthusiasm for books and reading, which has been felt not only by the young people in Baltimore, but indirectly by young people all across this country; her success in the skillful training of young adult librarians; her fine cooperation with library groups, especially the school librarians of Maryland" (cited in Hannigan 1996, 854).

Edwards Shares the Vision

It's easy to say that Margaret Edwards's success came because she was at the right place at the right time. Certainly she and her supervisor, Joseph Wheeler, were of like minds, which afforded her administrative support often lacking in library services for children and young adults. First of all, Wheeler took a chance on Edwards; he hired her, an untrained but enthusiastic young woman recently fired from her job teaching school in Towson, Maryland. He showed his confidence by staying out of her way, letting Edwards establish the young adult collection and programming even when he doubted that a particular activity would work. Like Edwards, Wheeler loved books, and there is probably no greater tie between people than a shared love of literature. Edwards remembers: "I never saw him leave the library for the day without books under his arm. Books excited him and he was daily in the order department laying his hands reverently on the new books, for any one of them, he often said, might change the plans and lives of whoever read it" (Edwards 1994, 94). He aggressively promoted books and reading through storefront displays and developed lists of books that were stuffed in with freshly laundered shirts, the milk delivery, and gardening supplies. In addition, Wheeler believed in "cradle-to-grave service" (Edwards 1994, 93) that brought the library's resources to every single person living in Baltimore.

Part of that population was the growing number of young adults given the luxury of adolescence as America moved from an agrarian to an industrialized society. Prior to the turn of the century, many youngsters went directly from childhood to adulthood, taking on the responsibilities of earning a living and raising a family during their teen years. Only when society demanded extended education or training for specialized jobs did circumstances allow teenagers time for this transition, thus signaling the birth of adolescence. As part of their development, teenagers had always experienced those physical changes often equated with adolescence, but as Ken Donelson and Alleen Nilsen remind us, "Puberty is a universal experience, but adolescence is not" (Donelson and Nilsen 1980, 2). Wheeler wanted to bring books, and the great ideas within their pages, to these teenagers; this was work Margaret Edwards wanted to do. It was a match made in heaven. Despite her deep appreciation and recognition of Wheeler's aid and approval, this support alone does not explain why Edwards's work is so widely known today.

Another viewpoint that attempts to justify the longevity of Edwards's ideas is that her thoughts about the power of reading and literature were ideas that apparently had come of age. Hearne and Jenkins (1999) conclude that works such as *The Fair Garden* were really the previously unexpressed "collective wisdom of the profession as a whole" (549). Margaret Edwards's philosophical underpinnings were not unique to her, although they were to young adult librarianship. Anne Carroll Moore's mantra, "the right book in the hands of the right child at the right time" (Hearn and Jenkins 1999, 551), repeated over and over both nationally and within the halls of the New York Public Library, where she served as head of Children's Services, clearly paralleled Edwards's conviction that readers' advisors dealt with individuals, learned their tastes and abilities, and used that knowledge as a base for beginning book suggestions.

Although Edwards expressed disdain for librarians overemphasizing one Dewey (Melvil), she nonetheless held strong philosophical ties with the intellectual descendants of another Dewey (John). G. Robert Carlsen, first as a high school English teacher, then as a student of Dora V. Smith, and later as professor of English (most notably teaching adolescent literature at the University of Iowa for over thirty years) and author of the influential *Books and the Teenage Reader* (Carlsen 1967), was sharing his views on the power of literature in the lives of young adults: "The things that stick in our minds, the things America means, are best seen through the concrete and dramatized experiences of men and women presented for us in literature—experiences selected for us by the writer and clothed in words of beauty, for literature has the power to carry a shining thing in the mind because it articulates the timeless quality in the living, the thinking, and feelings of people" (Carlsen 1994b, 111). Edwards was certainly at home with such ideas, just as she was with Carlsen's articulation of the concept that readers grew through certain stages moving from skill mastery in early childhood toward the ability in the high school years to grapple with themes concerning the wider world (Carlsen 1994a).

Concurrently, the belief in the education world of reading ladders, that adults gradually moved young readers to increasingly more complex books with each suggestion (which is best explained in Virginia Reid's *Reading Ladders for Human Relations*), goes hand in hand with

Edwards's convictions. Edwards knew her patrons had to be readers, so she was willing to put up with books offering even the most limited contents if they led to pleasure. She never saw getting teenagers hooked on reading, just for the sake of reading, as an end unto itself but rather the signal for the beginning of a process in which a skilled librarian would "know his readers and books well enough to be able to introduce readable, appealing adult titles at the propitious time and see that the young reader gradually moves into adult reading with all the enthusiasm he once had for teenage stories" (Edwards 1994, 63).

Edwards also defined sophisticated books as those works that contain multifaceted themes, complex characterizations, and introductions into the adult world into which the teenager would eventually move. Literary merit, while certainly a by-product of such works, did not represent the sole criterion on which she hung her recommendations. Similar ideas were also circulating within the ranks of English educators. Dora V. Smith, for example, mirrored Edwards's beliefs: "Books are not written to illustrate literary techniques, but to bring intimate revelation of human experience" (cited in Monseau 1991, 77).

Edwards understood that reading is a social activity, another notion that was gaining ground in the education world but one that yet hadn't been articulated (although there was some evidence of practice by the development of book clubs) in the library. As early as 1917, W. S. Hinchman expressed the idea that literature classes should be organized as "reading clubs," suggesting that members not only have a say-so in what they read, but also the opportunity to discuss that reading (cited in Beers 1990, 155). G. Robert Carlsen consistently held that teenagers were most willing to engage in that solitary act of reading if adults would allow them some kind of social payoff, typically repeated opportunities to talk about their reading in much the same way adults will gather around the water cooler at the office and share the particulars of the latest blockbuster movie or the events of their favorite television programs. Frank Smith, who popularized the concept of a community of readers, posits that real readers seek others with whom they can share their literary enthusiasms (Smith 1988). Edwards centered these ideas in the library, believing that "Young people often feel the need to talk about the books they have read. They will express themselves freely only to those librarians they trust to help them pursue an awakened interest" (Edwards 1994, 70). But to credit Edwards's influence by attributing it to her ability to voice ideas whose time had come is not only shortsighted, but also simplistic.

Occasionally individuals credit the staying power of Edwards's ideas to strong assistants, individuals she handpicked and trained to work with young adults. It's certainly true that many of these individuals continue, and continued, to espouse some of her fundamental principles during their careers. Frank Lee characterizes Lillian Bradshaw, a former Edwards assistant who left Enoch Pratt and eventually became the director of the Dallas Public Library and a president of the American Library Association, with the following words: "Bradshaw's activities have always [reflected] her key ideas, values, and beliefs . . . virtually every speech, publication or conversation begins and ends with the constituency of the public library . . . her focus on the individual has remained constant throughout her career, at the heart of her philosophy of service" (cited in Sheldon 1991, 30). And then there was Sara Siebert. As Linda Lapides, another outstanding Edwards assistant writes, "Sara Siebert was not only Margaret Edwards's patron at Enoch Pratt but her successor in the role of Coordinator [of young adult services, or Y services in Pratt nomenclature]. Dynamic and energetic, she possessed great leadership skills, clarity of vision, sense of humor and, like her mentor, the ability to challenge and inspire. Like Edwards, she, too, became president of the Young Adult Services Division and a winner of the Grolier Award. Siebert, in turn, inculcated a new generation of young adult librarians in the precepts promulgated by Edwards" (Lapides 2002b, 2).

These professional grandchildren live today as strong voices in present young adult services. Mary Kay Chelton, a Siebert assistant, cofounder of *VOYA*, and present library educator, stands out today as one of the strongest advocates for young adults, not only through insisting on direct service, but also by drawing attention to the ways in which the larger library world responds, and doesn't respond, to them. And Deborah Taylor, who also worked with Siebert but has remained at Enoch Pratt, capped her presidency of the Young Adult Library Services Association with a program centering on young adult recreational reading and went on to chair the Adult Books for Young Adults Task Force, organized to identify and publicize adult books for young adults from 1998 to 2002. (*See* appendix D.) While all of these individuals certainly embody some of Edwards's beliefs, to claim that they simply parroted them negates their real influences and their own philosophies. These assistants, and others such as Ray Fry or Linda Lapides, took their Enoch Pratt experiences into other times and frequently to other venues. Rather than consider these former assistants, and their assistants, as generations of Edwards clones, it seems far more realistic to recognize that a strong personality (Edwards) attracted equally strong personalities (the assistants) and that the latter simply ran with ideas encountered early in their education and training.

Yes, Margaret Alexander Edwards had strong administrative support. She developed a philosophy of service that blended well with others of the day. And she tapped and trained an incredibly strong cadre of assistants. While these forces certainly attributed to the acceptance and longevity of her ideas, they do not account for them.

Edwards as a Leader

Reading *The Fair Garden*, I am struck with several observations. Margaret Edwards clearly knew what she was about, knew how to translate her ideas into action, and knew when to abandon those ideas that didn't serve her overall goals. She knew how to communicate those ideas to others and how to garner trust through consistency in thought, word, and deed. These are leadership qualities she held in abundance and are ultimately the dynamics that led to her becoming such a force in young adult library services.

In 1991 Brooke Sheldon interviewed sixty library leaders and concluded that each possessed exactly the same qualities previously identified in leaders of the corporate world. Each had a vision and attended to it, was able to communicate that vision and expand it by listening to others, developed trust through consistency, and held a positive self-regard (Sheldon 1991). In interviewing these leaders Sheldon asked four basic questions: "What are your strengths and weaknesses? Was there any particular experience or event in your life that influenced your management philosophy and style? What were the major decision points in your career, and how do you feel about your choices now?"(Sheldon 1991, 3). Within the pages of *The Fair Garden* Edwards directly and indirectly answers each question. In turn, she reveals herself as a leader in each of these areas.

Toward the end of her career, Edwards quotes Kenneth Harrison on the subject of vision: "It certainly is a commodity in short supply at the moment" (Edwards 1994, 105). Perhaps, but that commodity never went out of stock during her tenure at Enoch Pratt. Edwards believed in libraries as social institutions charged with the responsibility of continuing education that would lead to the development of knowledgeable citizens, first of Baltimore, second of the United States, and third of the world. She believed books held the key for understanding the great issues that plague humankind. "There are on our shelves thousands of books that fight against prejudice, overpopulation, inhuman prisons, injustice, mistreatment of children, and all the other evils of our society. If we librarians feel social responsibility, books are our weapons. Our social obligation is to read these books and see that society reads them" (Edwards 1994, 104). In relation to young adults, she clearly believed that librarians were obligated to encourage reading because only through that reading would young adults grow up well equipped to face adult life. No ifs, ands, and buts; no alternative approaches; no hedging her bets. Every program, every booktalk, every reading list, every speech, and every article, in short, the sum of Edwards's career, were devoted to getting good books into the hands of teenagers. In 1919 William Warner Bishop offered this advice to librarians: "You will not succeed unless you do some one thing supremely well" (Bishop 1992, S4). Edwards did one thing extremely well: she held a consistent vision for service to young adults that guided her every activity and consequently her success and influence.

Edwards had a firm grasp on the big picture of library services to young adults and knew exactly how to compose the landscape. Some might say she painted by the numbers by requiring, for example, assistants to present booktalks in a structured, prescribed manner. But, for Edwards, these programs brought the desired results. "Time and again teachers and school librarians have spoken of the wave of reading that followed these visits, and certainly the public library has felt its impact" (Edwards 1994, 34). Edwards measured the effectiveness of her services by the amount of reading each generated. When programs, such as the Book Week parties, didn't bring in enough young adults requesting books to justify their continuation, Edwards abandoned them. In today's parlance, Edwards might well be characterized as a woman with an agenda and her eye always on the bottom line. However, as Sheldon (1991) notes, today's library leaders have a clear vision and are results oriented (11). And that was Margaret Edwards.

According to Sheldon, visionary librarians "have a deep and intense belief that what they are doing is not only satisfying, but deeply significant" (Sheldon 1991, 11). A recent interview with Lillian Bradshaw underscores how significant Edwards considered young adult librarianship.

"I was working in reference," she said, "and there was an opening in the young adult department. I really wanted to work with Margaret Edwards, so I asked around to see if I could apply. I found out I could, but I also discovered that she didn't think I was the best qualified—that I couldn't deliver booktalks with flair or maybe know all the books I should have. So I read, and I told myself, 'Honey, you weren't a drama major for nothing. You can make this work.'"

"And, so I did," she continued. "I went to see Margaret Edwards so I could 'audition for the part'" (Bradshaw 2002).

This phrase, "audition for the part," clearly shows how those working with young adults had to prove their mettle to Margaret Edwards. She underscores the value of such work by writing, "We must feel that the job is bigger than we are, that it calls for all the energy, time, thought, and devotion we have, and that is worth all we give it. . . . When one's work is bigger than he is, he constantly grows by trying to measure up to his vision" (Edwards 1994, 25). Sheldon (1991) concludes: "It seems that the leaders' tremendous confidence in the value of what they do is a powerful force in enabling them to achieve their goals" (13). That force was with Edwards at Enoch Pratt.

Sheldon suggests that the second aptitude library leaders possess is the ability to communicate with others. Edwards's written legacy in *The Fair Garden* attests to her powers of communication. Sometimes she writes succinctly: "In my preliminary thinking I realized that work with young adults is as simple as ABC. All there is to it is: (A) a sympathetic understanding of all adolescents; (B) firsthand knowledge of all the books that would interest them; and (C) mastery of the technique of getting these books into the hands of the adolescents. Simple" (Edwards 1994, 12). Sometimes she writes metaphorically: "Books are literary atom bombs capable of destroying stupidity, cant, insularity, and prejudice—if they are read" (Edwards 1994, 58). And sometimes she writes eloquently: "What can books do for these young people? Their most important contribution is to supplement experience, to intensify their lives. However long these young people may live, most of them will know few months or years that are filled with meaning. They will experience few passionate love affairs, few victories, few overwhelming griefs, few moments of insight and inspiration. Without books, they can live and die naively innocent of so much experience. But the young person who reads can live a thousand years and a thousand lives" (Edwards 1994, 57). While such communication skills are important, they cannot substitute for daily communication in which leaders clearly convey their vision so that all staff members will not only understand it but also believe in it.

Edwards's assistants shared her vision. They understood that the librarian who read books was the key to influencing young adults to do the same. They knew upon hiring that they had special qualities; after all, they had "auditioned for the part." And they knew that this work required rigorous training, like reading 300 books for starters. That Margaret Edwards required these librarians to read and read and read some more is legend. So are the stories about her talking with them about those books, to be sure they'd read them and they could in turn converse with teenagers about them. I asked Lillian Bradshaw about that portion of the training. "What did you do? Did you just have great book discussions in her office?" I wondered.

"Oh no, my dear," Lillian replied. "She grabbed us on the floor, right behind the current collection where the young adult section was, and she point-blank asked us about the books: the characters, the plots, the themes. Right there with everyone looking. And we had to know it." But, Bradshaw added, "We wanted to know it" (Bradshaw 2002). Anna Curry, "who went on to become Director of the Enoch Pratt Free Library and a trustee for the Margaret A. Edwards trust" (Lapides 2002b, 2), further comments on Edwards's power to inspire librarians. "My relationship with Mrs. Edwards was a very special kind . . . that transcended superior and fledging. It was a one-to-one relationship probing my intellect. For the first time, I thought about things and had an opportunity to express ideas . . . I began to be very proud of myself. It suddenly became important to be a good librarian, to open the doors of books, and to think clearly" (Braverman 1979, 197). Edwards communicated to those working with young adults the importance of their role in influencing their patrons' reading.

Communication also entails listening, and I suspect there were many people Edwards seldom listened to. But one individual who clearly had her ear was Mabel Williams at the New York Public Library. Edwards visited Williams and was energized by her time spent in New York. She returned to Baltimore "bursting with ideas" (Atkinson 1986, 39) for developing young adult collections in the branches. The genesis for young adult book reviewing *(You're the Critic)* came from "Back Talk," started by Margaret Scoggins, Mabel Williams's protégé and also at the New York Public Library. Clearly Edwards listened and learned.

Sheldon posits that library leaders garner trust because they are consistent. Edwards's admirers might refer to her as focused, her detractors as single-minded, but both would have to agree that she was consistent. While her opinions about the power of books and reading grew, they never wavered. She believed in books and teenagers so strongly, and her actions so steadfastly supported these ideas, that both her coworkers and her patrons could trust her to enable them to embrace concepts that expanded these beliefs and reject those that didn't. This trust in Edwards as an individual translates into trust in the library by extension. Consider how easily such trust leads to influence as generation after generation of young adult librarians read *The Fair Garden and the Swarm of Beasts.*

The fourth ability library leaders must possess is confidence. So sure was Edwards about the rightness of her views that this once timid young girl became equally sure about herself. Several essays in *The Fair Garden,* particularly those that deal with instruction in library organization and reference services, underscore that professional self-confidence. When Edwards wrote about what she saw as the futile teaching of the card catalog, for example, she adopts the stance of a passionate debater, confident in the rightness of her positions. When she gave instructions for delivering booktalks, evaluating books, developing a selection policy, and writing annotations *(see* appendix A), she does so forcefully and confidently. Edwards knew what she was about and that what she was about was right.

Edwards understood her strengths: her energy, her devotion to her program and ideas, her willingness to take risks, her ability to work with dedicated assistants. This knowledge characterizes library leaders, as does a willingness to learn. Edwards was a perpetual learner who continued to read throughout her career, and then she read some more. Leaders are learners; Edwards was both.

Edwards in Today's World

In writing about library foremothers, Betsy Hearne and Christine Jenkins discuss the near-spiritual messages that guided early library work with young people (Hearne and Jenkins 1999). Words such as *cannon, mission, vision, spiritual, humanistic,* and *idealism* either define or modify the beliefs and ideals of these pioneers. We can use all such words when discussing Edwards. The one we must avoid, however, is *saint.*

It is understandable that in reading *The Fair Garden* and being so moved by its ideas and themes that a librarian would automatically ask "WWMD?"—"What would Margaret do?"—at every contemporary crisis point. Such an approach would be shortsighted and fail to recognize that Margaret Edwards lived and worked and thought not in our time, but in another. Her work belongs to the ages, but her ideas are nonetheless shaped by circumstances of the second and third quarters of the twentieth century.

Edwards, for example, saw the new field of young adult literature as producing few great works and that such books merely provided literary way stations to occupy teenagers before they were ready for the "good stuff" in adult literature. But remember, she retired in 1962, and *The Outsiders* (Hinton), frequently considered the first contemporary young adult novel, wasn't even published until 1967. Her last article appears in 1974 (as does a revision of *The Fair Garden and the Swarm of Beasts*), the same year that Robert Cormier published *The Chocolate War*. Young adult literature as we know it today was clearly a creation of the future. As Lillian Bradshaw succinctly put it: "When I was working with young adults, adult books were about all we had to offer them. *Seventeenth Summer* had just come out, but most of the rest of the young adult books were called something like *A Career for Jenny"* (Bradshaw 2002). In her writing Edwards mentions a few young adult books, the now-classic *Seventeenth Summer* (Daly 1942) and *Two and the Town* (Felsen 1952), for example, but generally considers this genre as appropriate "to teach the apathetic the love of reading; to satisfy some of the adolescent's emotional and psychological needs; to throw light on the problems of adolescence; to explore the teenager's relationship to his community; and to lead him to adult reading" (Edwards 1994, 58).

Sure, I would like to think that after reading young adult literature, particularly those books cited for the Margaret A. Edwards (MAE) Award *(see* appendix F), that Margaret Edwards might relax her stand on such books. But how am I to know what she would do in such a case? In the final analysis, such hopes center around my own respect for the literature, rather than hers. If I wanted to know "WWMD?" I would have to be content to stock a present library collection mainly with adult books.

And those books would be told as story narrative. Edwards clearly believed, as did her contemporary Louise Rosenblatt, who published *Literature as Exploration* in 1938, that *aesthetic* reading (where readers live through a work) came with fiction, biography, and poetry while *efferent* reading (where readers carry away information from a work) was the by-product of the expository prose that characterizes nonfiction not cataloged by form such as drama, poetry, and biography. Again, remember the times in which Edwards worked; there is a good chance that she repeatedly had to defend fiction and to show that these books could influence readers' lives. While there may well exist a contemporary bias favoring fiction over nonfiction, at the turn of the century a reverse bias was just escaping institutionalization. Pleas from the late nineteenth century called for the abolition of fiction in the library, citing it as tasteless and harmful, and early restrictions on children's circulation patterns were an awkward attempt to limit fiction reading (Donelson and Nilsen 1980, 85–86). Edwards alludes to this history when she writes: "The fiction collection, dealing as it does with the emotions and feelings of people, is a kind of literary bastard since it does not fit into the library's philosophy of educating oneself by 'serious' reading" (Edwards 1994, 67).

While the Y collection at Enoch Pratt consisted of fiction and nonfiction, the latter was divided into that of "practical or recreational interest (rather than school assignment material) and the readable nonfiction that would touch the heart, stir the mind and enable a teenager to step in another's shoes and 'live' his/her life" (Lapides 2002b, 3). This "readable" nonfiction, as defined by the books Edwards discusses in *The Fair Garden* and those included in her Tool Shed *(see* appendix A), comes exclusively through story narrative with selections such as Gordon Parks's *A Choice of Weapons,* John Gunther's *Death Be Not Proud,* or Moss Hart's *Act One.*

It's interesting to note that about half of the fifty ALEX Awards, given to ten adult books every year that are considered the best available for young adults *(see* appendix D), are nonfiction. The great majority of those are biography, such as *Soldier: A Poet's Childhood,* by June Jordan, or books with strong biographical elements, such as Caroline Alexander's *The Endurance: Shackleton's Legendary Antarctic Expedition.* But others are not. Would Margaret Edwards share the same enthusiasm for expository prose in books such as *Lest We Forget: The Passage from Africa to Slavery and Emancipation* (Thomas 1997) or *The Secret Family: Twenty-four Hours Inside the Mysterious Worlds of Our Minds and Bodies* (Bodanis 1997) or *An American Insurrection: The Battle of Oxford, Mississippi, 1962* (Doyle 2001) that the committee did? Again, it is tempting to think she would, but there is no way to know.

If today's librarians ask "WWMD?" when selecting books for their collection, then they will be dealing with many out-of-date titles. There is no way to know which books Edwards would consider crucial for contemporary young adult librarians and their patrons. As she states in the introductory paragraph to her "Reading List" *(see* appendix A), her list is "not inclusive, nor is it a list for all time" (Edwards 1994, 134). Rather than discard the list completely, though, young adult librarians should look at the broad divisions (i.e., "For Younger Readers," "Useful Titles for Transferring the Reader to Adult Books," "Adult Titles for Good Readers," and "Advanced Reading") and consider creating their own. Appendix C offers a wide range of tools to help create such a personalized, useful, and modern list.

Margaret Edwards, in her drive to bring books and reading to teenagers, had little patience for what she called "technical skills": cataloging, collection development, administration, and reference work (Hearne and Jenkins 1999, 553). Wheeler believed that each was separate from the Y librarian's function, and Edwards concurred. Linda Lapides paraphrases Wheeler's stance: "The reference work for high school kids ought to be done in the adult reference room, where the trained reference librarians are" (Lapides 2002b, 3). She recalls that "in the central library, high school students were steered to the subject departments as well for assistance with their assignments" (Lapides 2002b, 3). Unlike other public librarians such as Jane Roos at Cleveland and Margaret Scoggins at the Nathan Strauss Young Adult Library in New York City, Margaret Edwards focused on her own agenda of introducing reading and fine books, which dovetailed perfectly with the Enoch Pratt philosophy.

Yet Lillian Bradshaw remembers that when an individual patron came in with a particular question and encountered Edwards, she would "tear up the library—the young adult collection, the children's room, the special collections—to help him find what he needed. Of course," Bradshaw added, "he would also always leave with a book to read"(Bradshaw 2002). Edwards may have eschewed the idea of helping teenagers with specific information questions, but she never slighted service to the individual.

Again, though, remember the time in which Edwards was working. It appears from her writing (which may be her skill at overstatement rather than a true reflection of the situation) that such reference work comprised finding the length of the Nile River or name of the twenty-third U.S. president. These assignments weren't the powerful "I Search" questions frequently developed today, where teenagers have a voice in defining their own research papers and in determining how such ideas affect them, which, in turn, often becomes the heart of readers' advisory.

Rather than ask "What would Margaret do?" it is more instructive to ask "WDMD?"—"What did Margaret do?" First, she established the book and the young adult as twin cornerstones of the profession. She gave legitimacy to many librarians working at that time and a near ethical dilemma to others. Contemporary librarians may well serve young adults in ways Margaret Edwards did not or did not want to, but her nagging voice on the importance of books and reading remains constant. Some librarians, like Michael Printz, tempered that voice, recognizing that "books have always been bonds between librarians and young adults" (cited in Gerhardt 1997, 462), but that other media and services are nonetheless vital in libraries. Those librarians who do not actively promote reading and books invariably respond to Edwards's voice as well. "I wish I had more time to spend with books" and "I know that reading is important, but my principal believes I should spend my time with technology" are but two often repeated phrases that offer some justification for not paying the kind of attention to books and readers that Edwards demanded. While her precepts may not be followed, they certainly still compose the collective wisdom of young adult librarianship.

Second, Edwards focused on the individual. That focus remains today, although it has undergone a shift. Attention breeds respect, which in turn leads to viewing young adults as resources and recognizing that young adults are well able to help solve their own problems (*New Directions in Service to Young Adults in Libraries* 2002). Would Edwards approve of that focus? Again, there is really no way of knowing.

Today's librarians reading *The Fair Garden* are, in many ways, like virtual assistants undergoing some of Margaret Edwards's training. Like those real assistants—Ray Fry, Anna Curry, and Sara Siebert, for example—these readers must take Edwards's ideas not as a simple blueprint for like action, but as a starting point for growing and developing their own philosophies about library services. Margaret Edwards asked teenagers to read books and use those themes when leading their own lives. We should expect no less from librarians.

What Margaret Edwards also did was show today's librarians how an effective leader works. While no one can "be" Margaret Edwards, we can all use her leadership qualities—developing a focused vision, taking risks, being willing to debate ideas, communicating with others, and exhibiting confidence—as models when considering our own work.

There's a catchphrase that reoccurs in library marketing: "Readers Are Leaders." I suspect Margaret Edwards would concur with this notion. She was both.

Works Cited

Alexander, Caroline. 1998. *The endurance: Shackleton's legendary Antarctic expedition.* New York: Knopf.

Atkinson, Joan. 1986. Pioneers in public service to young adults. *Top of the News* 43 (fall): 27–44.

Beers, G. Kylene. 1990. Choosing not to read: An ethnographic study of seventh-grade aliterate students. Ph.D. diss., University of Houston.

Bishop, William Warner. 1992. Changing ideals in librarianship. *Library Journal* 117 (2 November): S2–S4.

Bodanis, David. 1997. *The secret family: Twenty-four hours inside the mysterious worlds of our minds and bodies.* New York: Simon & Schuster.

Books for the teen age. 1975. New York: New York Public Library. Annual.

Bradshaw, Lillian. 2002. Interview with Betty Carter. Dallas, Tex., 11 April.

Braverman, Miriam. 1979. *Youth, society, and the public library.* Chicago: American Library Association.

Carlsen, G. Robert. 1967. *Books and the teenage reader: A guide for teachers, librarians, and parents.* New York: Harper & Row.

Carlsen, G. Robert. 1994a. The stages of reading development. In *Literature is . . .: Collected essays by G. Robert Carlsen.* Edited by Anne Sherill and Terance C. Ley. Johnson City, Tenn.: Sabre, 19–26.

Carlsen, G. Robert. 1994b. Understanding the American heritage: A classroom experience. In *Literature is . . .: Collected essays by G. Robert Carlsen*. Edited by Anne Sherill and Terance C. Ley. Johnson City, Tenn.: Sabre, 111–116.

Carlsen, G. Robert, and Anne Sherrill. 1988. *Voices of readers: How we come to love books*. Urbana, Ill.: National Council of Teachers of English.

Cormier, Robert. 1974. *The chocolate war.* New York: Pantheon.

Daly, Maureen. 1942. *Seventeenth summer.* New York: Dodd, Mead.

Donelson, Ken, and Alleen Pace Nilsen. 1980. *Literature for today's young adults.* Chicago: Scott Foresman.

Doyle, William. *An American insurrection: The battle of Oxford, Mississippi, 1962.* New York: Doubleday.

Edwards, Margaret A. 1994. *The fair garden and the swarm of beasts: The library and the young adult.* Chicago: American Library Association.

Edwards, Margaret. 1997. Taming the young barbarian. In *School Library Journal's best.* Edited by Lillian N. Gerhardt, Marilyn L. Miller, and Thomas W. Downen. New York: Neal Schuman, 52–53.

Farley, Martha. 1897. *Elsie Dinsmore.* New York: Dodd, Mead.

Felsen, Henry Gregor. 1952. *Two and the town.* New York: Scribner.

Fenwick, Sara Innis. 1976. Library service to children and young people. *Library Trends* 25 (July): 329–360.

Ferber, Edna. 1930. *Cimarron.* New York: Doubleday.

Gerhardt, Lillian N. 1997. In service to youth. In *School Library Journal's best.* Edited by Lillian N. Gerhardt, Marilyn L. Miller, and Thomas W. Downen. New York: Neal Schuman, 460–465.

Gunther, John. 1949. *Death be not proud: A memoir.* New York: Harper.

Hannigan, Jane A. 1996. A feminist analysis of the voices for advocacy in young adult services. *Library Trends* 44 (spring): 851–874.

Hart, Moss. 1959. *Act one: An autobiography.* New York: Random House.

Hearne, Betsy, and Christine Jenkins. 1999. Sacred texts: What our foremothers left us in the way of psalms, proverbs, precepts, and practices. *The Horn Book* 75 (September/October): 536–561.

Hewins, Caroline M. 1897. *Books for boys and girls: A selection list compiled by Caroline M. Hewins.* Boston: Library Bureau. Published for the ALA Publishing Section.

Hinton, S. E. 1967. *The outsiders.* New York: Viking.

James, Will. 1930. *Lone cowboy: My life story.* New York: Scribner.

Jenkins, Christine A. 2000. The history of youth services librarianship: A review of the research literature. *Libraries and Culture* 35 (winter): 104–140.

Jordan, June. 2000. *Soldier: A poet's childhood.* New York: Basic.

Junger, Sebastian. 1998. *The perfect storm: A true story of men against the sea.* New York: Norton.

Lapides, Linda F. 2002a. Margaret Alexander Edwards, 1902–1988. *Journal of Youth Services in Libraries* 15 (summer): 45–49.

Lapides, Linda F. 2002b. Letter to Linda Waddle, 25 June.

Madden, Michael C. 1967. An analysis of the American Library Association's annual list "Best Books for Young Adults," 1930–1967. Master's thesis, University of Chicago.

Monseau, Virginia. 1991. Dora V. Smith: A legacy for the future. In *Missing chapters: 10 pioneering women in NCTE and English education.* Edited by Jeanne Marcum Gerlach and Virginia R. Monseau. Urbana, Ill.: National Council of Teachers of English, 69–93.

Mülbach, Louise. 1867. *Henry VIII and his court, or Catherine Parr.* New York: Appleton.

New directions in service to young adults in libraries: Media sheet. 2002. Chicago: Young Adult Library Services Association.

Parks, Gordon. 1966. *A choice of weapons.* New York: Harper.

Reid, Virginia. 1972. *Reading ladders for human relations.* 5th ed. Washington, D.C.: American Council on Education.

Rosenblatt, Louise. 1938. *Literature as exploration.* New York: Appleton-Century.

Sheldon, Brooke E. 1991. *Leaders in libraries: Styles and strategies for success.* Chicago: American Library Association.

Smith, E. Boyd. 1910. *Chicken world.* New York: Putnam.

Smith, Frank. 1988. *Understanding reading: A psycholinguistic analysis of reading and learning to read.* Hillsdale, N.J.: Lawrence Erlbaum.

Thomas, Velma. 1997. *Lest we forget: The passage from Africa to slavery and emancipation.* New York: Crown.

Vandergrift, Kay E. 1996. Female advocacy and harmonious voices: A history of public library services and publishing for children in the United States. *Library Trends* 44 (spring): 683–718.

Preface

In *The Old Librarian's Almanac,* published in New Haven, Connecticut in 1773, Jared Bean advised his fellow librarians that the library, the Treasure House of Literature, "is no more to be thrown open to the ravages of the unreasoning Mob [the general public, especially young people], than is a Fair Garden to be laid unprotected at the Mercy of a Swarm of Beasts." This is the source of the title both of this book and of one of the essays toward the end.

The swarm of teenage "beasts" were my patrons at the Enoch Pratt Free Library in Baltimore for thirty years. In this book I have attempted to describe that enriching experience and to say what I learned from working with them and the young librarians who inspired them to read. Beauty learned that the Beast was a Prince, as all of us who really know him have realized for some time.

In my attack on the Weeds and Insects (Chapter VI) I may be a voice crying in the wilderness, as many public and school librarians will not agree with me. In fact, if I were not already retired, I might find myself, like John the Baptist, reduced to eating locusts and wild honey. I take consolation from the fact that though he ended up with his head on a platter, he was right just the same.

Sara Siebert, Coordinator of Work with Young Adults at the Enoch Pratt Free Library, and Linda Lapides, her assistant, helped me organize my thirty years' experience into a more coherent form than I could have done alone. Without their advice I might have ridden off in more directions than I have.

MARGARET ALEXANDER EDWARDS

I

Roots

According to modern educators, a child should not be taught to read until he shows "reading readiness." My family did not know about this theory, and shortly after I was able to dispense with the dictionary on my chair at meals, they taught me my ABC's. This was done by pointing to letters of the alphabet on the pages of books and newspapers and calling them by name until I could do my own pointing and identifying.

I learned to read by spelling out the testimonials on a calendar advertising Wine of Cardui. My mother liked this calendar, distributed each new year by the local druggist, because the numerals for the days of the month were placed in large squares, leaving sufficient room for records. By consulting the calendar she could tell when a hen would hatch or a cow come fresh, when one of us would have a birthday, or when the Ladies' Missionary Society would meet. Since Wine of Cardui was strictly a woman's medicine and some of the testimonials were a bit intimate, she hung the calendar inside a cupboard door where she could consult the farm records on a moment's notice and yet not make the calendar a part of the decoration of the living room. I was about four years old when I realized that the ABC's I had recently learned were arranged in interesting combinations suggesting words at the top

This chapter was first published under the title "A Little Learnin'" in *ALA Bulletin*, June 1956, 379–86. *Ed.*

of this calendar. My mother was always extremely busy, as she ran a farmhouse without a servant, so any questions I asked had to be answered on the run. I stood in the cupboard with the door ajar and called out words, asking after each, "Mother, what does this spell?" She would call back a quick answer, thinking I was looking over a book or a newspaper. I was well on the way to becoming a fluent reader when some of the words I was spelling out suddenly shocked her to attention. She hurried to the living room to find that I was in the midst of a rousing account of the change that had come over a woman in Iowa after taking one bottle of this magic medication. She immediately took me in hand and bought me some less interesting but more suitable reading matter.

The first book I ever owned was *Peter Rabbit* by Beatrix Potter, and I regret to state that I was puzzled by it. In our back pasture there were a great many cottontail and jackrabbits, but their lives were less complex than those of the rabbits in my book. To me the business of Peter's losing his shoe seemed out of character, and when Mr. McGregor undertook to put a flowerpot over Peter, I was amazed. It took a fast old dog and a lot of yelping to catch a West Texas rabbit, and the man didn't live who could just set an empty geranium pot over one. The sly humor and the artistry of the little book were lost on my practical mind.

Our farm was 250 miles from the noise and "temptations" of a big city. True, there was a small town five miles away, but generally speaking, we were "removed." However, an uncle and aunt and their five children lived only half a mile away on an adjoining farm and we frequently visited back and forth. Aunt Susan, who had nothing else to do but wash, churn, iron, cook, and keep house for her husband and five children, sometimes found time in the afternoons to read to us. I remember dropping in once when she was reading aloud *The Old Curiosity Shop* and how we all laughed when Quilp, the dwarf, stayed just beyond the reach of a vicious dog that was tied up and maddened him with his teasing. But as I look back upon it, I was more susceptible to grief than to flights of imagination or to subtle humor. I would like to say that I sensed style and quality, but alas, I succumbed to tears at the reading of *Whiter than Snow*.[1] All I remember about it is that I was met by my cousins as I came for a visit and was told that they really had a sad one this time—it was all about a girl who was sick and slowly dying. I was given the essential morbid details to bring me up to date and then Aunt Susan read us the last chapter where the girl really did get it. I began by merely shedding tears, advanced to sobs, and went on to howls. I soon became such a social problem that Aunt Susan suggested they all go outside and let me quietly get a hold of myself. They acted on her suggestion, but I felt the need of consolation and followed my hosts around out-of-doors, wailing until in self-defense they created a diversion that made things easier for all of us.

When I learned to read for myself, I did not peruse the best books with avidity, nor did I show indications of innate good taste. I had little access to the best books. In my childhood Childress, Texas, was cattle country in the process of becoming farmland. It had been settled by pioneer stock who refused to be beaten by drought and disaster but instead, by sheer courage and physical exertion, staved off starvation in the bad years and hoped for better times. These sunburned wiry people had neither the leisure nor the money necessary for the pursuit of the arts, nor was reading a habit with most of the people I knew. There was no reading matter whatever in the homes of most of our neighbors and the idea of supporting a public library was unthinkable. My mother and father had both been schoolteachers and our entire family had an understanding of the place of the book in society and had read and enjoyed many good books. Since their emigration to West Texas they had had no funds with which to maintain their family libraries, but they had brought with them complete sets of Dickens and Sir Walter Scott, *Paradise Lost* with Doré illustrations, a set of "complete masterpieces," and various other titles.

Of course, every family had a Bible—the King James version, thank God—and no one made better use of it than my mother and grandmother. Gramp's father, my great-grandfather, was a missionary to the Forty-niners. He packed some food, a little extra clothing, and his Bible in his saddlebags, mounted a mule, and followed the gold rush, exhorting those fanatical men to turn from their pursuit of earthy wealth in order to lay up treasure in heaven.

His daughter, my grandmother, inherited his religious fervor. She was one of the early pioneers to West Texas. In her forties she found herself a widow with six children and four step-children, holding a claim staked on the prairies of West Texas. Living off rabbits and wild turkeys, shipping wild horses, she and her big family fought off starvation and barely pulled through. Yet in her spare time she organized the Presbyterian Church of Childress County in a covered wagon and passed on what she termed "the Word of God" to the cowboys. If an encampment of cowboys had the bad luck to settle down anywhere near her claim, she bestrode a horse and rode out to devil the lives out of them about their immortal souls.

In later years, when she was bringing her grandson Edward home by train from his father's ranch in Oklahoma, she made use of the time to distribute religious tracts to the other passengers. After she had given out most of her "literature," two extra passengers showed up. Whether they had been to the washroom or in another coach I do not know, but their appearance was the signal for Grandmother to spring into action, tracts in hand. This time, to her surprise, she found herself jerked back to a sitting position. Edward had pinned her skirt to the green plush seat. He was very young but some instinct told him that the distribution of tracts, however sound religiously, was socially unacceptable. Gramps' slogan was "In season and out of season—serving the Lord." According to Edward's lights, the train episode was too "out of season."

Gramps lived most of the time with us and between her and my mother my religious training was pretty thorough. Among other things, I was exhorted to read the Bible through from cover to cover at least three times. When I was nine the two ladies decided it would also be a fine idea for me to know by memory nine psalms—one for each birthday. Since I already knew "The Lord Is My Shepherd" and "Make a Joyful Noise unto the Lord," I had only seven to go. In making the selections for me it was agreed that Number 19 was pretty long, but so lovely that we had better throw it in, too. Who could resist:

> The heavens declare the glory of God;
> and the firmament showeth his handiwork.
> Day unto day uttereth speech,
> and night unto night showeth knowledge. . . .
> In them hath he set a tabernacle for the sun,
> which is as a bridegroom coming out of his chamber,
> and rejoiceth as a strong man to run a race. . . .

The old girls were right. It really was lovely. They never fully explained the reference to the bridegroom coming out of his chamber, but I liked the sound of it anyway. I had a lot of trouble when I got to the part about the law of the Lord is perfect, converting the soul; the testimony of the Lord is sure, making wise the simple; the statutes of the Lord are right; not to mention the commandment, the fear, and the judgments of the Lord. Which came first or second or fifth? My mother explained that it was hard for anyone but good, and anything was worth memorizing that ended on the lofty note:

> Let the words of my mouth,
> and the meditations of my heart
> be acceptable in thy sight, O Lord,
> my strength, and my redeemer.

Gramps sometimes had me read the Bible aloud to her, instructing me to be sure and emphasize all words in italics. This ruined the meter because the words were italicized to show origin or a second possible meaning or something else that had nothing to do with emphasis. Since I seldom read her "daily readings" to her, this occasional offbeat accent did not hurt me.

My mother instituted "family reading" in the home. Each night the family must gather and read a chapter together. My father, who could take his Bible or let it alone, did not oppose the idea, nor did he exactly support it. He usually went to bed early and read the Fort Worth *Star Telegram*. We sat in chairs or on footstools about the bed, and when Mother began reading she would gently pull the *Star Telegram* aside, at which Dad would close his eyes and listen passively while my sister and I kicked each other or heard with martyred patience. Then Mother suggested that we take turns reading. She would read one night, then my sister, then I. Dad was not listed as a reader nor was Gramps, who went to bed early and listened with her bedroom door open. When this suggestion went into effect Helen and I spotted every short chapter in the Bible and proclaimed them our favorites. I must also confess that we found all the selections with words of obscene connotation. Somewhere in the Bible there is a character named Peleg, and I think Solomon used shittim wood in the temple, and David or some musician played a sacbut. When we came to these passages, deliberately selected, Dad, Helen, and I would roar with laughter until Mother was forced to censor the Word of God and ban certain chapters from our evening meditations. She could not understand how such irreverence was possible. When her evenings for reading came, she approached her chapter with a reverent tone and attitude that moves me after all these years. She honestly believed that just to hear any part of the Bible read enriched one's spiritual life. I don't know how true that is, but one thing I do know—there are few better ways to train a child's ear to the appreciation of style, rhythm, and cadence than to let him hear the King James version of the Bible read aloud regularly by a person who reads with expression.

Many people cannot distinguish between claptrap and style in writing, for they have never known truly distinguished writing at first hand. For those who wish to acquire an instinctive love of great writing, there is the King James version of the Bible.

Uncle John was the only one of us who actually hungered and thirsted for books. To our wonder, he even sat up late at night and read books. When I was permitted to spend the night in the "city" at their house, I might be awakened two or three times during the night to hear Aunt Daisy call, "Mr. Crawford, you come to bed!" He often read until two or three in the morning, when he would rise, stretch, and go milk the cow which he should have milked at sundown of the previous day. If the book were unusually absorbing, he might read until sunup, which meant the cow was milked twelve hours late. We sympathized with the poor cow, we commiserated with Aunt Daisy, we were outraged, but because Uncle John was so charming, we forgave him, and because he was so "cultivated," we were really quite proud of him.

He ran an insurance business and in dry years many people ran the risk of having their uninsured homes burn down in order to use the money intended for premiums to buy food and cottonseed for another bout with the Texas climate. In one such year Uncle John was low on funds, to put it mildly, and Aunt Daisy had practiced the most rigid economies in order to keep their three children and themselves fed and clothed. This she did cheerfully until the day she came home to discover he had bought from a book agent the complete works of Theodore Roosevelt. She was outraged and confided to us all that after this, when she left home she would have to lock the ass in the storm cellar. She also made it clear to him that she would escort the children downtown and fit them out in new clothes and charge the bill to him. We all thought Aunt Daisy was a wit and none of us could imagine why Uncle John had bought the books. The idea that in hard times a man would buy books was simply incomprehensible. Who was the old Persian who said:

> Had I but one loaf of bread,
> One would I sell,
> And buy white hyacinths
> To feed my soul.[2]

I have said that I had little access to the best books. However, I had access to *books* because Mrs. W. E. Davis lived in Childress. She came there with her clipped accent and fine education and set to work to raise the town's cultural level.

She was a leading spirit in the organization of the Childress Woman's Department Club, which has been the center of the city's cultural life for many years. When I was growing up, she determined that there would be some sort of library for the town. She found an empty room in one of the business houses and got permission to use it for a library. Then she scoured the town for books. Nothing offered her, I am sure, was refused and the selection was truly catholic. Here I found the *Little Prudy* series, *The Little Colonel* series, *The Five Little Peppers* series, *Pollyanna*, and *Anne of Green Gables*—a diet rich in sentimental sweets that did me no harm, furnished me with better recreation than I might otherwise have had, and above all else, did teach me that it was fun to read a book.[3] Since I have become a more discriminating reader, it pains me to think that I never once questioned the sweet stupidity of these books. I was not stirred by them, but as far as I was concerned, they were all right. I never remember showing the least critical ability except with two books. I enjoyed Horatio Alger's *A Boy's Fortune*, but when someone pointed out to me the absurdity of the poor boy's sudden rise to wealth and position, I was able to see that he was a bit too success-ful.[4] The second instance was a clear triumph and the first indication of any intelligence in my approach to reading. Someone gave me a title from the *Meadowbrook Girls* series.[5] I don't remember the heroine's name, but Jan will do. She and her girl friends went for a vacation where they met a fine young man who told them that a most important tennis tournament was to be held in about four weeks and made it seem quite urgent that Jan and her friends enter as contestants for the title, though none of them had ever played a game of tennis. They cleared a court and practiced, and when the tournament opened, there they were. After a series of tense moments Jan got to the finals, where she might have lost out to skillful and experienced opponents had she not hit upon the idea of looking at one spot on the tennis court and then volleying the ball to another. Even I knew that was silly.

But before I got to the *Meadowbrook Girls* I read four Dickens novels. I read them because there was nothing else to read and because, I think, I was showing off. *David Copperfield* fell before my onslaught when I was nine. I was encouraged by my parents who discussed it with me and made me feel brilliant for wading through it. As I remember, I mildly enjoyed it but was more impressed with myself than with the story. I remember the thrill and excitement I got from Andersen's *Ugly Duckling*, which by some mistake was printed in a school reader composed of duller material.

My grandmother subscribed to *The Youth's Companion* for me. I read it with avidity but it left no lasting impression except for the butterflies. I read an ad in the *Companion* depicting the rewards awaiting those who made a career of collecting butterflies and birds' nests. I bought the net advertised and set all my cousins to helping. We filled a back room of the house with a truly amazing collection of old birds' nests and jars full of badly handled butterflies before something must have happened to end my career as a naturalist.

I also read the comics, which we called the funny papers. They lacked the sex and shooting of today's comics, but they were stupid. Hans and Fritz played the most horrible pranks on people and always ended by getting spanked. Mutt and Jeff and Maggie and Jiggs were old friends of mine.[6]

At this point my mother traded a heifer for a set of Mulbach's novels and the complete works of George Eliot.

Since I have become more familiar with good writing I know that Mulbach is unreliable as a writer of history and is not mentioned on standard lists of fiction, but her *Henry VIII* was a terrific experience for me.[7] Brought up as I had been on the shorter catechism by parents who grew up with all the restraints of the nineties, I had never heard people talk of broken marriages or adultery. Henry's unrestrained amours set in the splendor of his court affected me in much the same way that the Pacific did Cortez. As I sat barefooted in the rocking chair on our front porch I wore satin gowns and ate exotic food. I saw Anne Boleyn beheaded and the Flemish Mary scorned, and I was completely spent when the book ended just in time to save Catherine Parr. From that day forward, I have loved history and historical novels.

I loved *Silas Marner* when we read it in school because I had a teacher who brought it to life for me. I then read most of the works of George Eliot but I needed someone to help me understand them. I also loved *Ivanhoe* when we read it in school and vowed to read Scott's complete works, but *The Heart of Midlothian* threw me for a loss and I did not read on. As for Shakespeare, I never knew the plays were powerful dramatic stories.

It was the custom of the English teachers in Childress High School to assign the various roles in Shakespearean plays to different students each day. We sat in our seats and made a kind of game of seeing if we could remain alert enough to read our parts when the time came. If I were Portia and she had nothing to say for two pages, I listened for the lines that would cue me while I laughed at the show-off in the class, and started to read when Portia spoke again. If I had no part, I paid little attention to what was going on. At the end of the play we went back and marked passages for memorization. One passed the exam on a play if he could quote thirty lines, and I always passed.

Imagine my surprise when I went to college and bought a ticket to a dramatic evening of entertainment by Charles Rann Kennedy and his wife, the actress Edith Wynn Mathieson. I remember nothing of the evening but the balcony scene from *Romeo and Juliet*. Miss Mathieson appeared in a flowing, heavenly blue Grecian gown with a golden girdle and began a conversation with Romeo. To my utter amazement, it all turned into lovemaking. This was not one of my male classmates and I sitting at our desks and reading lines, this was passion—these two people were violently in love and I was almost an eavesdropper on their intimate and moving conversation. I had not known that really nice people spoke and acted this way. I had not known that love was like this, and certainly Shakespeare was the last man who, up to now, I should have suspected of portraying it this way. I decided that from that time forth Shakespeare would bear watching.

The college I attended was located in Waxahachie, Texas, and was exactly the college I should have attended, for I was unsure of myself and needed confidence and it was small and friendly. The three years

I spent there were among the happiest of my life and I left the school a well-adjusted, self-confident person, but I do not remember meeting a single person either on the faculty or in the student body who was genuinely well read. I had a French teacher who was sophisticated and world-traveled and knew French literature. My English professor was an old darling who loved poetry, but I never heard him mention a novel or discuss modern writing. I worked as an assistant in the college library, which I thought existed for the sole purpose of helping students with school assignments.

When I left college and became a schoolteacher, I heard my cousins, also teachers, discuss some of the best sellers and I read a book once in a while. I had the good fortune to stumble onto Willa Cather and read almost everything she wrote. I also read my father's copy of *Les Miserables* and a few other titles. Then in my fourth year of teaching I met Eleanor Taylor.

I saw her first at the teachers' institute held in September at the county seat. She was overweight, unbecomingly dressed, and bare-headed; when we ignorant but becomingly gowned teachers from Vernon, Texas, heard that she was assigned to the English faculty, we looked at her critically. Obviously she was a maverick. However, when she walked up to me and made a caustic remark on the principal's address of the morning, I couldn't help laughing, as she was obviously not only intelligent but very witty. She hailed from Rice Institute and had been a newspaper reporter. She knew art and music. She brought with her a sensitive sketch made by one of her friends of a young cellist whose name was Hans Kindler. I never saw such pictures as she had on her walls. She had taken the trouble to bring books along, too. She was dynamite! I decided to room with her, and the dawn of my renaissance came up like thunder.

If Eleanor taught me nothing else she did show me that people could hold points of view quite contrary to mine and still be people of intelligence and character. She enlarged my point of view and began the dissolution of my extreme provincialism. She was also shock-proof. She read books that I had heard spoken of in whispers or with raised eyebrows, and she liked them. When my family and friends read Pearl Buck's *The Good Earth*, they asked, "Is nothing sacred?" Eleanor would read such a book, look me straight in the eye, and say how excellent it was! If a book depicted life truly, she did not throw it down and run like Chicken Little because sex was mentioned or some frontiersman swore. She did not wipe out in a few months the inhibitions I had acquired in twenty-one years, but she planted in my little provincial mind the idea that I could know people in print as I knew them in life. In Texas we ran tick-infested cattle through vats. I thought characters in books had to be similarly divested of sex and sin lest I become contaminated by reading about them.

At the end of two years with her in Vernon, Texas, I went to Columbia University to get a Master's Degree and then took a position teaching Latin at Towson, Maryland. After a few years my career there ended when I was escorting a class down the steps during a fire drill. I had reached the first landing when I thought about the implications of a question asked me by a visiting supervisor as the class and I had left the room. Before considering the matter carefully, I leapt back up the steps, gave the startled supervisor some free and unsolicited advice, and was fired.

Evidently my fall had been observed as closely as that of the sparrow,[8] for a special Providence guided me to Joseph L. Wheeler, then director of the Pratt Library, who was planning to move the library from its inadequate temporary quarters to the new building his vision had made possible. Interviewing me adroitly in his makeshift office, where he sat sweltering in his shirtsleeves, he soon discovered I was a "hot potato." But he played a hunch and allowed me to enroll in the library's training class. Moreover, to his eternal credit he never mentioned my questionable past to my critical supervisor.

Because I was a thirty-year-old woman who had been fired from my "chosen" profession and hired by a miracle, I was determined to make good. As I began working in this new field I fell in love with teenagers, whom I already knew, as well as with books, which I did not know. And so, under Dr. Wheeler's inspired direction, I undertook to do what I could to set up an effective program for library work with young adults at the Enoch Pratt Free Library in the city of Baltimore.

☙ II ❧

The Growing Season

Laying Out the Garden

When I finished the training class I was assigned, as I had hoped I would be, to work with the collection of teenage books for free reading that was located at the rear of the Popular Library in a room where the adult fiction and popular nonfiction was also shelved. I am sure the library hoped for nothing more than that I would be able to keep the teenagers away from the front desk where the adults were served. I took the assignment much more seriously and considered myself an amateur readers' advisor, attempting to make up in friendliness for what I lacked in book knowledge. To a degree, I succeeded, for a great many teenagers began to make use of the collection. Since many of my patrons were better acquainted with books than I, I realized I would soon lose them if I did not read ahead of them. I was a slow and inexperienced reader but I read with desperate determination. I took armloads of books home, piling them on one side of my chair to read and then stacking them, as finished, on the other. I read in streetcars, on buses, in my dentist's waiting room, and on lunch hours.

After a year or so I began to feel I was doing all right and decided to set up special collections for young adults in the branches. I worked

---

This section is taken from "A Long Way to Tipperary" in *The Library Reaches Out*, ed. K. M. Coplan and E. Castagna, New York: Oceana, 1965. *Ed.*

three nights a week in each branch for several weeks, assembling collections based on the votes of teenage patrons. When a book was endorsed by three people it was included and the written recommendations were signed and filed in a recipe box for all to read. This took a lot of time and entailed much paper work, but it advertised the collection and stimulated interest among the teenagers. However, if I were doing it again, I would be inclined to delay setting up a collection until I could find a staff member who was enthusiastic about it and wished to be responsible for teenage reading in his branch.

In those days the staffs in the branches were small and usually untrained. The concept of developing readers was not part of their philosophy. Answering reference questions and pointing out the location of books on the shelves were their idea of good service, and at that time I think I went pretty much on instinct rather than on any philosophy of young-adult work. I was incapable of explaining to my older, more conservative colleagues the importance of developing each young reader to his full potential. Yet the branch librarians allowed me to set up the collections and put up with me because I was young and enthusiastic. However, I know most of them thought it would be a lot easier for them to point out the locations of requested titles if every book were in its proper place. Fortunately, because I was so intent on the progress being made with the young people I never realized how much my activities disturbed some of the "ladies" on the branch staffs. I got some intimation of this one night when a hesitant boy came into one of the branch libraries. I engaged him in conversation and undertook to help him find a book he would enjoy. Suddenly I remembered seeing a new copy of Lowell Thomas' *Count Luckner, The Sea Devil* on a special shelf behind the librarian's desk. I hurried over to ask if I might have it for the boy, and she replied, "Oh, no. It's a new book and this is such a rainy night!"

In the meantime a few invitations were coming in for book talks in the schools. I was given my own telephone. Then one staff member in each branch was designated as the "YA" librarian. Work with young adults was gaining stature. These advances forced me to think through what I was attempting to do. I needed to formulate a philosophy, to set up proper goals, and to work with the branch YA assistants to implement these goals.

In my preliminary thinking I realized that work with young adults is as simple as ABC. All there is to it is: (A) a sympathetic understanding of all adolescents; (B) firsthand knowledge of all the books that would interest them; and (C) mastery of the technique of getting these books into the hands of the adolescents. Simple.

Teenagers (*The "Beasts"*)

Who are young adults? They are people in their teens for whom there is no adequate nomenclature. For years librarians have searched for a term that would best describe them. "Adolescents" is too biological and should be reserved for occasions when adults speak to adults on a professional level. "Teenagers," beside being a bit undignified, may sound patronizing or scornful and does not seem to include the more mature sixteen- to nineteen-year-olds. "Young People" has been used in many libraries, as has "Youth," but in the minds of the public both terms often mean children rather than people of high-school age and so call for endless clarification. As a result, the Young Adult Services of the American Library Association (ALA) has officially adopted the term "Young Adults" to define its clientele.

What are these young adults like? They are people in their teens who have outgrown the role of children and have become the eager, anxious understudies of adults. They are Angie Morrow of *Seventeenth Summer*, experiencing the poignancy of first love; they are Ken McLaughlin or Jody Baxter, learning through sorrow and pain that one must face up to life no matter what it demands; they are Holden Caulfield, the insecure; Dobie Gillis, the clown; or Cress Delahanty, gradually emerging from chrysalis to butterfly.[1] En masse they look as alike as the clothes they wear. They speak the same jargon and conform to the prevailing styles in dress and conduct, yet each is a distinct individual.

Someone has said that there is no time in life when a greater adjustment must be made than in the transition from childhood to adolescence. Everyone loves a baby. If he cries, adults come running to see what the trouble is. His bright sayings are repeated in his hearing and he may have almost anything he wants. But when he becomes an adolescent he is suddenly expected to get hold of himself. It is disgraceful to cry. No one will stand between him and trouble, for he is expected to meet his problems and solve them on his own. His cuteness suddenly has become impudence and he bores and irritates people who once doted on him.

In the face of all this it is no wonder that he is insecure. But because he is proud, he puts up a good front. On the bus en route to school he makes as much noise as possible, as if to notify all and sundry that he is present and going strong (only adults have enough self-assurance to keep quiet). Boys wear their hair in the style they have learned is most objectionable to adults. Girls go into hysterics over the current musical

---

This section was first published as "It All Started with Prometheus," *California Librarian*, April 1960, 93–96. *Ed.*

sensation. Clowning, funny hats, big badges, impudence, indifference, or even membership in a gang are often little more than manifestations of a feeling of insecurity.

Teenagers, the understudies of adults, wonder what kind of adults they will become and search constantly for patterns. When a model they have selected as perfect turns out to have feet of clay, they discard it and seek a new model until they learn that there is no perfect pattern for personality and that each of them must form his own with this man's wit, that one's charm, another's character and poise, and so on.

For the adolescent there is black and white but little shading of gray. On Monday Poe was a very dull and overrated poet; but that was before the reading of "The Haunted Palace." Now, on Tuesday, he is the greatest poet in the world. One teacher is the fountain of all wisdom; another is a drip, a square, a washout, or whatever the current term for absolute zero may be. To young people, right is right and wrong is wrong, and so they believe there are simple remedies for the complicated ills of society.

The teenager longs to be clever, different, and original, but does not dare break with any of his peers' conventions in dress or speech or manners. He is a bundle of contradictions to himself, his family, and his friends. With all his raucous, objectionable ways, the adolescent is at heart idealistic and would gladly dedicate himself to big causes. He is moved by heroism, self-sacrifice, and devotion to duty.

Only those adults he trusts and believes in know the adolescent as he really is and the rewards of his fine friendship. He is often frank to the point of embarrassment with the parent, teacher, or librarian he truly likes, pointing out to them their mistakes in conduct or dress so they may more nearly measure up to the highest standards. Best of all, he will comment with unreserved candor on books the librarian may have selected for him.

Nothing distresses the young adult more than the sight of an adult attempting to be young again. He does not want his mother and father to romp around with people their own age, and certainly not with the younger set. He wishes his adults to be dignified above everything else, for in his youthful insecurity dignity is the quality he covets most. The soundest approach to the adolescent is to treat him as though he were a reasonable, dignified, mature person. This kind of relationship, coupled with enthusiasm for books on the part of the librarian, will open up the world of ideas to many young adults who may never have become readers otherwise or who would have read on a level below their capacity to understand and enjoy.

There is no age group more important than the young adults, who in a few short years will be guiding the destiny of this nation, deciding among other things whether to drop the bomb or to use atomic energy for man's good. Fortunately they are impressionable, more open to ideas, more ready to listen to suggestions than are adults, and they are more likely to become thoughtful readers.

The YA Librarians (*Training*)

After the atom was split and Hiroshima was bombed, I read countless articles and books by thoughtful writers calling attention to the dangerous lag between man's knowledge and his emotional and cultural development. They convinced me that the destruction of the earth and the suicide of the human race were distinctly possible unless man became truly civilized. I was sure that the ideas to be found in books would help if the books were read, and I felt that as far as the adolescent was concerned, the library could not play a passive role, that the librarian should do more than just wait on these people and answer their questions. More young people needed to come to the library for voluntary reading and those who came should be introduced to better and better books until they were reading with enjoyment on an ever-widening range of stimulating and inspiring subjects. I realized that clever schemes, friendliness, attractive book lists, and gadgets alone would be ineffective without assistants trained to win the confidence of teenagers and to develop them as readers.

In other words, the training of the assistant has always seemed to me to be the key to selling the idea of reading. None of my assistants knew much about readers' advisory service to young adults. Even the library-school graduates were sadly lacking. They knew how to catalog books and answer reference questions, and some of them were fairly good at evaluating books. But most of them had little conception of the adolescent; they did not know how to talk to young people about books or how to develop a reader. Far too many of them had failed to develop themselves as readers. When they were assigned to work out on the floor of a busy branch, they would become paralyzed by such simple requests as, "Will you get me two good love stories?" or "What have you got that I would like?" So I began an in-service training program that had its repercussions.

Each hapless new assistant was initiated into this program on his first day at the Pratt Library when he came to my office after a general

---

This section is taken from "A Long Way to Tipperary" in *The Library Reaches Out*, ed. K. M. Coplan and E. Castagna, New York: Oceana, 1965. *Ed.*

indoctrination by the personnel office. During our conference I asked him to imagine himself in a situation where as a readers' advisor for young adults he had no problems. In this ideal setup there would be no apathy on the part of his patrons, the book stock would be completely adequate, and the young people would read whatever he suggested. Under such circumstances, what fields of reading would he emphasize? In other words, what do we mean when we say we want young adults to be good readers? When should we feel that a young person is on his way to becoming a superior reader?

Although these questions almost always produced a kind of consternation and often elicited some amazing replies, they did start a train of thought and paved the way for a discussion of goals. After some prodding on my part we usually agreed that our ultimate objective was to interest our readers in books that would help them become citizens of the world. This meant that they should come to understand through their reading that all men are brothers, that "no man is an island," that each is a responsible "piece of the main." We further agreed that our secondary goal was to concern our readers with the implications of citizenship in these United States. This meant introducing books that bring history alive and give the reader pride in his heritage, and books that deal with the problems that beset the nation and the responsibility of the individual citizen.

Subsidiary to these two goals was reading for personal pleasure on hundreds of varied subjects. I hastened to explain that no readers' advisor could lead all his readers to the big goals we hoped to achieve, but that each reader should be developed to his full potential if possible. For the younger, inexperienced reader, the important books were those simple stories that would awaken in him love for reading, especially stories dealing with matters that concerned him in his limited world. Each reader was to be met on his own ground and taken as far along the way as possible, with his cooperation and enjoyment.

It was pointed out to the new assistant, if he did not know it already, that the adolescent is almost always led to an interest in good reading through his emotions rather than his intellect. Stories about a Chinese girl whose love for a man is not returned, a German boy fighting and dying on the Western Front in World War I, a Zulu father keeping a lonely vigil on a mountain top the night his son is executed, are far more effective in promulgating the idea that all men are brothers than sound scientific disquisitions on the same subject.[2] *To Kill a Mockingbird* [Lee, 1960] or *Black Like Me* [Griffin, 1961] might cause a young person to identify with the suffering of others and lead him to abominate racial injustice. The adolescent is more likely to adopt a point of view as his own when he gets inside another's skin and loves, hates, and suffers with the character portrayed. Of course, to promote understanding through books it is essential that the librarian know at firsthand novels, biographies, dramas—any creative writing that will interest the adolescent and increase his understanding.

After the new assistant and I had agreed on these aims, he was asked to check the latest edition of *Books for the Teen Age*, compiled annually by the New York Public Library. Here some two thousand titles, old and new, are listed, about 80 per cent adult and 20 per cent teenage, under subjects of interest to teenagers. Seldom had any new assistant read as many as a hundred of the titles, though many of them were books any well-read person would be expected to know.

At this point we could agree that the assistant would not go far in promoting world citizenship and general enrichment on seventy or so titles, many of which had been assigned reading matter in high school and college and were now dim in memory. To help him become the readers' advisor I assumed he wished to be, I would check the New York Public Library list for titles it was most essential to read and ask the assistant to call my office as soon as he had read any ten of the checked titles so that we could set up a date to discuss them. This procedure would continue until he had read three hundred books from the list. Books he had read before joining our staff would not have to be discussed.

This program was not too popular. To those who had read almost nothing it was suggested that four books a week would be fine and two a week barely acceptable. Some of the assistants were unhappy, to say the least, and some branch librarians thought it was pretty hard to ask innocent young librarians to read a lot of books. Even the administration worried. A few of the new assistants transferred to fields where heavy reading was not required, a few resigned, but surprisingly, a majority stuck it out and eventually were grateful for the training. Some even asked to continue the individual book discussions after they had passed the three-hundred mark. The admiration and respect they inspired in their readers was rewarding ("Have you read *all* the books in the library?"); the staffs they worked with recognized their competence; the ensuing promotions were rewarding. But above all, they could see that the training program made sense. As a rule, all the books the assistant had read circulated constantly, while those he had not read sat on the shelves. The satisfied customers became friends who trustfully expected more and more suggestions. And almost always, to his surprise, the assistant found his own mind enriched by the reading he was doing.

It was my purpose in our discussions of each ten books read to teach the assistant to evaluate books, first for literary merit and then for usefulness in the development of a reader—to show him that many books that would never be classics could afford teenagers a great deal of happiness, enrich their experience, and broaden their points of view. We discussed ways of interesting a reader in a book he was likely to enjoy and titles to suggest as follow-ups if the reader wished to pursue the subject. Honesty and the folly of overselling a book were stressed. Prudery and overzealous censorship were ruled out. Ways of concentrating, reading rapidly, and skimming judiciously were pointed out. Suggestions were made for budgeting time so that it would be possible to combine wide reading with a social life. I suggested to girls who shared an apartment that it might be better to cut short long-winded conversations with each other about the men they had known in their past, instead employing that time to read and so have something to discuss with the men in their present and future.

Although this individual training took a great deal of time, it was more effective than a class for all new assistants would have been since in the conferences each assistant was compelled to do his own thinking and speak for himself. Individual talents were more easily detected and individual weaknesses minimized. Moreover, the rapport between us was better than it would have been in the more formal relation of a teacher standing before a class.

After our conferences ended and the assistant became a member of the "300 club," he became responsible for his reading. Almost invariably he kept going under his own steam, but if his steam pressure died down a bit, the young people with their trustful, confident expectations would start it up again.

The YA Librarian at Work

There is a theory generally accepted by librarians that people who come to the library know what they want, that if they need help they will ask for it, and that they resent the librarian who approaches them. This simply is not true of most adolescents seeking recreational reading. They do not know what they want. Most of them have a very limited acquaintance indeed with the world of adult books. Many have read a few books that delighted them and have come to the library for a "good book." They do not know enough about the authors of adult books to have any idea who the "good" writers are. They look over the

The above section was first published as "Introducing Young People to a Life-Long Pleasure" in *School Library Journal*, January 15, 1958, 218–21. *Ed.*

shelves filled with thousands of books and finally settle on one. If it proves to be a dud, they are discouraged, and if the experience is repeated, they will probably seek other forms of recreation.

When a book proves interesting the reader is likely to go through the entire output of its author, whose collected works may not be nearly as interesting or worthwhile as titles the young-adult librarian could suggest. Moreover, the teenager has latent interests of which he may be unaware. He does not know that he might be tremendously interested in art or sailing or satire, for he does not know about Stone's *Lust for Life* [1937], Heyerdahl's *Kon-Tiki* [1950], or Orwell's *Animal Farm* [1946]. He has no idea of the amazing resources of the world of books for his enjoyment. Certainly the teenager should not be beset by insistent busybodies, but the librarian who knows the art of salesmanship can become a respected, valued guide for the adolescent confused in a maze of unfamiliar books.

How does the young-adult librarian win the confidence of teenagers? By being friendly, by setting people at ease, by going to some trouble to be helpful. I cannot explain this any more than I can tell how someone walks into a room full of strangers and establishes rapport with them, or how a woman intrigues a new man at a cocktail party. I do know that an outgoing librarian who likes people can do it. Before long he convinces teenagers that he has an uncanny knack for selecting "good" books. Many years ago when I was in the most reduced financial circumstances, I went to the basement of a large department store to purchase a dress. A saleslady standing nearby watched me going through the dresses on a rack until she could estimate my taste, looked me over for size, and without a word disappeared to return with a little number that was exactly what I wanted. I bought it and returned when I had to have another dress and could get together $10 or $12. Each time I appeared she was glad to see me and asked about the last dress I had bought. When I told her the type of dress I needed, she recalled the color of my accessories and that I already had one red and one blue dress. She would not allow me to purchase an unbecoming garment and was determined that I would have the best the bargain basement had to offer. She never failed me. If she had told me to buy a bustle, even with my figure, I would have believed that she knew the latest styles, that she had reason to believe I would look well in one, and that if I gave it a try I would be convinced. A young-adult librarian works exactly like my saleslady.

An hour or so before school is out and the students descend on the public library the young-adult librarian should put his house in order, seeing that attractive displays are well stocked with books. He should look over the shelves to check for titles in demand, for unusual titles likely to fill a special need, and for popular missing titles that might be supplied from adult departments. As he scans the YA collection he should look to see what good love stories are in, what sport stories, novels, and biographies of social significance. This saves searching later while an impatient patron waits for the librarian to have an inspiration or is frustrated when a title enthusiastically recommended cannot be found. A quick glance over the shelves in the adult departments will often yield bait for unusual interests, such as a book about the different makes of cars, one on drawing cartoons, or a special cookbook. This is also the time to collect in one place all the volumes of international short stories for Miss Jones's current assignment, so that during the busy hours the librarian will not have to suspend the readers' advisory service to search for them.

In the few minutes remaining before the teenagers storm in, the librarian should repair the damage the day has done to his appearance. He should put out of his mind any worries and pressing problems he may have. No matter if his fellow staff members have been unpleasant, if the impending personnel shortages are critical, if his mother-in-law is coming for a long visit—all these things must be forgotten temporarily so that the librarian can present himself as well groomed, rested, and full of ideas. As the young people enter the room, of course, his interest will shift his weight from seat to feet.

The librarian cannot possibly remember all the books previously recommended to readers, but he can usually recall a title given out in an effort to lure a merry-go-round reader into another interest, or an adult love story given to a girl whose main interest has been teenage romances. To meet such a teenage reader with "How did you like *Mrs. Mike?*" will win the teenager's confidence when he realizes the librarian remembers the title of the book he borrowed and is interested in his reaction to it.[3] If a librarian can carry in his head the special interests of his readers and keep posted on new books coming out in special fields; if he can greet a reader, holding in his hand a long-awaited book, with "I was hoping you would come in today. Look what I have for you," it will warm the hearts of his patrons. The readers' advisor who makes his clientele feel that he especially keeps their interests in mind, is not pretending. He really does just that, letting faces come to mind when he is reading a new book and welcoming any idea that will broaden the reading of his patrons. These are not cheap tricks to win the friendship of teenagers; they are effective weapons to dispel apathy and persuade more people to enrich their lives with books.

There are different types of readers and they must be approached in different ways. There is the thirteen-year-old boy so shy he will run if an aggressive librarian bears down on him. It is a good idea to straighten shelves in his vicinity and to ask casually, "Did you ever read *Hot Rod?"* [4] If the librarian is relaxed and casual, the boy may soon unconsciously reveal his reading tastes. Whenever a title is suggested, watch the eyes of the teenager. A dull glance indicates that not only is the preferred book unappealing, but so are all books on that subject. If a girl who "doesn't like to read" comes in with a friend who is a reader, be sure she sees a popular teenage romance depicting a typical teenager on its cover and ask the friend who reads for her opinion of the book. If the friend comes through with the predictable effusive recommendation, the nonreader is likely to give the book a try.

With new readers it is best not to ask questions and probe for interests. Suggest generally popular titles and watch facial expressions. Instead of "May I help you?" ask "Have you read this book?" Love is the most popular subject with older girls and a book jacket featuring a modern girl is usually better bait for a reluctant reader than one with a lady in a hoopskirt or a rugged pioneer woman. For the shy reader it is a good idea to present three or four books in an interesting manner and suggest that he look them over and put those he does not want on the table. Then walk off and leave the reader to himself. When the librarian is new in a community and the teenagers are reserved, it may be a good idea to be friendly and not mention books on the initial contacts.

After the reading habit is set, after a relationship of mutual confidence has been established, the librarian can begin to consider hurdles. The young girl who has read teenage romances long enough should be introduced to adult love stories. These can be recommended with quick thumbnail sketches that present a girl in love who has a problem. Sometimes it is well to say the books are adult; sometimes it is better to wait until the girl in question has read and liked two or three such titles, and then commend her for her more adult taste. For many girls the next step after romance is biographies of women and girls, which may better he called "true stories" than biographies.

Boys have more interests than girls and do not need to be led carefully from one type of reading to another. With them it is more a question of deepening and maturing an interest and introducing new fields for exploration. After readers take these first few hurdles, the librarian will find that the best readers read on about the same level as the librarian and that some of them can read almost anything the librarian has liked.

If there is one secret to successful floor work, it is the reading of the librarian. Nothing can substitute for it. After a book is read, the librarian can work out a presentation for it and experiment until he is sure that it is effective. In speaking of a book to a prospective reader it is always well to avoid adjectives, particularly "interesting," exciting," and "well-written." Get the story moving with nouns and verbs. Be brief. Do not give away the plot. Be fair to both the book and the reader, i.e., do not overrecommend the book, and no matter how fine the story is, do not press it upon a teenager who may find it dull. Above all, be interesting. For example:

"Thor Heyerdahl believed Polynesia was settled by Peruvians. To prove his theory he persuaded five men to help him build a balsa raft exactly like the Peruvians might have built centuries ago. Then they all settled down on the raft with their supplies, a radio, and a parrot to sail four thousand miles across the Pacific [Heyerdahl, *Kon-Tiki*]."

"An old-guard Communist awaiting execution in prison thinks back over his past, remembering the girl he loved and the others he had betrayed for the sake of the party, trying desperately to reassure himself he had been right [Koestler, *Darkness at Noon*]."

"A white reporter darkened his skin by taking drugs and sitting under a sunlamp. Then he shaved his head and in the guise of a Negro traveled through the Deep South. He found out what it was like to have to ride in the back of buses, to be on a lonely road at night with no place to sleep, and to be unable to get a drink of water when he was in the white section of a town [Griffin, *Black Like Me*]."

A few don'ts:

Don't play favorites or encourage sentimental attachments. Cordial relationships should be built as far as possible on a mutual pleasure in reading.

Don't impose an opinion. Let the teenager think his thoughts and feel free to express them. Show him how to refer to the *Book Review Digest* and measure his opinions against the critics rather than lead him to believe the librarian is infallible. This does not mean that with tact and understanding the librarian may not help the teenager clarify his thinking.

Don't conclude a book is popular because it circulates. One of the most important features of floor work is the discussion of a book with the reader when he returns it. Ask constantly for reactions. The adolescent reader is pleased to be asked for his opinion, and the librarian needs to listen if he wishes to be an effective readers' advisor. In the discussion of a book recently read, the librarian has an opportunity to develop in young people sharper critical faculties and a better basis for enjoyment and to introduce to them new and related fields of reading.

Don't be too anxious to teach young adults to shift for themselves until they have made the acquaintance of many adult authors and have widened their interests. If the teenager continually asks for help in selecting books, the librarian has an opportunity to accelerate his reading and to introduce fields of interest that might never occur to him. Insisting on self-reliance too early is sometimes a way of passing the buck. To ask "Have you looked in the catalog?" in a certain tone can kill the germ of interest in a special book or in a new field of reading.

Don't take books away from young people. If they select books from adult departments, let them have them. Librarians are not policemen. However, the librarian should give the teenager planning to read a frank book a point of view for reading it, calling attention to the book's social implications, its weaknesses and strong points, and explaining what the author meant to imply.

Don't restrict young adults to the YA collection. While we stand behind the books included in young-adult collections, the young-adult librarian is, after all, introducing the adolescent to adult reading in the hope of transferring him to the adult section permanently in the near future, and an increasing use of adult titles makes the eventual transfer of the reader more natural and normal.

Don't think that all this, however difficult it may be, is not the most exciting and rewarding work in the world.

"The Rulers of the Queen's Navee"
(*Thoughts on Supervision*)

My husband, who was the principal of a big high school with a very large faculty, once told me that when a teacher came into his office to report what a stupid, lazy class he had and to say with some satisfaction that he had failed 50 per cent of them, that teacher was rated 50 per cent effective, for by his own admission, he had been unable to teach half of his class. While the teacher had probably sized the class up correctly, he had failed to remedy a bad situation. I often thought of what my husband said when someone under my supervision failed to qualify. I knew there was a very good chance that I had failed as a supervisor. This philosophy seemed to me to apply also to a branch librarian I knew. There was always a problem as to whom we would send to work with young adults at her branch. She was a very bright and efficient librarian who usually rated her assistants very low. It was difficult to argue with her as the failings she pointed out in her staff were evident, but all too often librarians on her staff resigned or asked for a transfer. That branch librarian was an excellent diagnostician but a failure at prescribing cures. A good supervisor not only detects weaknesses, but also finds ways to eliminate them.

To do this calls not only for understanding of people and a high degree of intelligence, but also for a lot of moral courage. All of us would like to avoid unpleasant situations. I don't know which is worse, a soggy handkerchief and tears or a flushed face and anger. The very possibility of facing either makes us all too often put off an unpleasant conference that should be held.

It is not fair to let an employee think he is performing well when he is not. No one under our supervision should ever be surprised at a low rating sheet or puzzled that he was not given an expected promotion. The annual rating sheet should be a summary of what has been said all along and no one should ever ask us, "Why wasn't I told?" Whatever might hold someone back from promotion should be discussed and remedied if possible before the employee is passed over. Probably the best way of telling someone the unpleasant facts of life is to convince him that we are sincerely interested in his rising in the profession, that we are impressed by his energy and intelligence, but that we find one or two matters blocking his progress and would like to suggest to him ways of overcoming these obstacles. Or we might say that we have an impression of the employee that is worrying us, and that before a final rating is made, we would like to discuss the matter to find out if the impression is correct. In such a conference the supervisor should make definite suggestions for improvement and persuade the assistant to try them. Whatever happens, the supervisor should never lose his temper or be sharp, and the conference should be completely private.

The young assistant not only needs correction, he also needs encouragement and constant stimulation. We owe it to our staffs to bring each member to the realization of his highest potential. However, on almost every staff there are one or two who have already reached their potential—mediocrity—and cannot go beyond it. These people, often over forty years old, are appealing, kindly, useful individuals who were created unequal. I believe in making life as pleasant as possible for them; I do not believe in calling them in to discuss their inadequacies when the only result would be to make them unhappy. If these people are ambitious and feel they are being passed over, the supervisor should call them in for one conference, where in as kindly a way as possible he gives them to understand that though they are appreciated, they are not likely to be given heavier duties nor will they be pressured to improve their performance. However, if a more exact definition of inadequacies is demanded, it should be given. Whether an employee is mediocre or superior, he should always be clear in his mind as to his rating in the opinion of his supervisor.

How often we supervisors look back with nostalgia to the time when we were rank-and-file librarians, working on the floor with people and books. Those were the days! How often we have secretly prayed, "Oh Lord, let me shuffle off these responsibilities and be free to share the pleasures of reading with patrons. I don't want to be 'the ruler of the Queen's navee.'"[5] But in the end a good supervisor knows that one of life's greatest satisfactions is to see the people working under him wake up and start going places, and all because the quality of his supervision made the difference in them.

So many library-school graduates and others begin their professional careers with the general idea of doing a good enough job to earn a good salary—to give value received for pay received—when if a fire were lit under them, they would become outstanding. In my library-school classes I often have two or three young people who seem to me to have special gifts and abilities of which they themselves are unaware. I sometimes write for the personnel file, "This girl has the ability to speak and write and establish rapport with people. She might become something special in the library world if she comes under the right supervisor." Because truly strong and inspiring supervisors are so scarce, many promising young librarians wither in the bud.

We have said the young assistant needs correction, that he needs encouragement and stimulation. More than that, he needs inspiration. Unless the supervisor is dedicated, he will have difficulty inspiring others to rise to great heights. We must feel that the job is bigger than we are, that it calls for all the energy, time, thought, and devotion we have, and that it is worth all we give it. We need to refresh ourselves ever so often by reading books about people who have felt this way about their work—such books as Jesse Stuart's *The Thread That Runs So True* [1949], Agnes de Mille's *Dance to the Piper* [1952], Kaufman's *Up the Down Staircase* [1964], and Hart's *Act One* [1959]. When someone asked Dr. Spock what he would like to be if he could come back for a second life on earth, he replied, "I would want to return as a young Negro man so I could dedicate myself heart and soul to something."[6] He meant, I think, that the very act of dedication does more than benefit mankind—it redounds to the good of the one dedicated. Like the quality of mercy, it is twice blessed. Certainly, if I could come back, I would want to be a librarian.

When one's work is bigger than he is, he constantly grows by trying to measure up to his vision. And if one is a person of spiritual stature,

it is reflected in his relation to those he supervises. Some evidences of
this are:

1. *He is not a glory hunter.*

Because the supervisor is not thinking of himself, he is not constantly
searching for personal recognition but in every way possible passes on
glory and credit to people down the line. He does not assign work to
underlings and have it published under his name. He is more likely to
work behind the scenes and to push the younger assistants out into the
spotlight to accept the applause.

2. *He does not nourish hurt feelings.*

I once heard a minister say that a sensitive person was a selfish person
always feeling his own pulse. In the minds of both supervisor and
assistants should be the idea that the work is what is important and that
criticism and frank opinions are expressed to further the effectiveness of
the work. This frankness should come from both directions—the supervisor and the supervised. The assistant should feel free to speak his mind
as long as he has the success of a project at heart. This can mean that if
he thinks the supervisor is making a mistake, he will feel free to say so
and will expect to be listened to as respectfully as he listens to the
supervisor when his mistakes are pointed out. I remember one such
lesson one of my assistants gave me. For our high-school book-reviewing
pamphlet one of the rules we laid down was that the teenagers could
review any adult book they chose as long as it had been purchased by
the Pratt Library. Things went along smoothly for years until a student,
in good faith, submitted a review of *Studs Lonigan* [Farrell, 1932–35]. I
feared parents and teachers would object and suggested that the assistant who sponsored the publication put the matter in the hands of the
high-school students who made up the board of the publication. Before
she did this she thought over my advice and came to my office to say,
"Mrs. Edwards, you are passing the buck to the youngsters." How right
she was! I found the courage to accept my responsibility, to abide by our
agreement with the teenagers, to publish the review, and to defend the
stand to the one upset teacher who called. Each assistant should be so
identified with projects on which the staff works and so anxious to keep
the ship sailing that he will feel concerned enough to offer helpful
criticism when he thinks it is necessary.

3. *He is not on the defensive but is honest enough and secure enough to admit a mistake.*

There is a temptation to feel that since we have risen above the ranks,
we are pretty good—that we know the answers, that we point the way.

This creates in the staff a feeling of hostility, a glee in proving us wrong, and hosannas when we bite the dust. Utter honesty is disarming. When a mistake is made, it should be freely admitted without too many alibis. Such an attitude will bring assistants to the rescue rather than the attack. No one should be a supervisor who is afraid he will betray a weakness. Few of us were made supervisors because of our many strong points, but rather because despite our weaknesses, hopefully, we have enough strength to keep out of the red.

4. He makes each member of his staff one of the crew.

The supervisor should formulate goals and plans for working toward them and should be sure each member of his staff understands and subscribes to them. Then each assistant should be made to feel he is a member of a crew that is sailing the boat to a certain destination. My parents made us children feel that way. If we bought six cows, we all watched to see how profitable they would be. If one died, we all grieved. When the cotton crop failed, we all cut down expenditures. We knew the state of the family finances and trimmed our sails accordingly. When I went off to college, my father gave me a checkbook—not an allowance. He told me what the bank balance was and instructed me to use my own judgment about what I bought. He knew I was a dedicated member of the crew and would think twice before I rocked the boat. The assistant should feel the same way and should be given opportunities to help make decisions rather than be treated as a galley slave who obeys orders and rows when the whip is cracked. If a supervisor heads a big community program, it is a good idea to have at least one meeting annually where the program is examined critically, project by project, and where the staff helps decide what might be dropped, revamped, or replaced, and what might be the nature of the replacements.

In the consideration of controversial titles, especially for young-adult collections, it is excellent training to have each assistant read them before discussing them in a meeting for value, appeal, possible effect on the community, and finally, rejection or purchase. This is one of the best ways I know to teach book selection; no one can ever say he was steam-rollered by his supervisor, for he had a voice in making the decision, and from the experience he may learn how to take a characterful and informed stand with his patrons. However, the supervisor should be the one to handle any ticklish situation where library policy is under attack.

A supervisor should be secure enough to have no hesitation about asking his crew to help solve a problem. Often my group thought a problem through and came up with a better solution than I would ever have found alone. One of my outstanding assistants at the Pratt Library was a Negro girl who was concerned that her ghetto community learn the joy of reading.[7] When a rock 'n roll radio station offered the library time on its program, she cut short her vacation to set up the program. She invited the teenagers of her branch community to participate in a discussion of books on the radio and received all the applications she could use. A few months after she had established the program she came into my office to say she was discouraged. Each week she had taken the disadvantaged youngsters who could not afford carfare to the station in her car. They had read the books she had assigned ahead of time, but because they spoke so incorrectly it took hours to cut a tape suitable for broadcasting. I could not think how she might solve this problem and suggested she present it to the young-adult assistants at the next meeting. When she did, someone came up with the idea that she restrict membership in the discussion group to those who spoke acceptable English. This solved her problem and offered an incentive to the young people of the community to try to speak better English. It was the group, not I, who had the idea, and the fact that they solved the problem made them feel identified with the project. This was not the only time that the assistants helped me decide what should be done.

When each assistant is a member of the crew the more experienced will feel a responsibility for helping to break in the new librarians. If an inexperienced young librarian can be sent to work with a gifted oldtimer, he will often catch fire. Older staff members have often dropped by my office to tell me what they thought was troubling a new person or to rejoice with me that he was so very promising.

Under this heading—making each member of the staff one of the crew—comes the need to allow the crew to try out new ideas whenever possible. Of course, some of the ideas are so far out we need to say no and explain very clearly why we say no. However, we should give the go-ahead sign when we are in doubt, for it is important to encourage initiative. I have been surprised time and again to see a plan work well when I was fairly sure it would never get off the ground. Even a failure can teach the assistant a lot. It is often a good idea to withhold a decision until the suggested project is discussed with the other assistants at their next meeting. Let the one with the idea present it to the group, and by the time it has been inspected for bugs either the original idea will be improved and seem acceptable or its originator will be convinced that it should be dropped and will not feel that a ruthless dictator never gave him a chance. Sharing decision-making welds a group together and accelerates individual development. This is not to say that in important matters affecting the system the supervisor should not take the responsibility for decisions.

5. *He is not afraid to establish standards and expect the staff to live up to them.*

In these days when librarians are so scarce, many supervisors go easy. The administration sometimes worries when people are expected to work very hard. Easier jobs with good pay are available elsewhere. I am thinking especially of the areas of librarianship concerned with the promotion of reading. What does a supervisor do with a new assistant innocent of books? In my thirty years at the Pratt Library almost every assistant who came to me was unread, that is, they had read *Silas Marner, Ivanhoe*, and the books assigned in high school and college, and sometimes about fifty on their own. In my library-school classes I hand out a list of one hundred titles that includes such authors as Pearl Buck, Remarque, Wilder, Baldwin, Aldous Huxley, Steinbeck, Dostoevski, and Hemingway, and ask each student to read five books. This is virgin territory to many of them and they scurry about to get their reading done. It is hard to believe how little they have read.

When such new assistants landed under my supervision at the Pratt Library, it was no soft landing. I always attempted to inspire them to read to improve themselves and for the good of their young patrons. When all else failed I explained to a girl who would not catch fire that in all likelihood she would get married, but on the outside chance that she might not it would be a good idea to insure herself for happy single blessedness. I told her an unmarried career woman with stunning clothes, a new car, and a beautiful apartment is the envy of many an overworked housewife, but the most pitiful woman in the world is the old-maid librarian who lives meagerly in an economy apartment with another librarian in a run-of-the-mill neighborhood. I advised her that if she thought there was the remotest possibility she would not marry a man of means, she should plan to make a very good salary indeed, and that the way to begin was to get a recommendation for a promotion from me, which would be impossible unless she read enough books to qualify as a first-rate young-adult librarian.

Although I killed off a few assistants this way, I think the library, the city, and the assistants benefited in the long run. I came to decide that more can be accomplished with ten experts than with thirty drones. We must remember, too, that the really able new assistants wish to be trained and resent a supervisor who is too easygoing. Those who want to take it easy may not like us, which is a bit of too bad. It is absolutely essential to have the respect of one's staff, and this comes only when one measures up as a person and as an administrator. Everyone wants to be loved, but the supervisor will not be loved until he is first respected. Respect is earned. Love is a gift that cannot be earned but is often the by-product of respect.

I accidentally tuned in on a TV program some time ago and I heard David Lilienthal being interviewed.[8] He said something that sums up in a sentence what I have written about over a number of pages. He said the highest quality of supervision is the ability to release talent. This set me to thinking of Joseph L. Wheeler and what it meant to work under his supervision. He took me on his staff when I was a school-teacher who had been fired for bawling out a supervisor and directed my uncontrolled temper and energy into creative channels. He found Kate Coplan in the preparations department and made her the renowned head of exhibits. He saw in a secretary qualities that he could turn into administrative abilities and schooled her to become the strong head of the branch system. He was so obsessed with the love of reading and with persuading the people of Baltimore to share this love with him that he left no stone unturned. He expected his professional staff to keep Baltimore's reading problems in mind and to think of new ways to enlighten the city. He demanded that every staff member serve every patron graciously—for reading's sake. He was a distinguished captain of the Queen's navee. Working for him meant constant application, grasping things you thought beyond your reach, developing talents you did not know you had. May his tribe increase!

✄ III ✄

Branching Out

In the Schools

The Baltimore high schools in the thirties were closed to visits from the public library. The superintendent of public instruction had told Dr. Wheeler that he did not intend for broom salesmen or any other outsiders to take up time in the schools. Nevertheless, I determined to attempt a gradual infiltration of the high schools. I cultivated individual teachers and school librarians and found an influential Pratt co-worker to say a good word for me to a supervisor. Despite all this, after ten years I was making only about ten classroom and assembly talks a year. Then out of the blue I was offered a position in a western city where I would be in charge of all young-adult work in both the public-library and the public-school system, under a librarian I knew and at a salary that seemed fabulous in those days.[1]

Since Dr. Wheeler was out of town at the time, I wrote a letter of resignation, thanking him for his many kindnesses. I was disposing of my few belongings when he returned to Baltimore and prevailed on me to remain. He promised to help resolve certain problems and was as good as his word. Among other things, we went to see the assistant superintendent of schools, who agreed to let me visit classes in the

---

This section is taken from "A Long Way to Tipperary," previously published in *The Library Reaches Out*, ed. K. M. Coplan and E. Castagna, New York: Oceana, 1965. *Ed.*

31

schools and promised that he would write Dr. Wheeler a letter confirming our conversation. It was not until several weeks later that I learned by accident that the letter, when it came, was a listing of what I could not do and that I was very little better off than before. Since I had not seen the letter, I pretended I knew nothing about it. Instead I went to see the principals of the various schools, told them that the assistant superintendent had agreed I might make talks on books in the high schools, and made it clear that I was available.

Gradually the invitations began to come in. Having learned about book talks on a visit to the New York Public Library, I began to prepare them. Any request for a visit was accepted, no matter what difficulties stood in the way. One February four high schools I had despaired of ever working with asked me to talk to all their classes. On the last Friday afternoon of that month I sank into a streetcar seat, clutching my modest collection of well-worn book talks with which I had regaled classes for seventy full periods that month. I was in the high schools for sure and I was careful to stay there.

No teacher ever asked me for a special book list that I did not prepare. As for the school librarians, there was nothing too good for them. I placed reserves on the books they wanted and held them on a special shelf until they could come in for them on Saturdays. I called their attention to books and magazine articles of interest and helped them find defenses when some book was under fire. If they needed help in compiling or annotating reading lists, I gave it. They, in turn, were good to me and defended me if any criticism arose in connection with a school visit. They were my friends and working with them was a rewarding experience.

When a director of school libraries was appointed, she and I worked hand in glove. She made out a year's schedule for our visits, which made it possible for us to plan ahead. She and I wrote articles in collaboration, attended each other's meetings, and felt we were working toward a common goal. Never in our school visits did I allow the public library to seem to be in competition with school libraries. We made it clear that as long as the students read books, it did not matter where they borrowed them. Pratt librarians always suggested to the students that they try to borrow the books we discussed from their school libraries first, and then when the supply was exhausted, they could try the Pratt Library.

Eventually the "Speakers' Pool" came into existence. It was composed of ten or so YA branch assistants whom I had trained to give effective book talks. As a rule, we spent a week in each of the city's large high schools, then covered as many ninth grades in the junior high schools as time allowed. We spoke in the school library to two classes each period, and covered every period of the day except the one reserved for lunch. Two of us went together each day, and we attempted to arrange the schedule so that no one gave book talks for more than two days in any given week.

When we visited schools, we took along copies of *Speaking of Books*, which was a listing of over two hundred titles of books on which our collective talks were based. Each student was given a copy of the list. We opened each session by introducing ourselves and explained that Pratt Library registration cards would be available at the end of the period for those who wanted them. Then we discussed the list, pointing out its various headings and offering the audience a chance to "stump the experts." They might call out any title by the number assigned to it to see if we could say what the book was about. Usually, a majority of the students wanted to get in on the game, and in selecting a title about which to ask and listening to our thumbnail sketches, they became aware of the readability of the books listed. It did the cause of reading no harm that we were seldom stumped.

While everyone was still interested in calling out titles on the list, we stopped and presented a well-prepared book talk. This usually consisted of relating a well-chosen incident from a book so skillfully that it would impel the listener to want to read the entire book. Two or three book talks interspersed with thumbnail sketches of about twenty titles filled the period. We often left the last ten minutes for browsing in the library, where we helped the students find copies of the books we had spoken about or made other suggestions.

Though assistants were often terrified before a first school visit, they soon thoroughly enjoyed talking and were unhappy if for any reason they were left off the schedule for one of the schools. We wrote out our talks so as to know them well, but we never read them, and so built up extensive repertoires that grew larger and richer each year. After an hour or so of refreshing our memories at the beginning of the school year, each of the experienced speakers would be prepared to give twenty or more talks. At the beginning of each period as the students came into the room, we learned all we could about them and planned our program as they were seated. A switch in the school schedule never upset us, for if we had planned to speak about a drag race to a class of apathetic shop boys and college-preparatory seniors came in instead, we were able to shift to *War and Peace*.

We never divided the city into sections, assigning each assistant to the community where his branch was located; all of us took the entire city for our province. No one assistant could be as effective giving book talks alone in the high school near his branch as he could be assisted by six other experts who had a repertoire of over twenty talks apiece.

Too, it enriched each assistant to learn to adapt his talks to the accelerated, the retarded, the vocational students, the audiences of all girls or all boys, as well as to average groups.

There is no doubt of the effectiveness of these school visits. Time and again teachers and school librarians have spoken of the wave of reading that followed the visits, and certainly the public library has felt the impact. Also, it is important that young people realize the importance of their public library, its reading resources, and the approachability of its staff. An informed acquaintance with the public library would seem to be an essential element of the education of youth and the Baltimore schools have come to believe this.

Blueprint for a Book Fair

In the spring of 1951 one of the branch librarians came into my office to say she had invited the seniors of a nearby high school to come to her branch for a visit and that she would like to turn the entire affair over to the young-adult librarians. We agreed to take over as we could not let her down, but after she left my assistant and I looked at each other aghast. We had already given book talks to all the classes of that high school, and there is a limit to the exciting revelations one can make in a little branch to a group of students who have been its patrons for years.

At a meeting with the YA assistants we decided to use the forty dollars the *Library Journal* had given us for a book-week article to set up some unusual displays.[2] When I discussed our plan with Emerson Greenaway, the director, he was not impressed. He was a member of the Rotary Club and knew their youth committee was looking for a project, so he thought it might be a good idea to see if they would back me and go in for something more elaborate. (*N.B.* Service clubs often have funds to invest in a youth project if it is well thought out and convincingly presented to them.)

The end result of my conference with the gentlemen of the Rotary youth committee was eight brightly-colored collapsible fair booths with awning tops, counters, and imitation-silk curtains hanging at the rear. There was also enough money for a large rack to display vocational materials and a small cart, which we decorated with pots of geraniums, labeled "The World on the Move," and filled with books about people in other countries.

There were eighteen YA assistants in the system at that time. They worked in couples to select a theme, decorate a booth, and choose the appropriate books. They all met on the Saturday before the grand opening on Monday, and with the aid of Kate Coplan, head of exhibits, and her staff, spent the day setting the fair up in the basement of the branch. The booths featured such subjects as Careers, Homemaking, College, Fine Arts (art, music, and dance), A Man's World, Humor, Personality (the usual etiquette and personality books plus books of sex information and marriage manuals), Bell Ringers (best sellers of today and yesterday), and Hobbies (displayed along a wall without a booth).

In the meantime we had scurried about to find added attractions for the booths: white rats from the zoo for the Hobby display; finger painting for all with easel and paint supplied; salad served at the homemaking booth by one of the assistants wearing a chef's hat. There was even a ballet dancer to brighten up Fine Arts, though one of the conservative teachers thought the dancer a bit too much. It took us almost a year to learn that these added attractions were subtractions. They called attention from the books and we eventually dispensed with them all. I became convinced from this that librarians should remember in any project to make the book the center of attraction rather than organize projects to entertain people or strain to prove that librarians are "real people." We also eliminated the Hobby booth. We learned the hard way that most busy teenagers are not hunting hobbies and that those who have hobbies have already read all they need to read about them.

From the beginning the fairs were a howling success. After the first year of experimentation we settled down to a regular routine. The fairs were set up in the school libraries. As the seniors entered the room we played a recording of the lively "Gaîté Parisienne," and then they saw the fair with all its light and color and hundreds of plasticleer-jacketed, new-looking books. They stood in the middle of the room while one of the three YA librarians present turned off the music and another addressed them in a style something like this:

"This is the Pratt Library's book fair for seniors. It occurred to us that most of you have no idea of the richness and variety of the books in the public library. In a few months or weeks all of you will do at least one of these five things: you will go to college, go to work, go into the armed forces, get married, or stay home and entertain your rich parents. Now whatever you do for the rest of your life you can find a book at the Pratt Library that will add pleasure and profit to your activity. We are going to take you on a quick tour of the fair to give you some idea of the kinds of books you might expect to find at Pratt. You stand and we walk. After we have completed the guided tour, there will be fifteen minutes at the end of the period for browsing. Each of you may borrow two books for two weeks, if you wish. Select the book you want, write your name, address, and homeroom number on the card in the back of the book, bring it to one of us, and we will exchange it for a card telling you when the book is due. Return the books to the Central Pratt Library or any of its branches. You do not need a borrower's card to take books from the fair."

Then the three librarians became barkers. Each had selected five or six titles from the booth to be introduced. He held each book high for all to see and spoke loudly. Examples of the spiel might be:

"Chapter Seven of this book is entitled 'How Can You Tell When You're in Love?' [Duvall's *Love and the Facts of Life*, 1963]. This big book, *The Occupational Outlook Handbook*, is put out by the United States Government. It devotes a page or so to each of over a hundred vocations, telling what a job is like, what it pays, how many people will be needed in that profession in the next few years, where to write for more information, and often, what part of the country offers the best opportunities in that particular profession. Here on this rack are job descriptions and sample civil service exams put out by the Arco Publishing house."

In other words, the spiel was brief, fast-moving, concrete, and designed to make the listener want to get hold of the book. The barker also pointed out the book lists to be given away at each booth.

When we finished the tour we usually found ourselves standing alone in the middle of the room while the students raced each other to the booths to get a book about which we had spoken. They did not know we had boxes of duplicate copies ready to supply heavy demands. We did a landslide business that lasted until all the seniors in the school had come in, two classes to a period. It was exhausting but it did get across the idea of the resources of the library and prove to almost every one of the students that there were books they wanted very much to read. And it was ten thousand times more effective than sending each graduate a form letter: ". . . hoping you will make use of the public library for the continuance of your life-long education and enjoyment."

It took four janitors working two hours each and two YA librarians working four hours each to assemble the booths and set up the fair. The pressure for time and money in recent years has meant that the plan had to be modified. Instead of the booths there are now two round tables and five rectangular ones—all with folding legs. They are covered with corduroy in shocking pink, bright orange, turquoise, mustard, and teal blue. There are posters on standards at each table to attract attention and advertise the subject displayed. For an exhibition of this type a wooden stick a yard or a yard and a half long can be painted black, nailed on the appropriate poster, and placed in a large jar of sand, or possibly sawdust. The posters may be cardboard in geometric shapes, clever signs, art cutouts, or whatever is creative and good advertising. For example, the Humor poster at present shows a lot of monkeys hopping out of a barrel with the inscription "More Fun Than . . ." The response of the students over a period of time determines whether to eliminate a booth in favor of a more appealing subject or to combine two booths into one.

In the early years of the fairs it was fairly easy to get all the books back, as the students had written the numbers of their respective homerooms on the book card and the homeroom teacher helped collect overdue books. But with the problems that beset the inner-city schools today, teachers find collecting books an added responsibility they are loathe to assume, and the heavy losses make it difficult for the YA department to stay in business. What a pity! This would seem a project made to order for teachers to teach young people civic responsibility. Moreover, these boys and girls deprived of a cultural background need the ideas found in books and it is urgent that reading have a place in their lives.

On those Friday afternoons when we spent four hours setting up the fair we often went home exhausted, wondering why we worked so hard. But Monday morning, when the "Gaîté Parisienne" was playing and the young people were all aglow over the books, we knew why we had done it. Any project that is truly effective may look easy but behind it is a lot of thought and hours of hard work.

Teenage Book Reviewing

Some years ago the New York Public Library began the publication of a mimeographed sheet called "Back Talk" made up of the frank opinions of teenagers about the books they read. It was intended as an honest reflection of the reading tastes of teenagers to which publishers, teachers, and others might refer.

A few years later we adopted the idea at the Pratt Library and began the publication of *You're the Critic,* a multilithed pamphlet that appears monthly during the school year. We attempted to follow New York's example and discourage any teacher participation in the project. For a few years we barely kept afloat, as it was difficult to get busy teenagers to sit down and write an annotation on a book when they returned it to the library, and they seldom wrote one of their own accord. We hesitated to press them too hard and sometimes thought of abandoning the project. Then we found teachers were encouraging students to review books for the pamphlet, giving extra credits to those whose annotations were published and seeing that their names were listed in the school papers. Interest in *You're the Critic* skyrocketed and students began to vie with each other to have their critical reviews accepted. We discussed the matter and decided there was no reason for us to aim at interesting publishers and other adults in the opinions of teenagers, especially since we were removed from publishing centers. We decided instead to take the gifts the gods provided and allow the teachers to help us when they pleased. The publication became so popular we could not supply the demand with the nineteen hundred copies we could afford to put out each month. From the first, copies were distributed through the school libraries and the Central Pratt Library and its branches.

The board of *You're the Critic* is composed of one representative from each public, private, and parochial high school in the city. Now that it has become an honor instead of a chore to serve on the board, the publication attracts popular student leaders. The head of the young-adult department at the Central Library is responsible for the pamphlet and supervises the young people who edit it. Four are assigned to each edition and one of the four must write the editorial. Some original poetry is included, as well as some announcements and movie reviews. Similar pamphlets are sprouting up in other cities. A display of books set up under the caption "Reviewed in This Month's *You're the Critic*" is always popular.

In setting up such a project it is necessary to have an understanding with the young people as to what the limitations will be. We agreed to accept reviews of any book purchased by the Pratt Library except childrens' books, which were ruled out to prevent sixth and seventh graders from crowding out the teenagers. All necessary explanations are printed in the first issue each fall.

When a protest is made by a parent or teacher, we reply that if we are ever convinced that the young adults are deliberately attempting to give the pamphlet a questionable tone, we shall discontinue its publication, but as long as reviews are submitted in good faith, we shall publish them. Since the teenagers know we will stand firm, they are delighted to feel they may explore the entire field of adult literature if they wish, and they do not abuse our trust.

A book-reviewing publication is good promotion for reading, since the recommendations teenagers make to each other are often more effective than those the librarian makes. Also, although books of all levels of difficulty are included, the teenagers often review books so complex that the librarian would hesitate to suggest them himself for fear of dismaying readers.

On the Wagon—A Grafted Branch

Some years ago I attended the annual conference of the American Library Association in Milwaukee where I heard Robert Blakely speak. At that time he was the editor of the Des Moines *Register,* and as one of the television commercials would put it, he was "tall, thin as a branding iron, and stood above the crowd." He addressed a general session on the ineffectiveness of librarians in a crucial moment of history, suggesting that we were overly feminine, segregated, timid people who should change our ways and get books into the hands of people, that we should go out into the highways and byways and hasten the day when books would be so available that there would be "wisdom crying in the streets." I was stirred and after a few months wrote an article for the *Library Journal* pointing out the implications of his remarks for YA work.[3] The article had no reverberations, but I fell victim to my own eloquence and began to consider what I might do.

When writing the article I had been thinking of one of the branch-library communities where juvenile delinquency was high and the circulation of books low. Upon consulting with the assistant working with young people at the branch as to the feasibility of operating a book wagon in that community, I met with such enthusiastic encouragement that I decided to make a private investigation to see how one could get hold of a horse and wagon and then lay the matter before those in authority.

True to my library-school training, I approached the matter through a reference tool, i.e., the telephone directory classified section under such headings as Stables, Horses, Mules. This led me to the stockyards where I found an enclosed wagon and a young mare, Sophie, not for rent but for sale—for $275. The difficulty at this point was that the library did not have an extra $275, but before abandoning the project completely it was decided that the branch assistant would find out if there were any stables in the neighborhood, and if there were, the probable cost of stabling a horse.

I was entertaining a last hope that there might be a chance to persuade the librarian that if we bought Sophie, surely she could be sold for the purchase price or maybe at a profit in the fall. That is how I discovered that horses and wagons in this city are for rent. I contacted a man named Stebbin who agreed to rent a pony and a wagon he thought might be repaired to suit at $2.50 per day, which price would cover the cost of feeding and stabling the horse. This seemed a mere pittance when

---

This section was first published as "Adventures with a Book Wagon," in *Illinois Libraries,* April 1944, 132–37. *Ed.*

compared with the $275 outlay for Sophie and had the advantage of affording an easy and inexpensive retreat if the project should fail.

Armed with figures and the most persuasive arguments, I presented my plans to the librarian, the assistant librarian, and the director of circulation. Though all those present, including the chief agitator, had many misgivings, the librarian consented to the experiment. I was given six weeks to put the idea to a test.

A week or so later I went back to make further arrangements with Mr. Stebbin. At this point he had decided to go to Pennsylvania with Happy Joe's Carnival and was sorry to say he could do nothing for us, but suggested we go to see Ernie Frank. Mr. Frank listened sympathetically to our plans. He had a wagon all right but was short on horses. I rather pressed him, as the library knew nothing of Mr. Stebbin's defalcation and I preferred not to go into the matter. Mr. Frank finally agreed to find a horse while I went on vacation and to rent same with wagon for $2.00 per day. I said nothing to him of Mr. Stebbin's price of $2.50.

The day before I left for vacation Mr. Frank brought the wagon to the library to be measured by our carpenter for shelves. It was a handsome, hawker's red vegetable wagon, low-slung with yellow shafts and wheels. Mr. Frank drove up to the rear of the stately Pratt Library building, bringing an amazed staff to the windows when the old gray horse whinnied loudly. (The catalog department said he laughed.)

After my experience with Mr. Stebbin, however, I had little faith that the promised horse would actually be on hand when I returned from vacation three weeks later; but there, standing in a stall in South Baltimore, was Betty, a sleek, pretty mare. In fact, Mr. Frank never once let me down.

The wagon was fitted on either side with red shelves and oilcloth awnings. The end gate was covered with a red board that could be lowered by a chain to serve as a charging desk. A red box with two shelves and a door that could be locked stood at the back of the wagon, so that when opened, all needed tools would be at hand. Supplied with a city directory, stamps and pads, and a telephone book, we stood ready to register new members and circulate books. We had everything but a noise gadget—which we needed to announce the book wagon's approach. For days friends and interested patrons searched the city in vain for a hurdy-gurdy or hand organ. Then our efforts were directed to finding a bell. Someone told me the B. & O. Railroad would probably have bells. I promptly went to Camden Station and looked about for a likely place to begin asking for a bell. After a fruitless search, I approached the information desk and asked half apologetically if they had a bell.

"What did you say, lady?"

"Can you tell me where I might find a bell?" I said.

"Did you say a bell?"

"Yes."

"Why, lady, *I* haven't any bell!" he said in a kind of frantic amazement that led to my hasty retreat and shed some light on why patrons sometimes sound idiotic to the librarian at *her* desk.

The problem was solved at last by the purchase of a xylophone with four notes, which served the purpose admirably but became unbearable if played too long and too near by strong-muscled and enthusiastic younger patrons. The instrument was stolen only twice. It was literally beaten to a pulp. At the end of six weeks its notes were loose and its handle grimy, but the children had had a glorious time with it and it had aroused many a block to come and read. A merciful Providence had saved us from a bell.

As the first day of the project approached, doubt and fear assailed me and faith waned fast. How foolish one could look, I thought, driving down the streets in a little red wagon playing a xylophone and looking expectant, if there should be no customers. Such a small proportion of the community used the branch library, how could anyone think they would read! There was some encouragement in the fact that when I visited the Sunday schools of the neighborhood to announce the project, there had been applause. Mr. Staples, the Episcopal rector who had effectively served this community with faith and works for forty years, told me when I wavered that I must go ahead believing—that this service would be so fine for the young people and that he knew they would like the idea. The Baptist and United Brethren ministers were gracious in allowing me to announce the project ahead of time in their Sunday schools. One minister was cynical and amused at such a silly idea. He suggested that there would be a better chance of success if I sold Good Humor ice cream to cool the people off. I was secretly inclined to admit he might be right.

The day before we were to begin, the book wagon was packed at the Central building with books sent in from all points of the system and from the Central departments. (Only $3.00 was spent for books.) That afternoon a man from the Frank stables brought a horse to take me down to the neighborhood to be ready the next day. As we rode through the main part of town, I felt more self-conscious than I had thought I might at the look of surprise and amusement on the faces of the people who saw the strange-looking vehicle and read the sign: "The Pratt Library's Book Wagon. Borrow Books Here." En route to the stables, Charles, Mr. Frank's driver, when he learned that I intended to drive the horse myself, gallantly showed me the tricks of cutting diagonally across streetcar tracks to avoid catching the wagon wheels in the car tracks. He also demonstrated the uses of the brake. As we drove through the community to be canvassed in the next six weeks, an older boy sitting in front of a store looked us over and guffawed loudly—not a very encouraging omen.

The first ride through the community took place in a late afternoon and evening of July. The branch assistant and I set out, escorted by swarms of little dirty-faced children and older boys—one of whom rode ahead on his bicycle, beating the xylophone. From the first the people of the community were generally enthusiastic, though there were some whose interest was never aroused to the point of borrowing books. When we stopped to wait on a likely customer, others approached, so that we remained sometimes for half an hour at one place. When this happened, the children, who soon learned that the easy books were under the seat, would come from all directions, ask for picture books, and perch on the steps all around, reading while we worked.

From the first day there was never any doubt of the success of the project. It soon became evident that one person could not handle the work alone. Too, Betty would move slyly toward the stables as evening fell. When volunteers were called for, the response from the staff was enthusiastic and many gave up more than one free evening or half-day to help. The boys of the neighborhood were only too ready to help with Betty, and soon the position of horseboy was open only to those who deserved special consideration for helpfulness or who had improved in behavior so much that they deserved a reward.

Because Baltimore people are accustomed to sitting on their famous white steps on summer evenings and because more volunteer help was available in the afternoons and evenings, the book wagon operated from four o'clock in the afternoon until it became too dark to distinguish one title from another. Ten routes were laid out and repeated every two weeks, so that in the six weeks' experiment each patron had the opportunity to borrow books from the book wagon three times. The books were returned to the book wagon if the patron preferred that to going to a branch of the library, until the last visit when the books were loaned with the understanding that they would have to be returned to a branch of the library. The cards were filed by blocks, with the name and address of the patron on each book card. On return visits of the book wagon each block was cleared for books borrowed and due before we proceeded to the next block. As a result, the percentage of books lost was negligible.

During the six weeks that the book wagon was operated, 480 people registered for library membership, of which 456 had no record of previous membership, 293 were young people and adults, and 187 were children. In the four hours the book wagon operated each day, it circulated about the same number of books as the branch did during its eight-hour day. Many children who had "quit" for the summer sent for the cards they had left at the branch. Many paid fines in order to borrow from the book wagon as their neighbors were doing. One Negro boy who owed fifty-four cents was told he would have to make at least a partial payment in order to borrow a book. He disappeared to return a few minutes later with fifty-four pennies taken, alas! from his little sister's bank.

The children dearly loved Betty. They pulled grass for her if there was any within a quarter of a mile. They petted her cautiously and fell into violent arguments over her sex. If there was a second to listen in the press of registration and circulation, we often heard from up front, "I'll betcha a million dollars he's a her." If this failed to silence some doubting Thomas, the children would appear, and leaning between the librarian's face and the charging desk, one would demand, "Miss, ain't it a her?"

The results of the project were provocative; they answered some questions and raised others. As for direct work done with adolescent delinquents, the results were not remarkable, since the young people were working or in the armed forces or married or maybe engaged in delinquency. Only about fifty of those who registered were young people. However, the project was a distinct success as a family affair, where possibly the library can make its most effective contribution to helping solve the problem of juvenile delinquency. The question was raised as to the legitimacy of taking books to people who lived within walking distance of a branch. It was said that these people did not want to read or they would patronize their branch library. These people *did* want to read. They enjoyed the books they borrowed and were steady customers for six weeks, recommending to each other the titles they liked. They expressed great appreciation that we had brought them books and lamented the ending of the project. For each month succeeding the book wagon's activities, the branch showed a rise in circulation, due at least in part to the summer's work. Why these people had not used their branch is something I cannot explain. It was said in some quarters that these people did not deserve to have books. By cold reasoning, maybe they didn't, but libraries are not in business to see that people get their just desserts, but rather to find how they can get more people in all communities to read more books.

Such communities as we worked in were the danger spots in our cities. These people were a prey to every slogan—good or bad. If the government issued a stirring call for defense workers, they responded at once, while many of us reasoned beyond the appeal to a realization that we were already in defense work. If radicals ranted, they made the same unhesitating response. Libraries must teach these people to read and think. This could not be done in a day nor in a six weeks' experiment. Our patrons read more Norris and Grey and less world affairs.[4] They were far more interested in *Gone with the Wind* than in *One World;*[5] but the fact that they read print with interest indicates that in the course of time, with inspired librarians and appropriate books, many of them would read far better books than they did that summer. If they would not come into a branch library for the books but would read them off a book wagon, it behooved the library to drive such a wagon down the streets of its city slums or to adopt some better means of influencing people to read and think.

A horse and wagon was certainly not the only solution to the libraries' problem; it was probably not even one of the best solutions, but our success seemed so closely connected with certain elements peculiar to our project that it might be of some profit to attempt to isolate and define these elements. In the first place, the slow motion of the equipage allowed time for many more personal contacts than would have been possible with a faster and better equipped gasoline-propelled bookmobile. The novelty of the project attracted attention, which made subsequent contacts easy. The friendly simplicity of the entire outfit made it quite easy to do away completely with institutional formality and afforded the librarian an excellent opportunity to "visit" with her neighbors and newly acquired friends.

Too often a wide gulf lay between our librarians and the people they wished to serve. In these poorer districts where tough-fibered men did hard physical labor and the women were too often the ill-nourished slaves of large families, our college-bred career girls housed in institutional buildings and representing "culture" had very little appeal for their possible clientele. There just was not enough in common between them. It was much simpler for a sunburned librarian driving a horse to quickly establish a bond of interest with the woman and her family seated on their doorstep.

While such a project seemed fruitful for the community, it was of inestimable value to the librarians. Those who worked on the wagon could understand why a Negro woman who lived with her eight children in a three-room apartment up a swaying stairway had not had time to broaden her cultural interests; why in such a family the older children returned the books. There just wasn't anywhere to put the book where the baby could not find it. The librarian could soon see why Mrs. Norris' *Angel in the House* [1933] was a fine book for this woman. Many matters that were merely irritating in the library became little human tragedies when seen against their backgrounds. These people had fine things to give us, too. They taught us much about courage and humor, strength and patience.

Mrs. Darden, a Negro who lived in a noisy run-down district, was anxious to have her five daughters read and love books. She herself had had books "when I lived in Virginia." She registered and sent for a book on United States history and had each of her girls take cards. When the book wagon drew up to her street, her five daughters appeared wearing freshly ironed dresses in celebration of the wagon's appearance and they all took books.

The white women who lived on the cobblestone alley where the stables were located loved the evening air, which seemed stale to us. They bathed their babies and made an occasion of sitting out until bedtime. The men at the stables were as gallant as the men who preside over cotillions. They had a rich sense of humor, too. One afternoon a man selling watermelons stopped us to say, "Hey! Why don't you buy a watermelon?" We replied, "Why don't you borrow a book?" He said, "If I borrow a book, will you buy a melon?" We traded and parted with amusement on all sides of the street.

One night I stabled the horse long after dark and started up the cobblestone alley towards the bus stop when I heard bare feet padding behind me and a woman calling, "Hey, Miss!" I turned to face the woman, who lived near the stable. "Say," she said, "have you got any books about being a woman?" I told her I would bring her one the next day. I brought her Zabriski's *Mother and Baby Care in Pictures* [1941], with which she was perfectly delighted, and she asked for more books like it. I brought her another dealing with "the facts of life," which she did not like. I brought still another, which she did not care for either. Then I asked her why she liked the first book but not the other two, saying she would have to give me some help in making the selections. "Well, you see, Miss," she said, "I can't read."

We librarians need to learn anew that people are the same everywhere. We are too inclined to go out to bless these people when we try to help them. We forget that we are often victims of a kind of precious insularity and that these people with fewer opportunities but more hardiness can often send us home with a greater blessing than we gave them.

The second summer I left this district for a crowded, all-Negro slum across town that was being given special attention by the Department of Public Welfare. In my first summer I had been dismayed by the number of white women who sat on their steps in the hot afternoons, preferring to stare out at their sordid surroundings rather than to read any book ever published. The men beat their children unmercifully. One woman whose son had stolen my purse begged me not to tell his father, as she could not stand to see the beating he would give the boy. With both men and women, interest was almost entirely in the physical.

I drove into the Negro slum the first afternoon, wondering what it would be like and fearful again of what my reception might be, when an old woman leaned out of a second-floor window and called down, "Do you have any poetry books?" When I said I had, she asked, "Have you got one with Rabbi Ben Ezra?" What a wonderful omen! From the beginning I met with warm friendliness and a far more heartening interest in books than I had encountered the first summer. There was a ready response to poetry and music. Young and old borrowed song books. Adults borrowed Bibles, religious books of many kinds, and collections of spirituals. There was an unexpected demand from adults for textbooks—geographies, histories, spellers, arithmetics "like we used to have in school." Two men wanted books on "how to talk right." One huckster left his wagon to ask for a book on the multiplication tables. Dictionaries and books by and about Negroes were requested. Evidently the motion pictures had influenced the demand for fiction, as better than half the novels borrowed were by authors whose books had recently been made into movies. The housewives were especially interested in cookbooks, and on my limited budget I could not begin to supply the demand. One afternoon I drove down an alley where some elderly women were sitting on their front steps. I asked them if they would like to look over the books on the wagon and one of the old women said, "I don't want any book in the world unless it tells me how to make watermelon pickles." Before I had started the season, I had gone to the gas and electric company for any giveaway materials they might have. I looked in one of their pamphlets and there by God's grace was a recipe for watermelon pickles. Amid general rejoicing I distributed pamphlets to all the old ladies to keep.

From four o'clock in the afternoon until dark the little red wagon moved up and down the streets. Since the horse was still stabled at Cross Street, when business was over for the day a lighted lantern was hung under the wagon and the trip across town was made.

The librarians who worked with the wagon were treated with the greatest kindness and help for any emergency was always at hand. My horse that second summer was named Berry for "liberry," and the afternoon he fell down on Gay Street was a tense moment. I was terrified that he might have broken a leg, and that if I forced him to get up, the leg just might be hanging by a tendon. However, several people recruited from the sidewalks and saloons by helpful onlookers got the horse up, straw hat and all, to reveal that he was in good condition and that his reluctance to get up was probably nothing more than boredom with a project others found more interesting.

In the thirty-eight days of that summer, 725 new members were registered, of whom about half were adults, and over four thousand books were circulated.

Librarians wonder why people living in a community with a branch library do not make better use of it. I could see by visiting with the women of this neighborhood why they were not members of the library. Many of them worked in a suburban household all day, returning at night exhausted to an unkempt house, children who were demanding attention, and a hungry, impatient husband. There simply was no time to make oneself presentable and walk even a few blocks to select a book, especially if one did not know what book one wanted and was timid about going into an institution that seemed a bit formidable. The men did not even know they wanted a book until they saw helpful titles readily available.

I worked the next summer in the same district, but after that, marriage ended the project. I was forty-two when a distinguished gentleman asked me to marry him. I had resigned myself to single blessedness and this was too much. It took about eighteen hours a day to keep the wagon rolling, and I was so in love. No other librarian could drive a horse or stand up physically to the work, so it all ended.

I should like to say in conclusion that I doubt if libraries will ever get books into the hands of the masses of the inner city until they get out of their institutions and onto the streets. I am not suggesting the book wagon as the only answer, but I am saying that librarians who know books and like people must go up and down the streets of slums selling the idea of reading and persuading people to reach out for books. We know from a century of experience that only a very few will take the initiative and come to us.

✕ IV ✕

Thinning the Plants

When the YA librarian considers undertaking a new activity, he should think over the activities in which he is already engaged to see if there is room for a new one or if the new idea seems promising enough to justify dropping an established project. Because I was inexperienced and sold on my job, I had to learn the hard way that there are only twenty-four hours in each day, that human beings have limitations, and that it is better to be effective than all-inclusive. I learned these things from three projects.

A Book Club

About the time I was setting up the YA collections in the branches, one of the younger trained librarians asked me if I would like to form a reading club at her branch and I jumped at the chance. Her community was roughly half Italian and half Jewish. From the gay Italians we recruited one brilliant girl.[1] The other members were the children of Jewish immigrants freshly arrived from Europe with scarves on their heads, large families, and little money, but with character and minds enriched by their Continental background.

This section is taken from "A Long Way to Tipperary," published in *The Library Reaches Out*, ed. K. M. Coplan and E. Castagna, New York: Oceana, 1965. *Ed.*

The librarian suggested we spend ten dollars monthly from her book budget to purchase books we thought would enrich the branch collection. To do this the club members and I read five or six books before each meeting, discussed them, compared them, argued, read reviews, and then took a vote to decide which to add to our collection.

As a book club it was a great success, but it just about finished me. I had to read every book, collect professional reviews, plan the reading for the next meeting, send extra copies of all the books to the branch for club members to read, and then lead the discussions. I took counsel with myself after a year and came to the conclusion that something had to give. Because I had to read all the books considered for purchase in order to make the discussions meaningful, I was falling behind in my reading for my patrons at the central library, as well as for those I worked with three nights a week in the branches. My book background was too weak to stand the strain and my good readers were outdistancing me. While the club was stimulating and obviously meant a great deal to the members, I wondered if it was fair to spend an evening with those few superior youngsters and leave fifty or so unattended at a branch. I was at that time the one readers' advisor for young adults in the system and there was no one to take my place when I was away.

There is the old story of Moody and Sankey that tells how the older of the evangelists, I think it was Moody, preached one night to an audience of one young man, but the youth turned out to be Sankey.[2] Maybe among the little group in the meeting room will sit the future Governor of the state. On the other hand, he just might be in the group wandering unassisted on the floor of the library. We have no way of telling, but the odds are in favor of his being in the larger group.

Many inexperienced young assistants wished to organize a book club but I often discouraged them. Certainly if large enough groups attend the meeting regularly, there is an argument in their favor; but most clubs are foredoomed to failure because teenagers do not read the books assigned for discussion. They are honestly too busy with school-work, homework, TV, sports, jobs, and dances to read for discussion and they usually drop out. Nor should YA librarians set up clubs that are not concerned with books, films, or library materials. Activities that keep youngsters off the streets, that give them games to play and entertain them, are the province of social workers.

I may be rationalizing here. While clubs seem unprofitable to me in comparison with other activities, another librarian might find them the best way to reach the young adults of a community. Each YA librarian decides for himself on what projects to spend time and energy in order to bring the most books to the most young people.

The UNY and I

When the United Nations Youth (UNY) was organized in Baltimore, I was persuaded to be its first sponsor. It seemed to me a good way to establish rapport with a large group of intelligent teenagers from most of the Baltimore high schools and at the same time to promote interest in world problems which, hopefully, might lead to reading. This seemed too good to pass up, and I went into action.

We prepared a float for a Navy Day parade; we attended a Chinese dinner where we ate chop suey with chop sticks and listened to Chinese speakers; we sent delegates as observers to Lake Success, to a Security Council meeting, and to other places. When they returned, they spoke to service clubs, school assemblies, and civic groups. We sent a large delegation to the New York *Herald Tribune*'s annual youth forum featuring students from South America and brought the visiting students back to Baltimore for a memorable weekend.

With all this, many of the UNY became better citizens of the world, but as I looked back over that year, I found it difficult to balance accounts. Under profits could be listed the breadth of vision and increased sense of responsibility for the state of the world that was fostered in many young people. On the other hand, I remembered the many Sunday afternoons when it was more urgent to attend a meeting of the UNY than to play tennis with a long-suffering husband. I remembered the endless telephoning and bookkeeping and extra quarters found among the papers on my desk at the library. There were the times when the youngsters did not show up as they had promised and I sealed and addressed important notices to get them out on time. But worst of all were the afternoons when crises arose, i.e., when the chop suey simply had to be sent to the changed meeting place by five o'clock or else. As I dialed numbers frantically on the telephone on my library desk, some youngster invariably edged up to ask, "Would you get me a book about an eccentric person?" Though never said aloud, my smothered answer to such a question was "I'll wring your neck!" How low can a librarian sink?

Some years ago two books were published at the same time. In one, *The Importance of Living* [1937], Lin Yutang said that the trouble with our Western world was its bustle and hurry. He described an old Chinese philosopher clothed in a white silk robe who stood for hours with an exquisite fan in hand contemplating a flower. In the other book, *Madame Curie* [Eve Curie, 1937], the discoverer of radium told how day

---

This section was published as "The Librarian and the United Nations Youth," in *Top of the News*, September 1948, 14–17. Ed.

after day she stirred a boiling cauldron with a stick almost as big as herself. "It was killing work," she said.

Now what is one to do? Contemplate a flower or be a ball of fire? And if one is too big a ball of fire, who is going to do the library work?

The Book Week Parties

For two years we celebrated Book Week with a teenage party. In the early forties when *Seventeenth Summer* [Daly, 1942] revolutionized teenage reading, we invited all the high-school students to a masquerade party at the central library, with Maureen Daly and the editor of *Seventeen* magazine as speakers. The guests were to come disguised as characters in books. There was apprehension in some quarters, as this was to be an integrated party and in Baltimore at that time such a thing was almost unheard of. The affair was quite successful but it was the ninth and tenth graders rather than the juniors and seniors who came in the largest numbers. For Southern High School it was truly a gala affair. An understanding high-school librarian helped the students with their costumes, which took most of the prizes and gave the students courage to make their first trip across Baltimore Street into the heart of the big city. The autographed copies of *Seventeenth Summer* were the first books most of them had ever owned. One of the Baltimore *Sun*'s best photographers took pictures of the most attractive costumes for the photogravure section on the Sunday paper. It was a big night.

The next year's Book Week party featured the sportswriter and author John Tunis. The day of the event was a rainy Sunday afternoon. There was a fair crowd, the boys loved Mr. Tunis, and the guests had a good time, but it seemed to me these parties were too difficult to plan for, too time-consuming, and too unrelated to reading. Here again, an evaluation of our program seemed in order. In making decisions about which projects to eliminate and which to keep, there are always intangibles to consider. One never can measure the extent to which readers have been inspired or enriched. However, circulation figures give us a pretty good indication of the effectiveness of a library activity. Although our guests enjoyed our parties and they were good public relations, they did not influence young people to read books as had some of our other activities, so we eliminated the Book Week parties.

❧ V ❧

Provender for the "Beasts"

What Is the Best Food for the "Beasts"?
Classics? "Pleasant" Books? Realism?

Years ago in a Texas town a doctor I knew was returning from a sick call late at night when he heard the sound of running feet. Soon a young man came tearing past him, only to be outdistanced by a black cat that streaked across his path. "Son of a gun!" the outraged boy shouted. "Son of a gun!"

For years adults concerned with the reading of teenagers have been racing another kind of black cat—this one not so much a symbol of bad luck as of personal corruption. These adults cherish certain beliefs about what teenagers should or should not read. When these beliefs are violated, they are outraged. What escapes them is that these precepts, while seemly, are not always sound.

Let's look at a few of these precepts.

Give him a classic! Any literate person is heartily in favor of the classics, but because a book is a classic it does not as a matter of course become a rich reading experience for everyone. In fact, the depth of philosophy, the subtle probing of complex human motives in the great

---

The first part of this section was originally published as "A Time When It's Best to Read and Let Read," *New York Times Book Review,* May 8, 1960. *Ed.*

books, often dismay the inexperienced reader. The teenager who has never known consuming passion cannot understand how Anna Karenina could desert a good husband and a sweet child for another man. Many teenagers like *A Tale of Two Cities* but are bored by Dickens' leisurely progress through the adventures of *Dombey and Son* and *Martin Chuzzlewit*. With the exception of *Ivanhoe* and some of the Waverly novels, Scott has little interest for today's teenagers. This is not to say that young people do not like classics. They adore *Jane Eyre, Pride and Prejudice, Wuthering Heights*, and others they can understand.

Is it possible that some librarians insist on the classics in order to play safe, to avoid reading widely and forming opinions on modern writing, and to escape criticism when recommending to teenagers books to which their parents might object? For example, if Shakespeare writes a sonnet to a beautiful boy, we pass over it lightly because the master is above censure, but if Mary Renault touches on the same subject in *The King Must Die* [1958], we hope no parent will protest its inclusion on a high-school list. Marriage without benefit of clergy is one thing for Hester Prynne but something else for little Teale Eye in Guthrie's *The Big Sky* [1947].

We must make the best writing of all time available to teenagers. We should offer them the classics they can understand and then seek out the best of modern writing, defending it when necessary.

Keep it pleasant! Though the floods descend, some well-meaning adults would intone this old chant:

> It is not raining rain to me,
> It's raining violets.

We do not want our adolescents to see the seamy side of life. We do not want them to suffer pain and unhappiness, and if we could, we would prolong the age of innocence indefinitely. Of course, if we should succeed in our efforts to do this, we would at the same time rob our young people of the opportunity to build strength of character and incapacitate them for the crises they are sure to meet.

Hunger and pain are the lot of millions of people; war has ravaged the earth periodically; love is not always constant; and death will end us all. But *mirabile dictu*, the spirit of man can rise above every disaster. Young people are not devastated by reading about unpleasantness. (Even as children, they applauded as the little pig boiled the big, bad wolf alive for supper.) We must let teenagers read of life as it is and learn how people of courage get the best of it. *A Tree Grows in Brooklyn, The Good Earth, Hiroshima, All Quiet on the Western Front, Manchild in the*

Promised Land, and other books that present life truly are part of the heritage of the adolescent.[1]

One good book can work a miracle. Americans are people of faith. We believe the product recommended on TV is as superior as the commercial announcer says it is. If a writer on health is enthusiastic about blackstrap molasses, we eat it until another recommends honey. We have been told and do believe that one "good" book can work a miracle while one "bad" one can guide the reader down the wrong path.

There are no reliable studies on the effects of reading. However, psychiatrists tell us that if children are given enough love and a sense of security by their parents, it is very difficult indeed to upset their emotional balance. Children who do not gain this sense of security are likely to be upset eventually by the first bottle of beer they drink, the first encounter they have with sex, the first "bad" book they read.

We want teenagers to read the best books for we feel sure that one's accumulated reading has a decided effect. But if one or two "bad" books find their way into the adolescent's hands, it is likely their effect will be neutralized if many good books are also read.

Facts are better than fiction. Certainly we get essential information from factual books, but it is experience we need most. If we would live richly, we can expand our lives more by sailing down the Nile with Cleopatra, looking at the cherry trees with Housman, or sweating it out to triumph at long last with Moss Hart than we can by gathering all available information on Egypt, raising cherries, or writing for the theatre.

Sex isn't necessary. Many adults seem to think that if sex is not mentioned to adolescents, it will go away. On the contrary, it is here to stay and teenagers are avidly interested in it. They will find out all they can about it and wise adults will make available reliable books that tell them what they wish to know. There are excellent factual books on the market, but the best novels on the subject go beyond the facts to the emotional implications of love. *Of Human Bondage, Wuthering Heights, The Cruel Sea, Love Is Eternal, Winter Wheat, Gone with the Wind, Bridge to the Sun, Three Came Home*—all these have something to say about love that cannot be learned from informational books.[2]

Too many adults wish to protect teenagers when they should be stimulating them to read of life as it is lived. When a story is true to life and well-written, the teenager will do well to arm himself with whatever experience such a book has to give him.

The section "Sex Isn't Necessary" was first published as "Mrs. Grundy, Go Home" in *Wilson Library Bulletin,* December 1958. *Ed.*

Once I was standing in the fiction department of my library when a teenage girl came up to ask about a novel she had heard of which dealt with homosexuality. A charming, well-bred woman patron who overheard the request was aghast. She said, "I do not see why she wants to read that. I read it and found it very strong fare indeed." The girl and the woman had the same reason for reading the book—they wanted to know about this strange no-man's-land of sex. Adults need not look far for answers to their bewildered questions about teenagers' curiosity about sex. It is the same curiosity they once had and never quite outgrew.

The best books, old and new, have a richer and more subtle message about sex for the adolescent than he will hear from his peers. Certainly they will supplement whatever truths he may glean from a conscientious but sometimes tongue-tied parent.

All well-meaning adults and certainly all librarians want to "do right" by adolescents. I am one of those who was done right by, as many people would interpret the phrase. Brought up on a Texas cotton farm, I was protected from the evil world by two devout, educated, Presbyterian parents and a characterful grandmother, all eager to make me a lady, a Christian, and a good citizen. No intoxicants were allowed in our home, except when the doctor prescribed them for Grandmother in her old age, and then the bottle of whiskey was hidden in the back of a clothes cupboard and was not referred to by word or look. Since gamblers and toughs played cards, I had no association with them. Sex and dancing also seemed too closely connected to risk allowing me to sway to music in the arms of some panting male, so I didn't dance either. When a boy winked at me in the fifth grade, Mother told me not to wink back; as I grew older, I was told it would be perfectly all right to kiss a man after he had asked me to be his wife. Sex was *out*—out of our conversation and out of my reading matter.

From home I went to a college supported by our church and I graduated *summa cum laude—et puritate*.

After five years of teaching in little Texas towns, at twenty-six I betook myself, unsullied from the world, to Columbia University and a professional career in the East.

It took me ten years to become a normal human being. I beat off the men who tried to kiss me and was so unable to show the poor brutes affection that I would never have been married had not a kindly older man taught me, at forty, to love him. I had to learn that sex was normal and fulfilling, and that those who pervert or suspect it are pitiful. I wish that in my teens someone had given me *A Tree Grows in Brooklyn* to read, so I might have sympathized with "Sissy" rather than scorned her. I wish I had read *Of Human Bondage* earlier, for I was inhibited, too, and I needed to understand the effect of a love such as Philip had for Mildred.

Had I read *Ethan Frome* sooner, I might have lost any prim assurance that all one had to do was be good and characterful and one would be happy.

I desperately needed to have read the adult books that were kept from me, for I was not ready to cope with life and was merely amusing to people whom I wished to interest.

Of course, no one is reared so strictly any more, but even now too many adults would like to keep before adolescents only the good, the true, and the beautiful. Let them read of knights and ladies, of courage, of goodness. I agree; but I insist that we have a duty to teenagers that extends far beyond protection. We must be more positive than that. To become an adult citizen of America and the world requires an understanding of all sorts of people and the feelings that motivate them. It requires an acquaintance with people of all the other countries on the globe, and some conception of treating with them. It is important that young people read books that will help them meet these demands. It is a disservice to a young person, who must live dangerously, to acquaint him only with good, innocuous people in ideal situations.

Clifton Fadiman[3] has said that if a young person cannot understand what he reads, it will not harm him, while if he can understand what he reads, he is ready to read of life situations truly presented.

At what age are we to allow a young person to know of unpleasant things and sex? Many European libraries allow young people adult privileges at twenty-one. Is there some magic age at which one suddenly may be allowed to know of life, and shall we let this knowledge hit a youth at one fell blow?

Some adults honestly think average adolescents will understand when we tell them that they are not quite ready for the stories of adult experiences presented in serious fiction and that they will be content to wait. Like fun they will! Those with spirit will beat it out of the library to the nearest corner drugstore to inquire for the specific titles they have been refused, and to search there and in their friends' collections for juicier items. Theodore Roosevelt was told as a boy that he might not read Ouida.[4] Did he calmly accept the opinion of older wiser people? He did not. He read Ouida.

Young people mature at different rates of speed and many a teenager is better informed and more knowledgeable than the average adult. As he becomes interested in the adult world and its problems, he should not be recalled to more puerile interests and simplified writing. The readers' advisor for young adults should help the accelerated teenager find his way gradually among adult books, showing him how to develop critical ability, how to distinguish between sham and truth in writing, how to become acquainted with the great literary heritage that is his, so that when he finishes high school he will be already on the way to broadening his limited experience and enriching his understanding through adult books.

One swallow doesn't make a summer and one book will neither destroy nor save a reader—unless he is psychotic. It is the accumulation of a lifetime of reading that affects us for good or ill.

We heavy-footed adults might just as well slow down and let the black cat run. He will eventually win the race anyway—with no harm done.

"Let the Lower Lights Be Burning"
(*The Teenage Novel*)

Many of the young people in our cities are culturally deprived, trapped in a slough of frustration and despair. They have little understanding of what public property is. They have never sat down to a well-set table or heard an interesting conversation or known a father to love and respect. A resounding slap takes the place of a quiet discussion of good manners. They live in ghettos isolated from the mainstream of American life and their ideas are provincial in the extreme.

While the children of suburbia are more fortunate, many of them are also provincial. They do not see beyond their pretty little communities to the larger world or even to the slums of the nearby city. Surveys of suburbia usually agree that what the parents of these children want is two cars, membership in the country club, their children in private schools, and isolation from the problems of the poor. The children of both the ghetto and suburbia are living in a world growing constantly smaller of which they have very little understanding.

What can books do for these young people? Their most important contribution is to supplement experience, to intensify their lives. However long these young people may live, most of them will know few months or years that are filled with meaning. They will experience few passionate love affairs, few victories, few overwhelming griefs, few moments of insight and inspiration. Without books, they can live and die naively innocent of so much experience. But the young person who reads can live a thousand years and a thousand lives. In a few hours, at any time, he can add to his meager experience another whole lifetime condensed to its meaningful moments, with all the dull, uneventful days left out. He can go back in time three hundred years before Christ to travel with Theseus in *The King Must Die,* dancing on the backs of

---

"Let the Lower Lights Be Burning" was first published in *English Journal,* November 1957. *Ed.*

charging bulls, threading the labyrinth to slay the minotaur, and winning Ariadne's love. He can learn what it means to be consumed by a dream when he reads of Jesse Stuart,[5] Moss Hart, Gordon Parks, and Agnes de Mille. He can experience the overwhelming passion of Anna Karenina, weep over Anne Frank or George's anguish for Lennie. He can understand the poignancy of living from *Our Town* and struggle with bewildered Holden Caulfield to adjust dreams to harsh reality. But why go on? Here in books is life a thousand times more various and richer than anyone could ever live it.

Books are literary atom bombs capable of destroying stupidity, cant, insularity, and prejudice—if they are read. The trouble is that not enough people read books at any time, and so the ideas contained in them, like our supply of bombs, are stockpiled. One reason for this is that we have killed off many young readers by our determination to give them only great books too complex and deep for younger, inexperienced readers to fully understand. We should first teach the youngest teenagers, who have limited imaginations and scanty experience, to love to read, and this can be done by giving them books they can thoroughly enjoy—teenage novels, for instance.

At the appearance of teenage novels the literary critics went into tailspins and vied with each other in expressing their scorn. Some librarians agreed with them, while others who have read and circulated these books and listened to the reactions of young readers have come to believe that the public library can make good use of teenage novels: to teach the apathetic the love of reading; to satisfy some of the adolescent's emotional and psychological needs; to throw light on the problems of adolescence; to explore the teenager's relationship to his community; and to lead him to adult reading.

To Teach the Apathetic the Love of Reading

People who read books are enigmas to some young people. They wonder why anyone would withdraw from the hurly-burly of the street where he can converse with people to go off alone with a book. These adolescents have no interest in distant places, interplay of character, or man's struggle against fate. The girls are interested in growing up and dating; the boys like sports, space travel, cars, adventure— whatever affords an entree to a man's world.

If a younger girl whose friends are unread speaks of going to the library because she loves to read good books, she may arouse only concern for her eccentricity, but on the other hand, if she shows her friends that she is returning *Seventeenth Summer* by Maureen Daly and *Double Date* [1952] by Rosamond Du Jardin, it is quite likely that one or more of her nonreading friends will look these books over, listen to her warm recommendations of them, and return with her to borrow them from the library. Moreover, these girls will tell others about them and constantly increase the number of younger teenager patrons of the library.

A teenage boy is quite likely to be intrigued by the science-fiction novels his friend is reading when he looks at the jackets portraying ant men, robots controlled by the laws of robotics, a spaceship buried in a sea of moon dust, humanoids, hive-hearts, men from Mars. Though a boy may be a reluctant reader, if he reads one of these stories, he will find that writers of science fiction can take the earthbound on flights of fancy to distant planets and out into the incredible void. Outrageous as some of these plots may sound, they are the fairy tales of this techno-logical age and they intrigue readers because no one can prove they are impossible. If we had been told a quarter of a century ago that children might vacation on the moon or that mankind would possess the instruments of its own destruction, who would have given credence to such wild tales? *The Three Musketeers* and *Moby Dick* are better literature than science fiction, but they do not lure the nonreader to make a first contact with the library.

If there is one subject dear to teenage boys, it is automobiles. All of them either own their own cars or hot rods or dream of owning them. In Felsen's *Hot Rod*, one of the earliest stories on the subject, Bud Crayne's race with the policeman, his insolent attitude that brakes are only for sissies, and the results of his folly make a story beloved by boys despite the obvious lesson driven home at the end. They like stories that go into some detail about mechanical problems. They want the feel of driving an MG or a Jaguar with their tremendous power, remarkable maneuverability, and manner of burning up the track in the big races. There is also a great need for stories of motorcycles.

Few teenage novels will ever be classics, but they speak to young people in a language they can understand on subjects that interest them. For that reason they are bait for reluctant readers. Unless the adolescent can be convinced that reading is fun and that he must make time for it in his busy life, he will never become a reader. No books accomplish this more quickly for the masses of younger teenagers than teenage novels.

To Satisfy the Adolescent's Emotional and Psychological Needs

Why does a teenage girl rush to the telephone after school to call up the friends she saw all day and with whom she rode home on the bus a little while ago? Why does she talk for hours and hours on the only telephone in the house? Why does she giggle so much? Why is she such a pain in the neck? Because she so desperately wants to be popular. She must find out how to be attractive to boys before old age overtakes her. She is only six or seven short years from twenty, when old age sets in, and if she does not succeed in being alluring, she may end up as a "brain" with a career and never know the meaning of love or have children or anything! She is so beset by her own worries and fears that she is often callous to the rights and privileges of others and indifferent to the advantages of a really good education or the charm of culture. However, in the midst of her feverish turmoil, she will go to the library and borrow teenage romances.

The warmest defender of these stories would not recommend them for the Great Books list nor ask to be marooned with them on a desert island, but they do have their good points. They are as wholesome as oatmeal and they are invaluable standards of taste for the girl whose association with boys consists in gathering with the crowd at the corner drugstore and engaging in friendly pushing and shoving. These teenage romances give younger inexperienced girls a glimpse of the dating world, of good manners, of fitting into one's family circle with respect and affection.

The adolescent is just discovering the appalling fact adults know all too well—that we are all essentially lonely. He has an idea that his unformed worries and fears, as well as those clearly defined, are peculiar to him. In these simple little stories he welcomes the discovery that what he thought were his individual problems are common ones that other teenagers have met and solved. He takes courage and makes a quicker and better adjustment. There is yet another psychological factor to be noted here. The technical term for it is probably "wish-fulfillment." The more awkward and shy and unglamorous a girl is, the more interest she may have in reading about a girl who is the embodiment of what she herself wishes to be. Certainly a steady diet of stories of happy people leading happy lives may dull the senses over a long period of time, but a few books of this type may be no more harmful than the child's fairy tales if the individual's reading is directed eventually to a more balanced realism.

To Throw Light on the Problems of Adolescence

Besides the difficulties of growing up and learning to get along with one's family and peers, other problems are dealt with that may not seem so important to adults but are crucial to adolescents. Modern authors of teenage stories have depicted skillfully the girl whose lovable father is an alcoholic, the girl suddenly faced with the fact that her parents do not love each other and that her warm circle of love is an illusion. There is the father coming home from prison, the mother who wants people to think she and her daughter are like sisters and who is always the star with both the boys and girls among her shy daughter's friends. We read of the compulsive eater, the basketball player sensitive about his height, the "select-girls-school" type who learns that the protection her family's wealth has given her has also made her a snob. And again and again there is the study of values between the glitter and the gold of which Mary Stolz's *Pray Love, Remember* [1954] is probably the best. In this story Dody Jenks escaped from her dull life and prosaic family to glamorous Oyster Bay and a rich household for whose little boy she was responsible. Strange to tell, the Oyster Bay family wasn't much better than her own and Dody's sense of values was confused until a Jewish boy with whom she fell in love showed her, before he died, how to measure life's intangibles and to attain inner strength.

For the boys, sports stories often deal with the importance of subordinating one's desire to be a star to the good of the team and frequently the relative importance of winning and playing fair is weighed.

To Explore the Teenager's Relationship to His Community

One of the first teenage novels to deal with the boy and girl who "had to get married," Felsen's *Two and the Town* [1952], shook up conservative librarians. What happened wasn't any more Buff's fault than Elaine's. It just happened. The two respectable middle-class families saw that the children were respectably married and sent them off on a pseudo-honeymoon. The boy's resentment at losing a chance to play college football, the girl's embarrassment at being asked by the school principal not to come back to school, and the coming of the baby are skillfully handled, and though the ending holds out hope that the boy may grow up to his responsibilities, the beating the two took for a year or more would surely dismay any adolescent.

The book came off the press in the fifties, a few weeks before the American Library Association met in New York City. There was to be a preconference on young-adult work in the public library, and I was to sit on a panel where I expected the book to be questioned. I immediately bought a copy for each young-adult branch collection in the Pratt system with the request that each librarian give it to a teenager to read and get his honest reaction. One of the librarians said he gave it to a boy whose mother charged into the branch one evening to ask, "Did you give this book to my boy?" The librarian was looking for a hole to crawl into when the woman explained that she, the boy, and the boy's friend had read and discussed it. She thought it really very good, but only for boys as mature and well read as her son. (Parents often think their children are superior to the herd.)

All the reactions from young people had been favorable, and I set out for the ALA panel meeting. Sure enough, *Two and the Town* came up for discussion and the panel seemed agreed it "was not up to Felsen," which simply meant they thought it too hot to handle. I came to the book's defense saying we had no other book that dealt honestly with this problem, which was of interest and concern to teenagers, and asked what they would give a young person who wanted a book on this subject. One of the true-blue ladies drew herself up and announced, "I would give him *The Scarlet Letter!*"

Times have changed and most librarians accept such books as a matter of course. One of the best is *Mr. and Mrs. Bo Jo Jones* [1968] by Head. Here the death of the baby makes it possible for the two families to engineer an annulment of the marriage, but it also brings the boy and girl together in grief and gives them a realization of the true meaning of marriage.

Years ago John Tunis undertook to show the workings of democracy through sports stories and succeeded admirably. Many sports stories today depict the sports-crazy town that cries for the blood of the coach who loses, whatever the justification, and deal with prejudice against Negro, Jewish, and foreign players.

All sorts of problems that bother teenagers are dealt with in contemporary teenage novels. Many adolescents who are worried about matters they hesitate to discuss find what they are looking for in teenage stories. Most of these are adequately written; they are neither pornographic nor Communistic, they hurt no one, and they afford a great deal of pleasure to a lot of young people.[6]

To Lead the Teenager to Adult Reading

The problem in the library world is not teenage novels but the librarian who allows them to become ends in themselves and fails to make use of them as simple, effective tools in the development of readers. Teenage stories should not be shelved as a collection in themselves, since this tends to develop dead-end readers. They should be shelved with adult books for teenagers and not represent over 20 percent of the

From left to right, Margaret's sister, Helen, her mother, Hadena Alexander, and Margaret at Seven Falls in South Cheyenne Canyon, Colorado

The book wagon in the first year of circulating books in the streets of Baltimore, ca. 1943.

Edwards and her assistant checking out books to neighborhood young people, ca. 1944.

The Bell Ringers Booth at the first book fair for YAs at Pratt, 1951.

Pratt book fairs were given for every senior English class in every public high school in Baltimore, ca. 1951–1955.

Pratt YA librarians at an annual gathering at Edwards' farm, 'Ed Ache, where they all performed skits and put on "roasts," ca. 1952.

Edwards on tractor, sometime in the early sixties.

On the day of her retirement, October 9, 1962, Edwards greets staff and friends in her office.

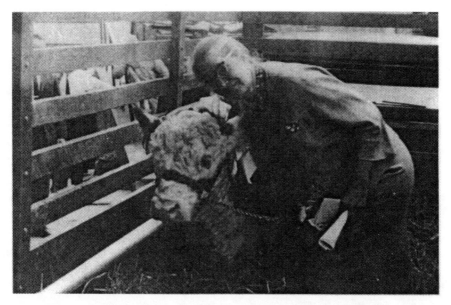

For a retirement gift, the staff decided to go big. They purchased a bull from Nicholas Merryman's farm. But Bullie Sol Edwards did not perform as Edwards had hoped, so Mr. Merryman gave her a new one—called "Pappy," after Hemingway—who did very well and increased the herd.

Edwards in the door of the hay loft at 'Ed Ache, ca. October 1963.

Phillip "Doc" Edwards, ca. 1965.

Annie Oakley takes aim at a nest of blade snakes in an enormous oak tree at 'Ed Ache to the amusement of children and adult guests at a picnic, during the late sixties.

Edwards and Emerson Greenaway in Pratt's central hall at the celebration of the 100th birthday of Pratt, fall 1986.

The 1986 or 1987 Christmas card from 'Ed Ache. Edwards with Tammy Faye and Fawn Hall.

Margaret Alexander Edwards
October 1902–April 1988

titles in the collection. The librarian should know his readers and books well enough to be able to introduce readable, appealing adult titles at the propitious time and see that the young reader gradually moves into adult reading with all the enthusiasm he once had for teenage stories.

In America provision must be made for gifted students, but the public schools and the public library are rightly committed to the enlightenment of the masses. If the masses are to recognize demagogues as they arise, if they are to vote as individuals instead of as city blocks under the rule of a political boss, if they are to understand the problems of this country and its role in world affairs, they need to avail themselves of the wisdom in books. Certainly teenage novels will not solve the world's problems, but if they lead more people to a first understanding of the pleasures and profits to be found in print, they have a place in the reading program.

❧ VI ❧

Fighting Weeds and Insects

The Strange Device . . . *"Excelsior!"*

Some years ago I went for my summer vacation to the Poconos and put up at a summer hotel. On one Sunday evening of "my week" a young minister came up to hold vesper services. After two hymns and a prayer he spoke briefly, presenting the hardships of the Christian life and explaining that he had given up "the world" and its temptations to preach the Gospel. As I looked at this overly earnest young man, I wondered how much deprivation he was suffering. Had he remained in "the world," would he be dancing down the primrose path, clinking glasses, and tempting pretty ladies? I also did not like his attitude toward his profession. The ministry is surely more than denial and hardship, and he was probably doing better financially than if he had hit Wall Street. I should have respected him more had he taken pride in the ministry and spoken more of fulfillment and less of denial. All in all, I got a meager blessing from the vesper service.

Why do people go into the professions? Because they want to. Most intelligent college graduates have to choose between business and the professions. Those who elect to enter the business world want the position and security money can give them. They are interested in the world of commerce, are well suited to it, and are willing to work hard for what they want. It is to their credit and better for all of us if they enter the business world.

Other young people elect to go into the professions because they wish to work with people and ideas. They cannot find rich fulfillment in the business world and feel their modicum of financial reward is compensated for by the personal enrichment they receive from professional life. They honestly want to bear through snow and ice a banner with the strange device "Excelsior." [1]

Unfortunately, the public generally has the impression that librarians are not so interested in carrying the banner as in getting out of the snow and ice to find a warm place. I believe this is because we are more technicians than professionals. Our activities center largely around manipulating book collections and buildings and staffs so that queries can be answered. We stress skills and the performance of them rather than our relationship to the individuals these skills are supposed to help. If the day ever comes, as it surely will, when computers answer questions related to schoolwork and most other general inquiries, the public library can be set up like chain stores with a general manager, one or two assistants, and clerks to put the books in order on the shelves.

Most professions center their activities around the individual. When misfortune strikes a home, the minister is often notified. He comes with sympathy to hold one's hand and say a little prayer, attempting by word and look to soften the blow. Many a teacher has so identified with his individual students that he has increased their vision and changed their entire lives for the better. Clifton Fadiman said that in John Erskine's class one did not so much learn something as become something. [2] The lawyer enters into the personal life of his client to see that he receives justice. We love and trust the physician as our personal protection against pain and death. The librarian, more often than not, is impersonal. So while other professions, centered as they are on the individual, must fill their ranks with personalities strong enough to win confidence and persuade people to go along with them, the library profession can absorb numbers of colorless personalities so long as they can organize and administer a book collection and reply to the questions of the few patrons who approach them.

The library profession hopes to improve its image and seems to feel this can be done by proof of efficiency. We even set up workshops on the operation of computers. Library schools train for efficiency, as is witnessed by their catalogs listing page after page of courses in descriptive cataloging, subject cataloging and classification, advanced classification, indexing and abstracting, automation of library services, reference and bibliography, advanced reference and bibliography, government documents, research, administration, principles of book selection, and one or two electives on materials for children, and rarely, adolescents. Over half of the required courses are not really necessary for public and school librarians. In place of those that could be eliminated, the schools might set up courses designed to train students in the promotion of reading among people of all ages and types, and in the meantime, make readers of the library-school students themselves.

A survey of the Baltimore-Washington metropolitan libraries showed that half the patrons of the public library had come to it simply for a good book to read.[3] The general public, even the unread portion of it, has a deep and abiding faith in the moving power of the book. The public is so sure books are dynamite that they often burn those they believe to be evil to keep people from falling under their spells. Yet patrons who come to the library are seldom accosted by a librarian who has thought enough of books to read very many of them, or if he has read extensively, cares enough to recommend books to others searching for good reading.

The library-school graduate often lacks a professional attitude. He is inclined to think he has learned what he needs to know and is now ready to fill a professional position. He really is ready to perform fairly well as a technician, but in young-adult work he is sadly lacking, for as a rule, he does not know books nor has he been taught how to work with people. Furthermore, he does not feel he should be asked to remedy these deficiencies on his own time.

How often I have been asked why the library does not provide time for reading in the daily schedule and not ask the assistant to read books at night. A new assistant, duly certified by a library school, felt the required outside reading under my administration was an imposition, at least when he first learned of it, though he was at a loss to answer such simple requests as for a story about the American Revolution that was easy to read. He complained to his branch librarian, who sometimes came to my office to plead for these new people, reminding me they "were so young" and should be having a good time. I do not know any other profession where people expect to work eight hours a day and always have the remainder of their time free. Ministers comfort the bereaved and bury the dead on their days off; doctors answer emergency calls day and night; lawyers work extra hours to prepare briefs; and teachers grade papers and make lesson plans almost every night. A professional is not a blue-collar worker who punches a clock. He works when he is needed and he renews himself constantly. This renewal by reading is generally overlooked by librarians, old and young.

Some years ago I was very ill in the Johns Hopkins Hospital. Since I could not sleep well at night, the young intern assigned to our ward usually called on me around midnight to chat a while and lift my spirits before he went off duty. The next morning at six o'clock I would see him walking briskly through the halls, half dead but going strong. One morning while he stood by my bed, almost asleep on his feet, I stormed, "The Hopkins Hospital should be ashamed. It has hundreds of applicants for internships from all over the world yet it takes only a few interns and works them to death. They should take at least twice as many and not treat you this way." He took me up quickly to say, "Oh no! That way I wouldn't see as many cases!" This was a professional dedicated to perfecting himself to serve people, even at the cost of physical suffering. I could not help thinking of those nice young assistants who were so unhappy at being asked to read books. It is my belief that the young-adult librarian's love of people can be measured by the amount of reading he is willing to do for them.

When the time comes that library schools train readers' advisors as well as technicians; when administrators make the promotion of reading as important as the informational services; when staff members render creative professional service to individuals, we shall not have to worry about our image.

YA—The Library Bastard

According to the Baltimore-Washington metropolitan survey mentioned previously, 50 per cent of the patrons who come to the public library have in mind only a good book to read. Now, these people are a problem, as so many of them like to read fiction—which might run the circulation figures for fiction higher than those for nonfiction, thus leaving the impression that the library's patrons are not "serious" readers. It would never do to have more people reading for enjoyment and enrichment than for information. If this should happen, it will not be the fault of the librarian, who seldom calls attention to fiction but stresses educational reading with such displays as "Know Your State" or "Understanding Missiles." The fiction collection, dealing as it does with the emotions and feelings of people, is a kind of literary bastard since it does not fit into the library's philosophy of educating oneself by "serious" reading.

But the biggest bastard in the library family is the young-adult department. The work in this department cannot be done by technicians or colorless people. It is centered around service to and enrichment of the individual. Its pedigree reads: "*Out* of service to the individual *by* the promotion of reading." This sire and dam are not fully recognized in the library's stud books and their offspring has been disowned in some quarters. It is time we reexamined the bastard's relation to the family to determine his eligibility for recognition. Here I serve as his advocate.

My assistants and I believed that we should attempt through books to take each individual, whatever his reading level, and develop him to his full potential as a reader, widening his interests and deepening his understanding until he came to know that he was a member of one race—the human race—and a citizen of one planet—the earth. This was a big undertaking and required highly developed professional skill. It would have been impossible to have implemented our goals by simply shelving books in order and letting young people browse around. It required on the part of the assistants a very rich reading background, sincere liking for teenagers, energy, dedication, and mastery of the art of interesting young people in reading. They had to become real people with hearts open to experience and minds capable of absorbing it. They were warned against becoming like the two little librarians who share an apartment and go into hiding from the city.

These two typical little librarians waste hours sharing their limited experiences and bemoaning the scarcity of men. For entertainment they go to dinner at the apartment of two other little librarians, where they discuss the queer characters that come into the library every day, their most effective methods of squelching troublemakers, and the breakdown of the charging machine. And they bemoan the scarcity of men.

This kind of isolation from the community is like sitting alone at a gourmet banquet eating crackers and milk. In every community, large or small, there are intelligent, stimulating people interested in living. They race horses, take part in politics, join little theater groups, grow roses, paint, watch birds, hike, swim, play tennis, work with the League of Women Voters, raise funds for the symphony orchestra, and so on. No librarian has time for all these activities but he or she should be interested in at least one of them and get to know people who are concerned with something beside the breakdown of the charging machine. Too many librarians are anemic. When their library joins the blood bank, it is difficult to find enough donors with sufficient iron in their blood to renew the strength of the least-depleted donor. This anemia may be the result of holing up in that little apartment.

By his performance on the floor of the library, the librarian leaves a very good impression with patrons of the kind of person he is. Too often the patron in the library sees the librarian sensibly dressed, seated, earnestly sorting cards or reading. If someone gets up enough courage to ask him a question, he looks up patiently and says "Yes?" Or if there is noise, he raps on the desk and stares down the offenders. If the noise continues, he yells "QUIET!" This does not "send" teenagers—or anyone else.

When patrons are in the library, especially if they are young adults, the well-dressed, well-groomed librarian should be up on his feet, looking friendly and approachable. Think how impatient we become when we stand in a shop waiting for a clerk to assist us. When teenagers come to the library after school the librarian should move about among them, helping old customers and making friends with new people. As one high-school girl put it, the relation of a librarian to young adults should be that of a hostess to house guests. This girl went on to say that a gracious hostess would not tell her guests provisions are in the refrigerator, assuming they know how to cook and can prepare their own meals. Emily Post says good manners are based on common sense and kindness of heart. These are the same guidelines a young-adult librarian might follow in establishing good relations with teenagers.

We should have enough faith in ourselves and enthusiasm for books and people to make the initial contact rather than leaving it to the insecure, often inarticulate, young person. By our social grace and tact we should set all young people at ease and make their trips to the library an experience they look forward to and enjoy. This same grace and tact will lead us to let alone the youngster who wishes to be let alone to help himself. But most adolescents are so overwhelmed at the sight of all those shelves holding hundreds of books written by authors they never heard of that help from someone who does know is more than welcome. It is good to have a friend at court who will go to great lengths to help one with a difficult problem and who keeps smiling, no matter how rough the going gets.

In our monthly meetings we seldom reviewed new books. When twenty or so new titles had been read by the assistants, they were assembled in one place with written reviews attached and each assistant looked them over and made his purchases. This left the meetings free for more important matters. We studied how to interest reluctant readers as well as the accelerated college-bound students. We decided what positions we would take on controversial books of interest to young people. We planned programs to feature reliable books of sex information for teenagers who were getting their knowledge of sex in back alleys. We viewed and discussed films and constantly evaluated the effectiveness of our special projects such as book fairs, school visits, the young-adult program for which we were responsible on a rock 'n roll radio station, or our book-reviewing publication by and for teenagers. When an assistant discovered a new approach that seemed effective, we shared the idea, and if there were doubts about it, we did some experimenting.

Not every assistant was a howling success with the young people, but most of them were. They did not impinge on the privacy of teenagers or oversell them. Teenagers crowded around them after school and it was evident that they held the affection and respect of their clientele. Many a mother who read in the young-adult department as a high-school girl has dropped in to tell about her children and to say she hopes that when they are older someone will make reading as meaningful for them as it was made for her.

And yet I was told by the dean of a library school, and I have heard administrators and staff members say the same thing with assurance, that any staff member can help young adults just as well as a special assistant. I never saw a general assistant who had the background or understanding to work as effectively with young adults as did my trained assistants. Of course, he can do as well if we define the word "help" to mean operating as a technician, i.e., if a girl asks for a romance, tell her to look under "Romance" in the catalog or give her the H. W. Wilson *Standard Catalog for High School Libraries*. If she persists in asking what the books are about, she can be shown the annotations in library references. Few assistants untrained in young-adult work can satisfy teenagers who ask, "Will you find me two real good love stories?" "What is *Mr. and Mrs. Bo Jo Jones* about?" "Will you help me find a real thin little book about going West?" "I loved this book. Will you get me one like it?" "Would you be willing to speak at our assembly next month?" "My teacher said to ask you if *Manchild in the Promised Land* has been approved for high-school reading." "My teacher sent this note to you. She is coming in Saturday morning to ask you to help her bring up to date the unit our ninth grade class has on 'The Lure of the Middle Ages.' "

Young people often feel the need to talk about the books they have read. They will express themselves freely only to those librarians they trust to help them pursue an awakened interest. A general assistant could not possibly attend to his other duties and read widely enough in this field to function effectively.

Many administrators disband YA collections to make room for more "serious" adult reading. In serving young people it seems to me important to keep together those books most essential to the introduction of adult reading. This collection serves the same time-saving purpose as the ready reference collection in the reference room. There are a few hundred books that are used so much that it is a waste of time to run over the library constantly searching for them. Also, when the young-adult librarian is away from the library it is a great help to the youngster to know there is one place in the library where he is pretty sure to find something he will like to read.

When administrators eliminate YA work they usually compliment themselves by saying, "We treat the teenagers just as we do the adults."

I'll say they do. They make it possible for the teenagers to join the 84 per cent of all adults who never speak to the librarian, who have learned to shift for themselves whether they know their way around or not, and who can always rely on the catalog for advice and inspiration.

In winding up my case I admit that under the prevailing standards of public librarianship the bastard YA cannot claim legitimate membership in the library family, but the fault is with the system, not with the bastard. As long as public librarianship is concerned primarily with collecting and making available information and educational materials, it seems arbitrary to ask a college graduate to take another year off and spend a large sum of money to get another degree in order to learn to perform little better than he would if he were trained on the job. Since trained librarians have been in such short supply, many a large public library has been forced to employ untrained college graduates and in the process has learned that they are quite acceptable without a B.S. or A.M. degree in Library Science. Administrators keep this secret well and insist that promising people leave to get a degree, for they know this union card is essential for advancement to the big money and the big jobs and they also wish to keep alive the idea that librarians belong to a profession in which extra training is necessary. In some large libraries thought is being given to employing trained heads and supervisors and filling all other positions with staff who will be trained on the job.

Many a library-board member thinks it is folly to pay high salaries to library-school graduates when they do not see librarians who have been so trained doing anything that seems too difficult for any intelligent college graduate to learn. However, if they saw trained librarians up out of their chairs and on the floor, sought after by young and old, handing out books and discussing them with people; if their children came home from high school excited about books the public librarian had described to their class, or had in their hands attractive book lists and were saying what it meant to go to the library and find a friendly expert who knew just the kind of books one would love to read—then a board member might conclude that special training was worth paying for. But before this happens, public libraries will have to change their philosophy and library schools their curricula.

If, however, we continue to confine ourselves to administering collections, to making information and materials available, to answering questions but remaining unconcerned for the individual, then we should be honest enough to admit we are technicians, cease insisting on professional status, disown the bastard YA, and catch up with our work. After all, we librarians are not to blame that Americans are the worst-read people of the world's democracies . . . or are we?

Once a young man named Moses who was herding sheep in the Egyptian desert looked up and saw a burning bush and, "Behold, the bush burned with fire and the bush was not consumed." When he turned aside to investigate, a voice called to him out of the bush and said, "Put off thy shoes from thy feet, for the place whereon thou standest is holy ground." Many administrators and librarians wander about in the desert and never look up to see the miraculous burning bush. Instead they devote their attention to taking care of the sheep, a useful occupation, but it was the voice from the burning bush that inspired Moses to lead his people from the bondage of Egypt to the Promised Land.

The City Kid and the Library

During the last of the four summers when I was sweating out a library degree, I was slated for a seminar in library administration that I was sure would kill me. So I borrowed the notes of a fellow librarian who had previously taken the course, read them over on the train, took the exam, and got a C. This enabled me to enroll for the same number of points in the adjoining university, where I took an exciting course in philosophy—a symposium introduced by Morris Cohen.[4] This was before World War II, when I and other innocents believed that despite a few slips, man was climbing the ladder rung by rung from the lowly earth to the vaulted skies. Morris Cohen said this was not so. Man was getting neither better and better nor worse and worse, but as the individual had his ups and downs with some good days and some not so good, so the race maintained something of a norm.

If this is so, is it not as true for teenagers as for others? As a group, are they basically different from what they always were? Socrates said the teenagers of his day were simply impossible. Two thousand years later the young people of my generation were enthusiastic over the theory of companionate marriage. They drank bathtub gin from girls' slippers, whispered over Elinor Glyn's *A Bed of Roses*, and sang "The Sheik of Araby" with deep emotion while their mothers tore the buttons off Lawrence Tibbett's clothes.[5]

Certainly some teenagers do terrible things today, but it is quite likely that Morris Cohen was right—that basically man does not change. Man's activities may fall into new patterns, his conception of the world and the universe will be as new each year as the discoveries

---

"The City Kid and the Library" was first published in *Top of the News*, November 1967, 62–71. *Ed.*

of science, his habits of work and play will be altered by electronics, but his concerns will remain constant. He will still need love and security, he will still seek for identity and fulfillment, he will still wonder about the meaning of his own and all existence. Though he may die without realizing it, the answers to many of his questions are in books. It is especially important that the adolescent learn this, for his search for meanings is especially intense.

All over the world young people are interested in politics and society's welfare. But their eagerness to take up causes and protest, their readiness to overthrow the established order and set right what seems to them wrong, their potential power in sheer numbers, mean they desperately need a sound attitude toward life, civilized feelings, an understanding of people and cultures. They need something to go on besides emotion. There are various sources where they may find understanding, ideas, and enrichment, but the most reliable, never-failing source is the books on the shelves of the public library.

What is the public library doing to interest adolescents in reading these books? In too many cases, nothing.

Generally, librarians have been content to supply factual material and technical help, but this is not the case in some cities where provision is made for the adolescent and special services are offered. Detroit has conducted programs for young adults on TV for years with success; Philadelphia has worked with delinquents and probationers; Dallas and Seattle have worked effectively with schools; New York City has led the way in work with manual-minded vocational students; Boston, Pittsburgh, St. Louis, Los Angeles, and other cities have set up special services for young adults, while Baltimore in addition to its program in the schools has been an innovator with new ideas such as book fairs, in-service training, and at present, experimental programs in the war on poverty. Other cities I have not mentioned are also doing good work, I am sure, but the present social crisis in our big cities calls for a general breakthrough. It is extremely important that city kids all over the nation find out that the public library has a lot more to offer them than material for school assignments. Because this is so very urgent I am going to make five charges against the public library, not in a spirit of hostility or carping criticism, but with a firm faith in the potential of the public library for influencing the thinking and feeling of the adolescent. By pointing out what seem to me to be failings, I may stimulate thinking on new courses of action. I should like to cite as state's evidence for the charges I shall make the recent *Survey of Metropolitan Public Library Users of Maryland Baltimore-Washington Metropolitan Area* by Mary Lee Bundy, Associate Professor of the University of Maryland School of Library and Information Services. The urban district surveyed is organized, supported, and patronized well enough to seem as representative, up-to-date, fair an example as we might find of the city library we are here discussing.

How Has the Public Library Failed the City Teenager?

1. It has failed in the relationship of the majority of the staff to adolescents. (Young-adult librarians and those innately gracious staff members are not included here.)

The ALA Ad Hoc Committee on Instruction in the Use of Libraries in the report it presented at the San Francisco Conference in 1967 made this statement: "One of the greatest blocks to the total use of public libraries has been the attitude of generations of public librarians toward students." The Bundy survey cited above shows that though adults were not unusually critical of the staff, 25 per cent of the students complained. One said, "I appreciate the librarians who can tell when you need help and offer it to you in a pleasant manner without making you feel ignorant." Another wrote, "Kindness is a virtue and I hope in the future we will have kinder librarians."

For years I have attempted to figure out why so many librarians dislike teenagers. Is it that these librarians are insecure and feel there is more status in working with adults? Are they afraid of adolescents? Is it a little touch of sadism that leads a librarian to humiliate the defenseless young person, bawling him out for a stupid assignment his teacher gave him, interrogating him in a seemingly polite way that undermines his confidence? Though adolescents make up about half our patronage outside the children's department, many librarians still consider them an interruption to business. It is not only the 25 per cent who write out complaints who resent the staff. Even those not mistreated resent seeing librarians bully-rag their friends. Yet we wonder why there is such a shortage of librarians and put out more attractive recruiting material to explain to these young people what an opportunity for service librarianship affords.

2. The urban public library is off-balance. Its concern is with its informational services to the neglect of other needs of its patrons.

Since the simultaneous explosions of scientific knowledge and the population, all hands have been put to work to get the facts to the people as expeditiously as possible and to deal with the never-ending, everbroadening school assignments. Some cities have eliminated young-adult work above the ninth grade and have transferred positions calling

for special skills in introducing reading to the adolescent to more utili-
tarian uses. Some cities have kept token YA work, assigning the head of
young-adult work to a subsidiary position and regarding this special-
ization as a kind of extravagance. Most administrators cannot see why
capable librarians should be talking about books and reading to teenagers when several students are waiting for material on the mineral
resources of Hawaii. Even those administrators who believe in the
promotion of reading have no system for promoting outstanding young
librarians in this field except to remove them from their specialty and
make them branch librarians. The money is in administration rather than
in the promotion of reading. It should be in both. With our microfilm,
indices, teletypes, catalogs, and impersonal staffs, the machine is truly
our message and for high-school students it is also a massage.[6] Yet
according to the survey cited above, the percentage of people who come
to the library for general reading is exactly the same as that of those who
come for materials or information on a subject. So our services are geared
to the needs of half the patrons who come to the library.

One day during the summer when I drove the horse-drawn vegetable cart loaded with books through the streets of a Baltimore slum I
pulled up in front of a hovel where a Negro mother was ironing. Her
little boy wanted to borrow a book and when I showed him a fairy tale
we were ready to clinch the deal. But first I called to the mother, "Is it
all right to let Henry have a book?" She looked very doubtful but
eventually said, "You can let him have a book if you give him something that will do him good." She meant I could give him a speller or
an arithmetic book, but the fairy tale was out. Her philosophy of
reading is shared by many librarians.

3. The public library is passive rather than active.

The Bundy survey asks, "In all the areas it attempts to cover, is the
library's role a passive supplying one or should it undertake active
programs and services of its own?" As far as the adolescent is concerned, it is time the public library answered this question. Do we or
do we not believe that it is important enough for teenagers to read
books that it behooves us to bestir ourselves and not lay the problem
entirely in the laps of other institutions? Polls and surveys tell us what
we already know, that adolescents do very little unassigned reading.
Are public libraries willing to let it go at that?

Once I was walking through the exhibits at a librarians' conference
and my eye happened to fall on a panel in a booth where I read, "The
time has come for the library to recognize that its primary responsibility today is to the other agencies of society and only secondarily to
the individual who walks through the doors."

It seems this was a quotation from a talk made by someone in the book world. If this view is widely held, we will become the only profession not concerned primarily with the individual. Does it not follow that when we agree to this, we will cease to be a profession and become the warehouse of other professions?

We run too many of our libraries like Helpy-Selfy supermarkets. You put it in the basket, we check it out. As a result, the adolescent often arrives at the checking-out point with an empty basket or with a book he selected by its title or cover, which may turn out to be a bad bargain. The Bundy survey says 47 per cent of the library's patrons leave without being completely satisfied. At present, librarians generally believe that if books are in order on the shelves, the reader in search of a good book to read has been served. If he needs help, let him ask. The supermarket, the automat, and libraries are agreed on this method. Many other institutions that serve the public and believe in their product put skilled salespeople on the floor, not behind desks filing cards or reading book reviews and waiting for the customer to approach them.

A short while ago I was teaching a course on the adolescent and his reading in a well-known library school. I was lecturing the students on the fine art of floor work when one of them said, "Mrs. Edwards, I am confused. You speak of what you call floor work as if it were a generally accepted practice. In all my life I never had a librarian approach me and suggest a book I might like to read." I was horrified and asked the class if any of them had also never been approached by a librarian, and all but four raised their hands. I have taught courses in three library schools and held workshops over the country for many summers. With each group, I would ask how many were ever approached by a librarian with a reading suggestion after they outgrew the children's department, and as a rule, two or three hands would go up. Often students would drop by the desk after class to say how they went to libraries for years without a glimmer of recognition, let alone a suggestion for reading from a librarian. They remember this with resentment. One of my students, reared in a large midwestern city, said, "I remember getting my adult card. When my juvenile card expired and I went to renew it, the clerk asked my age, said I was old enough now for an adult card, and gave me one. No one suggested where to begin reading in this alien land." How can it be possible that librarians would not wish to share their pleasure in reading? How could they not help talking about books to patrons? Yet in city after city public librarians have not suggested an enjoyable book to a single teenager. The Bundy survey says, "In the day-to-day operation of a library, librarians talk to only a small number of users." And again,

"The library user is apparently on his own; only 16 per cent sought help from a staff member." (And we can be sure many of those who contacted the librarian lived to regret it.) The machine is our message.

The promotion of reading calls for intensive, skillful training. Most library schools ignore this field or give it the once-over lightly in favor of training research technicians. The training is in library science rather than in the art of librarianship. This makes sense because college and special libraries want this kind of training for their employees. For that matter, that is the type of librarian most in demand in public libraries. If library schools turned out specialists in the promotion of reading, they might have difficulty placing them. Incidentally, this is the basis of many complaints about library-school training. Those students who enter the library profession because they love books and wish to work with people soon discover they are being trained for technical services and become bored and disillusioned. But readers' advisers can be developed by in-service training if the administrator believes in the service and if he has a staff member who knows books, likes people, and is an inspiring supervisor. To be honest, isn't the root of our passivity the fact that so many librarians do not read books outside their own interests and do not like people?

4. Our obsession with the catalog is a boomerang that has sailed back to harm our relations with the teenager and to diminish his joy in reading.

I hesitate to make this fourth charge for it is heresy and is likely to end once and for all my activities in the library world, but I shall make it anyway. After all, no one can fire me since I am retired, and if worst comes to worst, I can eat my Hereford cows.

Before I touch the holy mountain, let me say that college-bound students should be taught enough about the catalog and reference tools to make it possible for them to do the research they will need to do in college. However, we should take a critical look at our plan to train all other high-school students. In 1965, the latest year for which there are complete statistics, 28 per cent of the high-school graduates of Baltimore went to college. In addition, 2.6 per cent enrolled for part-time courses. This 30.6 per cent of high-school graduates should have been taught the use of the catalog and reference tools. To the remaining 69.4 per cent we have done more harm than good by our insistence on teaching them how to use the catalog and tools of reference and research. The arguments against such instruction as I see them are:

(a) It cannot be taught successfully. The ALA Ad Hoc Committee on Instruction in the Use of Libraries says, "The great majority of students do not master library skills, and do not feel impelled to gain proficiency

in them." The committee, however, does not despair. They plan to "Hit 'em again harder" with new devices and more instruction. For many years the schools of the Baltimore-Washington metropolitan district have given tireless instruction in the use of the catalog and reference tools all through high school and to some extent in the lower grades. The surveyors working with Dr. Bundy looked for this trained patron who needed to do simple research, and where do you think they found him? At the shelves, looking through rows of books— hoping to wrest from them the information needed. The survey says, "He browses through the shelves hoping to find what he wants but is not likely to use reference books, library catalogs, or to seek help from a librarian. He is even less likely to make use of other library services and resources such as periodical indexes." If the survey is correct, how many hours, days, and years of instruction have failed to pay off! Methods of teaching this skill may change and improve, but however many variables we introduce, one constant remains—the student who does not wish to learn, and so, cannot be taught. Moreover, if the library world keeps abreast of the times, surely computers will eventually supply the material needed for school assignments. Meantime, the public library could make available instruction in the use of the catalog and reference tools for those who wish to learn. Attractive instructional devices such as those used by the National Geographic Society in Washington, D.C., might lead many patrons to wish to teach themselves the skills of research.

(b) Our burning passion to force the adolescent to use the catalog has damaged our relations with him. I have seen librarians demand that a youngster look up a book in the catalog when it was within arm's reach of the librarian. Probably the most hated six words in these United States of America are "Look it up in the catalog." Here is what some teenagers say in the survey: "In general, the librarians are fairly helpful as long as you never make the mistake of asking where a book is. Do this, and the librarian 'sweetly' says, 'What's the matter, don't you know how to use the catalog?' " Another: "I feel library service could be improved in that sometimes the librarians are too lazy to help you. Many times I have asked where a certain book is and she will say, 'Look it up in the catalog.' I feel this is not right. . . . Thank you for letting me express my opinion." One of the adult patrons spoke of librarians who, like some tradespeople, showed "the tyranny of petty authority," which, right or wrong, seems to be the idea in the heads of teenagers.

Further bound by our obsession, if a class from a neighborhood school comes for a visit to a branch library, we often entertain them royally with a lesson in the catalog when we might, instead, have interested them in Dostoevski's analysis of the criminal mind, A. B. Guthrie's depiction of the mountain man, or Van Gogh's passion to capture the essence of life in paint and color.

(c) Our argument for teaching all students to use the catalog is based on a fallacy. Library literature puts it this way: "The student should acquire proficiency in the independent use of library resources as an essential part of his formal education, and in support of his continuing self-education." We public librarians have honestly convinced ourselves that students now in high school will avidly continue their self-education throughout their adult lives, for which they will need to make continued use of the tools of research. The fact of the matter is that very few of these people will ever put foot inside the public library, and as was said above, half of those who do come want a good book to read rather than informational material. Most people live out their lives unaware of a need for books. No one ever inspired them to read for pleasure and they get along without looking up information. As for continued self-education, that is the last item on their agenda. I would guess that not one in a thousand citizens in any of our big cities is continuing his self-education to the extent of needing to know how to do research, and these we can continue to help or teach how to help themselves if they wish to know. Nor is it just the unread masses who fall short here. It is possible that librarians let a day slip now and then when they do not pursue "continuing self-education." A faculty member of a well-known university recently sent out a questionnaire to library administrators that contained a question on their professional reading and was surprised to find that few of them had read any books in their field in the last year or two.

(d) If we gave up our futile attempt to teach everyone to use the catalog, the time saved could be spent in the intensive promotion of reading. We could use the time for more class visits to talk about books, assembly programs on reading, book lists, reading clubs, and above all, work with individuals on the floor of the library. Even if we agreed that it is desirable for the 69.4 per cent who will not go to college to master the catalog and even if we succeeded in teaching all of them to do so, we would still have misused the time if instead we might have engendered in them a love of reading. The principles of education hold that the teaching of a skill has less value than the development of a cultural attitude.

5. We are not meeting new challenges with new ideas.

It is common knowledge that in the last twenty years the population of the American city has changed. In the past the public library catered to the well-heeled middle class to which most of us belonged. Today most of these people have fled the city, leaving behind the poor, the disadvantaged, the culturally deprived. Instead of college-bound, well-fed, well-mannered young people, we have thousands of adolescents who live in ghettos on relief, without a father and with a mother who never finished the third grade. In their homes these people are unlikely to hear what we think of as interesting conversation. There is little mention of good taste, little talk of ethical standards. Too many of them drop out of school, commit crimes, take dope, join mobs, and hate all authority and established institutions. The whole concept of voluntary reading is foreign to them. These conditions have made little difference in the public library's mode of procedure. The books are still on the shelves for those who wish to borrow them. This method, which never was too successful with the middle classes, is doomed to failure with the masses. Our new social crisis calls for new solutions.

An article entitled "Schools Make News" in the *Saturday Review* (May 21, 1966) began, "Pleasure books, books to read just for fun, are seldom seen, much less owned, by children and adults from disadvantaged areas. None lurk on shelves in their homes to be picked up and browsed through at off moments. Books are largely alien to their environment." The article went on to say that to counter this deprivation the Fund for the Advancement of Education had granted $200,000 to VISTA to equip them with portable paperback libraries suited to the needs of the people with whom they work.[7] I understand this project has not yet realized its full potential, but it seems the sort of undertaking in which the public library should be engaged.

Is it not possible that the solution of our problem may lie in going out to the people instead of waiting for them to come in to us?

Has not Dr. Fader's experiment with the delinquent boys of the Maxey School something to say to us? His *Hooked on Books* [1966] sounds like the beginning of a breakthrough.

There should be a regular national program on TV sponsored by ALA that would dramatize books and reading in such a highly professional, effective way that libraries all over the nation would feel its impact. Surely we could be as interesting as the family wash, bad breath, and tired blood.

Solutions for our problems could be found. But we need administrators concerned with the problem who have the ability to release talent. Then we need young-adult librarians dedicated to establishing rapport with the city kid and convincing him that the public library can furnish him not only with the informational material he needs, but also with the wonder and joy of reading. The book is our message.

Ho! every one that thirsteth, come ye to the waters,
and he that hath no money, come ye, buy and eat;
yea, come, buy wine and milk without money and without price.

[*Isaiah 55:1*]

The Fair Garden
and the Swarm of Beasts

In *The Old Librarian's Almanac* [1773] Jared Bean sets forth some guiding principles for his profession. Among them we read, "So far as your authority will permit it, exercise great Discrimination as to which Persons shall be admitted to the use of the Library. For the Treasure House of Literature is no more to be thrown open to the ravages of the unreasoning Mob, than is a Fair Garden to be laid unprotected at the Mercy of a Swarm of Beasts.

"Question each Applicant closely. See that he be a Person of good Reputation, scholarly Habits, sober and courteous Demeanor. Any mere Trifler, a Person that would Dally with Books, or seek in them shallow amusement, may be Dismissed without delay."

Jared Bean also has a message for those of us concerned with the teenager and the library: "No Person younger than twenty years (save if he be a Student, of more than eighteen years, and vouched for by his Tutor) is on any pretext to enter the Library. Be suspicious of Women. They are given to the Reading of frivolous Romances, and at all events, their presence in the Library adds little to (if it does not, indeed, detract from) that aspect of Gravity, Seriousness and Learning which is its greatest glory...."

Dear Jared, hordes of young adults are pouring into our libraries, devouring the information in books. Indeed, the Treasure House of Literature has been thrown open to the ravages of the unreasoning mob and your fair garden lies "unprotected at the Mercy of a Swarm of Beasts."

Some have tried locking the teenagers out in the evenings; others have isolated them in certain rooms without access to the library as a whole; still others put up with them, crying inwardly and sometimes outwardly at the desecration. Young hands are reaching out for books and more books. Students are asking endlessly for help in finding

---

The above section was first published in *Library Journal,* September 1, 1965, 3379–83. *Ed.*

material for school assignments. Unhappy librarians say with some justification that adults are so dismayed by this invasion of youth that they do not make use of the library. If we could only get rid of these youngsters, our libraries would be more like Jared Bean's, the books protected from use, and unhappy librarians would find their problems solved. They wouldn't be librarians any more, for staffs could be cut from 50 to 75 per cent.

Certainly, there are many librarians with vision who are delighted to have the young people. They realize this invasion of young people could be quite meaningful for the future and wish they might serve teenagers better. But what is better? What is the best we might do for them?

These questions bring us to a serious consideration of the function of the public library as it serves youth. For the moment, suppose we had no problems of space, of book stock, of staff. If fairy godmothers and rich citizens and generous budget directors gave us carte blanche, how would we proceed? More than likely, we would purchase new encyclopedias, history reference books, everything we could find on the Elizabethan theatre in duplicate, more foreign language records, more about the UN. We might provide more individual study tables, more trained staff, more people who could take the daily grind. In other words, we would greatly enlarge our reference services. This would be wonderful; but would it be enough?

In this speeded-up civilization when people send in reservations for seats on the first moonflight and Mars has been on *Candid Camera*, big business and the institutions of society are reexamining their policies and procedures to see if they are adequate for the space age. I should like to propose this question for consideration by those concerned for the public library: If the library answers the inquiries it receives with courtesy and reasonable speed, if it provides a rich collection of books on all subjects for the reader to select from as he chooses, if it provides a staff able and willing to answer questions requiring research or knowledge of books, has it discharged its full duty to society? In other words, is the provision of a building, staff, and books enough, or is the public library in any way responsible for the fact that though we have one of the best library systems in the world, Americans read less than any other Western democratic people? That a very small percentage of the adults in most of our large cities are registered in the library and that a smaller percentage of those registered use their cards very often? According to polls taken, citizens of this country do not read on the average more than four books a year and many of those books are of a very poor quality indeed. Here are the nonfiction best sellers of 1963 as listed in *Publishers' Weekly*, in order of popularity:

Happiness Is a Warm Puppy
Security Is a Thumb and a Blanket
J.F.K.: The Man and the Myth
Profiles in Courage
O Ye Jigs and Juleps!
Better Homes and Gardens Bread Cook Book
Pillsbury's Family Cook Book
I Owe Russia $1200
Heloise's Housekeeping Hints
Better Homes and Gardens Baby Book[8]

While the many book clubs and the proliferation of paperbacks have stimulated reading, we cannot by any stretch of the imagination say that the citizens of the United States, who are expected to lead the free world, are reading enough to make them worthy of the trust. We can't derive much understanding and vision from cuddly children's books, cookbooks, and Bob Hope.

Perry of Harvard said, "The test of society is the quality of the persons who compose it."[9] Books can enrich the quality of the reader but informational books alone are not enough. Books that teach us are important but books that change us are wonderful. As a barefoot child on a Texas cotton farm, my first acquaintance with nobility came when my mother read to me the story of Ruth from the King James version of the Bible. Her "entreat me not to leave thee" expanded the horizons of my spirit as did David's lament for Absalom. When he cried in despair, "O Absalom, my son, my son, would God that I had died for thee," I wept with him. In my later years I have become a bigger person since my vigil on the mountaintop with Kumalo the night his son was executed in *Cry, the Beloved Country*. Agnes Keith set me thinking of the wonder of being able to identify with the other person whoever he is and wherever he lives.[10] She established perfect rapport with the natives of Borneo, the sophisticated guests she entertained, with the sad little Filipino boy singing in his shabby slum, even with the Japanese who imprisoned and tortured her. Baroness Blixen's *Out of Africa* [1964] gave me a new perspective on the African—not as a savage or a pathetic primitive but as a remarkable man with a different heritage. From her first sentence, "I had a farm in Africa at the foot of the Ngong Hills . . . " I felt I was in the company of a sophisticated, wise, humorous woman who saw life more clearly than I. *The Education of Hyman Kaplan* and *Life with Father* showed me how much richer humor is if it has an undercurrent of sympathy or poignancy.[11] From James Baldwin I have learned the deep suffering prejudice inflicts on the intelligent, sensitive Negro.

When I read Saint-Exupéry's *Wind, Sand and Stars* [1939], I found expressed the philosophy I had begun to feel but had never formulated for myself. His long, lyrical definition of man ends with, "To be a man is to feel that in setting one's stone, one is contributing to the building of the world." Alfred North Whitehead in his *Aims of Education* [1957] summed up what I have been attempting to say when he wrote, "Culture is activity of thought, and receptiveness to beauty and humane feeling. Scraps of information have nothing to do with it. A merely well-informed man is the most useless bore on God's earth. . . ."

I am grateful for my schooling, and the facts I learned were important and necessary, but I would be poor indeed if my reading had stopped with my schooling—and that is exactly what does happen to most high-school and college graduates. In a Gallup poll taken a few years ago, it was reported that half of our high-school graduates and a fourth of our college graduates had not read a single book in that year. The Deiches survey recently made states that Baltimore high-school students read while in school to complete assignments, better their grades, or please their teachers, and that when their schooling ends, all too often, so does their reading.[12]

Reading for understanding and enrichment has always been important, but today it is urgent. John Ciardi says modern man is really Neanderthal man with a push button. Someone else has said he is the old barbarian with vast new instruments to use. We must make Neanderthal man into a citizen of the modern world very quickly before be blows himself to smithereens; the old barbarian must become a gentleman fast, before he swings his club. All social institutions must work to this end, but libraries have a heavy responsibility, for it is within the covers of books that man may find the ideas and understanding that will civilize him.

Just making books available is not enough, just helping with school assignments is not enough. Neanderthal man must look on books as more than the tools of formal education. He must taste the flavor of rich, unrequired reading, as Lamb's character tasted the flavor of roast pig and found that it was good.[13] The best time to persuade the barbarian to read is when he is young, for this is when he is most receptive to ideas and most responsive to them.

Dora Smith, a distinguished reading specialist in the National Council of Teachers of English, discussing high-school and college reading, wrote, "Left to themselves, young people tend to read within a narrow area and in materials which afford them little real challenge. They need the guidance of sympathetic and widely read adults in identifying, extending and intensifying their interests. Many of them have problems which they could solve if they were but aware of them. Others have latent interests which need only to be challenged. Still others know specifically what their interests are but are unaware of materials available for pursuing them."

Not everyone can persuade the young barbarian to undertake the voluntary reading of books. And here is where the special librarian for the young adult enters the picture. To work successfully with young adults he must understand and like teenagers and be able to establish a rapport with them based on mutual respect and liking. He must be a genuine person with a sense of humor and emotional balance, outgoing rather than self-centered. Above all, he must know books—hundreds of them—on a wide range of subjects and on various reading levels. He must know how to make books seem interesting and important to all readers, from the most deprived to the most fortunate and accelerated. He must be able to discuss books after they are read and constantly enrich and enlarge the quality of reading done. Just waiting on people pleasantly is failing them. He must develop readers to their full potential.

Someone has said, "Paradoxically, as the world grows smaller, men must grow larger." If we sit tight in our chairs when young people come into the library, pointing to the catalog, answering questions when asked, encouraging teenagers to browse around and find a book but never approaching them or making suggestions for voluntary reading, we are doing very little to ensure that they will grow larger. We fail the boy who finds Erle Stanley Gardner and plans to spend the winter reading all his mysteries if we do not interest him in *All Quiet on the Western Front*, people of other countries, or such books as Horgan's *Distant Trumpet* [1960] and Braithwaite's *To Sir, with Love* [1959]. Nor can we allow meaningful, moving books to sit on the shelves indefinitely because their titles do not attract casual browsers. The young-adult librarian must be an artist. He must have the original passion or capacity for feeling that any artist has. Then, he must learn how to perform—the technique to make his work effective.

The young-adult librarian must be creative. He must devise ways to sell the idea of reading for reading's sake not only to individuals but to groups. He must make of himself an effective speaker and visit schools to talk to classes informally of books to read for pleasure. He must learn to dress windows and make displays of books to catch the eye. He must think constantly of new ways to advertise the world's best product.

To be a successful young-adult librarian takes some doing. It calls for fertilization of the mind, enlargement of the spirit, identification with the community, constant reading, dedication, and old-fashioned hard work. But all these qualities are not enough without a sympathetic administration. In these days when libraries are besieged by Jared

Bean's "unreasoning Mob," when there is not standing room in the reference department, when the staff is literally inundated with requests for materials for school assignments, it seems to many administrators a kind of extravagant luxury to assign one of their most gifted librarians to hand out books for pleasure and to talk to young people about books when everyone else is working at fever heat to find the height of Mount Blanc, the structure of the frog, a picture of the uniform worn in the U.S. army in 1812. How can the administrator justify a staff member's taking full time to talk to a young reader about the underlying philosophy of *1984*, Golding's concept of man's nature, or what Griffin learned about prejudice when he lived his *Black Like Me?* [14] To some administrators, this is not as urgent as answering questions related to school assignments. Maybe it isn't so urgent but it might be more important. The public library must be more than the handmaiden of the schools.

So far we have discussed our cultivation of what Jared Bean called "the Fair Garden," suggesting better seed and more fertilization, with emphasis on more effective layout. Let us now look at an adjoining patch of weeds. There are 38 million people in this country who live in poverty. Many are unemployed, living on relief to the third and fourth generation—slum dwellers and dropouts who are more than problems. They threaten our economy and constitute one of the gravest dangers to our security. Unless they are reeducated, retrained, absorbed into the labor market, and taught how to live, there is trouble ahead. The government realizes the seriousness of the problem. More than that, the schools are reconsidering the kind of education that has failed these people. It is essential, it seems to me, for the library to revise its middle-class approach and devise new ways of making books a part of the lives of these people who desperately need the ideas found in books. We must study to find books that speak the language of young people from fatherless families where the mother didn't finish the fourth grade, where no one reads or discusses ethics, where work is a strange concept, where only the relief check is real. For young people from such backgrounds the simple teenage romance or baseball story scorned by literary critics may have a great deal to say about wholesome family life, sportsmanship, codes of honor, good manners, and so forth. If we have no suitable books, we should find out just what we need and get publishers to produce them.

Then we should master the technique of introducing these people to reading and study to lead them eventually from simple books about the world they understand to books that will interpret to them the world they never knew. James Baldwin was one of these people who, as a despairing child of the Harlem slums, went to the library in his neighborhood and systematically read every book in it in a desperate search for identity with people outside the wretched world he knew. He found it when he read the great books and discovered he was bound to other men in suffering. Too few of these young people come to the library of their own accord, but we must not abandon them.

We must not be content to work only with people who happen to come to the library, excusing ourselves by saying it is hopeless to make readers of most people when often it is ourselves and our methods that are at fault. For too long we have waited on young people rather than developing their highest reading potential. For too long we have been satisfied to furnish information only, when enriching books were standing on the shelves.

In an annual report of the Toledo Public Library I read, "Man is not the only animal that talks. Monkeys chatter and signal to each other, crows caw, bees direct each other to new sources of nectar by intricate dances. But man is the only animal who can talk from one century or millennium to another. And he does it through books and libraries." Our assignment is to make sure that when mankind tells the story of his struggle to the light, of his suffering, his failures, his joy and love and faith—that the message gets through to the people here and now.

Let the Beasts In

With all its machinery for charging out books, organizing, preserving, and dispensing information, with all its technicians trained to operate the machinery, the public library is as new as tomorrow. As for professional services to the individual and the community, however, the library is becoming an anachronism. Never effective in dealing with the nation's reading problems, the library is slipping further and further behind the times.

In most school libraries the promotion of reading is a lost art. Many school librarians do not go beyond doing reference work, supplementing the curriculum, and teaching the use of the catalog and reference tools. As a librarian attached to a state department of public instruction put it, "Many schools have felt a need to indicate the change in the image and role of the school library by changing the name of the area to Media Center, Instructional Materials Center, Resource Center, etc." Whatever happened to the book and the pleasure of reading it? Hey, miss, where is the library?

In the past, middle-aged people were in the majority. It was the well-to-do, established, conservative "pillars of society" who called the tune. In this new era, it is the young people who are in the majority. They are alive, concerned about society, active in politics, intolerant of sham and hypocrisy. They look at society's institutions with critical eyes and force establishments to offer proof of things previously accepted without question.

Industry and the professions are becoming increasingly aware of the importance of youth. *The New York Times* says Macy's now aims its advertising at the twenty-five-year-olds. The movie industry has found that over half its patrons are under thirty and they have had something to think about since *The Graduate*. This unheralded, inexpensive picture had something to say and spoke to youth in youth's language. As a result, waiting lines formed for blocks down the streets of cities and towns all over the nation and many young people went to see it five or six times. The reaction of young people will have a marked effect from here on as far as the motion picture industry is concerned.

Lawyers are beginning to say that they must cease to rely so heavily on decisions made in the past for this is a new age with new problems. High schools are seeking to interest more young people in finishing their educations and colleges are reexamining their philosophy and curricula to gain the confidence of young people. Ministers and priests often join with youth to protest injustice, and the Catholic mass has been set to the music of young people.

In the face of all this the public library, like the Southerner waving a Confederate flag, lives in its past and continues to center its planning around the solid, middle-aged citizen. It resents the fact that high-school students fill up the chairs and wear out the books in the reference room, hoping the day will soon come when the students will disappear to be confined more and more to the school library. Public librarians consider young people an interruption to business, yet they *are* the business, more so than the middle-aged adults the librarians are waiting for.

We know that young people make the heaviest use of our reference services, and evidence points to their being the majority of our readers as well. In a recent Gallup poll, it was found that 58 per cent of the sample of 1,510 American adults said they had "never read a book from cover to cover," 11 per cent said they had read a book during the last eleven months, and 5 per cent said they remembered reading a book more than a year before, not since. But the poll found that far more young adults (in their twenties) had read a book than older adults. Evidently there is a correlation between age and reading books.

Yet the public library puts its emphasis on adult services, making young-adult work subsidiary. It purchases its books and arranges its services primarily for adults, allowing young people to make use of its books and services if they must but without attempting to make them feel welcome, without, with a few exceptions, making special provisions for them, and without delegating a well-read, friendly staff member to make books meaningful and to share with them the joy of reading. As a profession, the public library is "stuck fast in yesterday," still protecting the fair garden from the swarm of beasts. It is time to let them in.

❧ VII ❧

I Once Did See
Joe Wheeler Plain

On July 1, 1926, young Joseph Wheeler arrived in Baltimore as the head librarian of the Enoch Pratt Free Library, probably the worst public library in any large city in the U.S.A. It was housed in a gloomy old Victorian dwelling on Mulberry Street with an overflow in three private dwellings around the corner on Cathedral Street and a patchwork of branches. The staff was made up mostly of genteel women of fairly advanced years who suddenly became librarians when Enoch Pratt endowed the library and offered his friends' daughters a chance to make pin money in a ladylike way. In the entire system, there was not one trained librarian and only five college graduates.

Though all the books were out of sight in the stacks, the oldest ones were in a dark basement along with mice and rats, which, the timid "slip chasers" avoided by writing "out" on the call slips and themselves remaining on the floor above. Only two books—one fiction and one nonfiction—could be withdrawn at a time. My husband, who was a patron as a boy, said the borrower was given two "asks." If a book came up but was not what he wanted, he had to take it anyway for he had asked for it, hadn't he? If neither of the two came up, he went home as he had had his "asks." Kate Coplan remembers that on the counter

---

This chapter was presented as a paper at the American Library History Round Table in Dallas, Texas, June 1971, under the program title "How Firm a Foundation: A Tribute to Joseph L. Wheeler." It was added in the 1974 edition of this work. *Ed.*

of the room known as the "delivery room" stood a small glass case holding about two hundred books. The reader could point to a book he wanted to take home in addition to the two borrowed. If, on examination, the reader decided he did not want the book, he could choose another but no third choice was allowed if the second were declined.

When Joe Wheeler arrived, he put seven thousand of the best books on open shelves. He brought in two trained librarians, one to head childrens' work and one adult work. The book collection was weeded, reorganized, and expanded. He radiated energy, cheerfulness, and enthusiasm for the job. He was everywhere, encouraging, showing appreciation of work well done, and enlisting ideas from the staff. News stories about the changes appeared and Baltimore, which previously had had little regard for or interest in the library, began to sit up and take notice. Before long Pratt's circulation had increased 113 per cent. When Joe Wheeler pointed this out to the municipal authorities in an attempt to obtain a large appropriation, one of the officials asked, "Who the hell told you to increase the circulation 113 per cent?"

Meantime, the trustees were not helping. Enoch Pratt had appointed a self-perpetuating board of upper-class gentlemen of fine old Maryland families who worried over this brash young librarian. For one thing, the band around his straw hat was too loud and they felt obliged to tell him so. But they were worried even more by his irritating insistence that they should provide the city with a new library building. He brought the matter up at every meeting, and each time they told him it was "being considered" until they could stand it no longer; then they told him not to bring the matter up again, that it was closed.

He simply had to have that building and could not let go. He went to the mayor and found there was a remote chance that the legislature would pass an enabling act allowing funds for the building the very next day, the last of the session, but only if pressure was brought to bear. Dr. Wheeler figured his only hope lay in enlisting the aid of the one board member who seemed sympathetic, a prominent surgeon. He rushed to the Hopkins hospital, found the surgeon in his underwear preparing for an operation, and started talking. The surgeon said he would think it over while he operated, decided to help, rode with Dr. Wheeler to Annapolis at the crack of dawn the next day, and got the money.

Dr. Wheeler had his own ideas about that building. It was not to be located in a quiet suburb approached by a winding, tree-bordered drive. It was not to have a lot of steps or a marble enclosed vestibule. He wanted the building in the very heart of the city, where the people were—on the street level so women could wheel their baby buggies into it. There would be show windows across the front, and the first thing the patron would see would be books, thousands of them out in view—everywhere—and there would be color and light and beauty all around. In this building, businessmen and others who approached the service desks would be waited on by smiling, efficient, pretty girls. He used to stand in the central hall and smile and look at them. It did him good to see them at the desks, just as Samuel Pepys said it did him good to see Nell Gwynn's underwear hanging on the clothesline. It did the city's businessmen good too.

When the library got settled in the new building, he brought a secondhand printing press and hired an inexpensive, tobacco-chewing printer to run it. He composed broadsides of brief biographies of great men who achieved success through reading and persuaded a laundry to put them on cards inserted into freshly laundered shirts. He had a dairy delivering lists with the milk and seed merchants distributing lists of books on flower and vegetable gardening with seed purchases. In 1929, Baltimore's anniversary year, at one of the largest department stores two pretty girls in colonial costume with baskets filled with library book lists stood at the store's main entrance handing out leaflets to all. When he heard a live tarantula had been found down at the docks in a cargo of bananas, he got the tarantula and featured it in a display of books on spiders.

But his greatest achievement in the beginning was the creation of a truly professional staff, starting from scratch. He had an uncanny knack of sizing up people and in his quiet, friendly way, making them experts. He set up a training class for promising young applicants where the students were given basic courses in working with children and adults, understanding the catalog, doing reference work, and becoming acquainted with a wide range of books. On his frequent rounds about the library, he watched among the patrons for young people with the personality and potentiality he needed for members of the staff. One of the department heads told of the time her attractive cousin came to take her to dinner. As they left, the girl said, "While I was waiting for you, a man came up to me and asked me if I would like to work in the library. I told him no, that being around all those books was like being in a morgue." What a blow that remark must have been, for it was his anxiety to make the library a beautiful, joyous place that had led him to ask her if she would like to work there.

Soon after he arrived at the Pratt Library, he looked over his untrained staff to see who had possibilities. For one thing, he had a secretary who had no college training; but she was so vibrant, charming, and efficient, he decided she did not belong behind the scenes but should be shared with the public. He transferred her to the Circulation Department, from which she advanced to a branch librarianship and, eventually, to head the branch system.

Kate Coplan was a young assistant replacing old, dirty, wornout books in the order department. She had no college training; but because she was eager and had ideas, he decided to see if he could teach her to handle publicity. She had no idea of public relations but he lent her his *Library and the Community* with his philosophy of making the library and its resources as useful as possible to every segment of the city and to every individual—a cradle-to-grave service. Before the new building came into being, he sent her into the heart of Baltimore's business district to borrow vacant store windows. The library had no truck, but Kate had the part-time assistance of a seventy-three-year-old janitor who carried the basket of books in one hand and a pail and cleaning equipment in the other. After borrowing a bucket of water from a corner drug store, they would wash the window to be used and set up the display. Kate says Dr. Wheeler taught her how to plan displays, write news releases, and compile booklists. With his encouragement and guidance, she became nationally known in the field of public relations, won the friendship of the city's newsmen, and was frequently offered positions with commercial firms.

As for me—in 1932 I entered the training class by God's grace and because of Joe Wheeler's gambling instincts. I had just been fired from the teaching profession and was under a cloud, to put it mildly. As he could not resist the impulse to see if he could make a silk purse out of a sow's ear, he agreed to let me enter the training class. When I taught school, the supervisors who paid surprise visits always looked first at my window shades, no two of which were ever at the same level. Then they looked at the thermostat, which was either too high or too low. Dr. Wheeler never told my library supervisor of my dark past. He never checked on me but assumed I was intelligent and well meaning. He encouraged me to be creative and to discuss my ideas with him even if they seemed far out. He let me try doubtful schemes and never reproved me by word or look if I came a cropper. When I asked him if I might drive a horse-drawn book wagon in the slums in the summertime, he said, "I don't think it will work, but you can try it." I was drunk with his confidence and worked my head off. We all worked, but so did he.

Soon after I was put in charge of the young adult collection at Central, I edited a vacation reading list with what seemed to me a very clever design for the cover. A few months after it was distributed, my supervisor showed me a crude copy of the design on a list some little library in another state had used without asking permission. I was furious. I took the list to Dr. Wheeler in his office and laid it on his desk in high dudgeon. He looked at it and smiled and said, "Well?"

I replied with some heat. "They copied my list and did not even ask my permission!"

"I don't understand why you are mad," he said. "Isn't your aim in life to get teenagers to read books?"

"Yes," I replied.

"Well, if you have an idea that works, aren't you glad for it to be used anywhere it will help?" After working under Joseph Wheeler for a while, one could say with the Psalmist, "I will lift up mine eyes [Psalm 121:1]."

I never saw him leave the library for the day without books under his arm. Books excited him and he was daily in the order department laying his hands reverently on the new books, for any one of them, he often said, might change the plans and life of whoever read it. I remember when a prison requested a list of books for its library, I was assigned the compilation of the list because in my work with young adults, I was supposed to be familiar with readable books in various fields. Along with the request had come a listing of the prisoners' many interests and as most of them fell in fields with which I was unfamiliar, I leaned heavily on the department heads. I added what little I knew and took the pack of some five hundred slips to Dr. Wheeler. I sat open-mouthed as he went through the slips, commenting on almost every title with such remarks as: "There is a better book on orchards by Jameson." "There is a later edition of this book." "Try the government pamphlet instead of this book." "This is newer, but Floyd is better."

He was obsessed with service to the individual and kept an idea list on his desk of ways to serve the city better. He spoke of the great pleasure he felt in watching people, each with his individual background, lined up at the loan desk—each getting the same attention, regardless. He defined librarianship as the fascinating profession of helping all kinds of people get the information, ideas, convictions, and encouragement they seek in every aspect of their lives. A few weeks before he died, an interview with him was recorded on tapes, to which I have been allowed to listen. There were long pauses and extraneous reminiscences, for death was staring him in the face and it was difficult to concentrate. After one long pause, he called out clearly, "Service! Service is a wonderful word." Later he said, "Censorship, automation, regionalization, and such are today the concerns of the staff while the poor customer stands on one foot on the other side of the desk and who cares about him?" He saw to it that every person who entered the door of the Pratt Library was given the best possible service with courtesy and grace.

I remember there was on the staff a brilliant girl with a marvelous book background who was unsurpassed at her best; but at her worst, she could be rude. One day when she was at her worst, an old lady fell into her hands in the fiction department and was given the works, at which she went to Dr. Wheeler's office and reported the matter. He sent for the assistant who returned thoroughly chastened. She told me confidentially,

"He made me feel like a fool. I was expecting to be bawled out but he was calm and looked sad. He said, 'Lucy, you know that old Mrs. Jenkins you waited on this afternoon? Poor old thing. She walked clear across town with her feet hurting saying to herself that if she could just make it to the Pratt Library, she would get help and when she got here, you hurt her!' By the time he was through, I thought I would die."

"Listen," she continued, "If you ever see me starting to be mean to anybody ever again, for God's sake, stop me!"

He not only worked to make the Pratt Library effective. He wanted all the libraries of the nation to be effective. He encouraged Mary Barton to compile the booklet *A Guide to Reference Books* when she was head of the Reference Department. It is now in its sixth edition with Marion Bell as coeditor of the last edition; 80,000 copies have been distributed. Virginia Kirkus has often spoken of what his encouragement meant when she was hesitating to launch her project of prepublication book reviewing. Father Kortendick, head of the Catholic University Library School, told me of running into Dr. Wheeler at an ALA conference and the lift he got from Dr. Wheeler's praise of two of his projects. These are only a few examples of his ranging librarianship.

But back to the Pratt Library. St. Exupèry said, "A rock pile ceases to be a rock pile the moment a man of vision contemplates it, bearing within himself the image of a cathedral." And so, in ten years, this man of vision changed one of the worst urban libraries in America to one of the best in the world. He said once that in those years, he often felt a giant had him by the hand running with him so fast his own feet touched the ground about every five or six steps. He might have added that in this wild dash, he had his staff by the hand, and their feet, too, just touched the high spots. Despite the pressure, librarians often came to Pratt at a reduction in salary for the opportunity to train under him. It is remarkable how many who worked under his supervision became leaders in the profession. Among them are: Emerson Greenaway, Harold L. Hamill, Harold V. Tucker, Francis St. John, John Humphrey, Paul Howard, Joseph Shipman, Richard Sealock, Lillian Bradshaw, Stewart Sherman, Thurston Taylor, Amy Winslow, and many others. What public library is training such administrators today? Where is there available inservice training for librarians with potentialities? I was told recently that eight city libraries are searching for directors and even with the great surplus of librarians now available, the eight cities cannot find administrators with a vision of service who are book lovers, innovators, dedicated people who can excite a staff and through them, a whole community with books and the ideas they contain.[1]

But of all Dr. Wheeler's qualities, to me, the most inspiring was his concern for youth. When I took the entrance exam for the training class, one of the questions was, "If you were waiting on a young person and a U.S. senator came to your desk, what would you do?" Had I answered that I would let the child wait while I attended to the senator, it would probably have been curtains for me. One of the first things he did as the new librarian at Pratt was to change the borrowing privileges of children so that a child could always have one adult book if he wanted it. He told me he did this to protect children from those old maid librarians who did not realize the potentialities of some children.

Because there was no doubt in his mind of the power of the book and because he was challenged by the tremendous potential in youth, he felt there was no more important function of the public library than to cultivate and promote the voluntary reading of teenagers. In his last interview he said YA work was so horribly important, for at this time in their lives, young people must learn to love books; it would be tragic if they did not. He put some of the best read and most creative people on his staff on the floor of Central and the branches to win the confidence of teenagers and sell them the idea of rich voluntary reading. These librarians talked to classes in the schools, put on TV and radio programs, spoke to parents and teachers, and constantly devised ways of enriching teenagers with books.

He felt administrators of public libraries did not understand the importance of young adult work, did not see how obvious was the need for it. In his last days, he kept writing me that something was going on in New York state that bothered him. "There is a report," he wrote, "that is all wrong." For the public library to wash its hands of young people was to him unthinkable.

The public library's departure from Dr. Wheeler's conception of the importance of work with young adults could be the death knell of an institution fast losing vitality. There has always been hostility to teenagers in public libraries over the nation. Insecure librarians have always wanted to be identified with adults, not youth. They have kidded themselves into believing that if it were not for young people, captains of industry, industrialists, union leaders, directors of theaters, editors of newspapers would swarm into the library. We serve the bulk of our clientele, people under twenty-five, only as much as we must and are even considering making the public library off bounds to them. If we implement the report of the New York committee and the adults do not swarm in, we shall have committed suicide.

We have been frightened for years of the little old lady in tennis shoes, realizing our public image was too close to hers to be comfortable. In an effort to disprove any association with her, we have embraced every new advance in technology—the computer, charging machines, teletype, AV. We have done every new thing possible but have neglected the book and the individual. Along this line, W. H. Webb of the College and Reference Library section of the Canadian Library Association wrote recently, "Just as the 'little old librarian' of recent memory was written off because she could neither comprehend nor accept computer manipulation of library problems, so the 'modern academic librarian' is in imminent peril of being ignored by the new spirit on the campus. The new spirit does not demand ever larger libraries, ever larger and larger computers. . . . Rather, the new spirit suggests that the purpose of the librarian is to help explain, with all the tools available, mankind to man and each man to himself. If the library and its librarians fend off the questioners and avoid confrontation with the new consciousness, then surely they will lose the opportunity of coming close to the concerns of present day students. They will not touch reality and they will surely be forgotten."[2]

I hear that some of the young librarians of this sonic age of Aquarius consider Wheeler old hat—no computer, no AV, too much emphasis on books. Nor was he impressed with them. He called them McLuhanatics. So far, these McLuhanatics who allow technological gadgets to take precedence over the book and reading have not shaken up present day society or even one city as Dr. Wheeler shook up Baltimore by the simple but more difficult procedure of persuading people to read books. We are withering on the vine with our failure to produce leaders and with young librarians becoming disillusioned with the profession. A return to Joseph L. Wheeler's philosophy might save us. That is, if we had faith in the book, read it as he did, believed in youth, and turned heaven and earth to put books into the hands of people. If we got out on the streets, if we won the hearts of the young and made an impact on the masses, we might hold our young assistants and develop leaders to renew us in the future. Whatever methods we are using today are not effective enough. Possibly if we followed the trails Dr. Wheeler blazed, we might convince the people of this country that libraries and the nourishment of the mind are as essential as physical necessities. If we do not, we may be reduced to a few little old ladies in tennis shoes stuffing computers; for in the future there will be more and more people and less and less money and idealistic young taxpayers of tomorrow will probably not support us when the masses of people are hungry, ill clothed, and imprisoned in ghettos.

Joseph L. Wheeler, the activist, not only set the city of Baltimore afire with books as bombs, but he revolutionized librarianship over the nation in the almost two hundred administrative and building projects for which he was consultant as well as by his writings on buildings and the relationship of the library to the community. Among his more important books is *The Practical Administration of Public Libraries* written with Herber Goldhor. In order to keep the price of the book down to $7.50 so that even small libraries could afford it, he volunteered to accept only minimal royalties.

This man was also a "character." His daughter, Mary, wrote me that he loved to drive a car and could not resist speeding. He had a lot of trouble with cops over stop signs. When Mary was a little girl, in the days when cops could collect fines, he was arrested for running through a stop sign. The cop demanded a fine and Dr. Wheeler told him he did not have in hand the fee demanded. "All right," the cop said. "It's jail for you." Mary cried so loud and hard, the cop let him off. "As we drove away," Mary wrote, "guess what he pulled out from between the cushions?" You see, he didn't actually have it *in hand*. When he was eighty-two, he drove from New Hampshire to Wisconsin and was clocked going one hundred miles per hour for ten miles. He reported that he and the policeman had a nice visit and he was let off with a warning.

Tact was not his strong point. When he saw other librarians mismanaging libraries, he sometimes gave them free, unsolicited, and unappreciated advice. When he was consultant for the Dallas Public Library many years ago, he told them they should get rid of some dead wood and put Lillian Bradshaw in charge. She was fairly new at the library and a low man on the totem pole at the time. The remark did her no good with the staff and she had to talk fast to keep in their good graces. While his suggestion was not tactful, the idea was not so bad—just a bit ahead of time as were his other ideas. When the city fathers denied him funds and his board would not help, he blew his top. His daughter says he would have been in one controversy after another if her mother had not forced him to "keep his cool." In his eighty-sixth year, he plunged into the fight over aid to parochial schools by writing red-hot letters to the local paper. On his deathbed, when Mary told him the hospital had put on his tray a dish of spinach which he despised, all he said was, "Hell!" And of course he willed his eyes to the eye bank. It is interesting to speculate on why he was never made president of ALA. Did he give some person in authority unsolicited advice? Was the establishment afraid he would rock the boat? At eighty-five, when Castleton State College in Vermont was without a librarian, he stepped in to fill the job until a librarian could be found. Then, he became head of the college's reference department under the same circumstances. Three of his sons became PhD's and John won the Fermi award in 1968.

I should like to close with a brief account of his last days gleaned from the diary he kept in 1970 when he was eighty-six. That year he achieved one of his heart's desires, something he had worked for long and hard—a grant of over $34,000 to the American Association for State and Local History for the preparation and publication of a manual on the collecting, handling, and servicing of local history materials in public and college libraries and here is the clincher—to be carried out over a twenty-eight month period by Joseph L. Wheeler with a committee to assist.

Though his strength was failing and he was having painful circulation problems, he spoke at ALA in Detroit to over seven hundred people on cataloging-in-source, another of his special interests. Fearful he might not have the strength to complete the reading of his paper, he asked Emerson Greenaway to stand by and take over if he failed but, he wrote in his diary, "I was able to finish by slowing down and a few waits."

The problem of circulation became more and more acute and he was in and out of the hospital; yet he kept up a flourishing correspondence about library matters, sometimes writing ten letters a day, such as one to a librarian in the South: "Why don't you write to the Superintendent of Documents about a half dozen indexes by major subject field of the detailed contents of the U.S. documents, organized just like the Wilson subject indexes? I realize this should go through some ALA committee but am so discouraged about the time it takes to get *anything* underway through ALA committees." He suggested to others that reading lists on U.S. history be prepared. And who could fail to be moved by his asking the Pratt Library in these times of frustration and despair to publish a reading list he called "Lift Up Your Hearts"?

July 30th, he wrote in the diary: "I wrote some letters. Very wobbly and weak today." August 19: "Pretty tired and foot ached." August 21: "Working on Building Manuscript." October 24: "I mailed 20 letters yesterday, not including letters to second hand booksellers." And again, "Working on Building Manuscript."

As Browning said:

> That low man seeks a little thing to do,
> Sees it and does it;
> This high man, with a great thing to pursue,
> Dies ere he know it.
>
> [from "A Grammarian's Funeral," 1855]

When he resigned from the Pratt Library, the *Baltimore Evening Sun* said in an editorial: "It is customary nowadays to speak of 'library science'! Ah, but the administration of a great library is still an art rather than a science. If there were in fact any such thing as library science, the impending resignation of Dr. Wheeler would be a matter of little moment, just install a new library scientist and let the wheels continue to turn. But since public library administration is an art, indeed one of the great arts, thousands of people in Baltimore will be wanting to know whether an artist of comparable stature is to succeed Dr. Wheeler."

In *Wind, Sand, and Stars,* St. Exupéry tells of an old gardener who lay dying. Thinking back on his lifetime of working with the earth and growing things, he called out, "And who will prune my trees for me when I am gone?" St. Exupéry extols him as a great soul "for he was bound by ties of love to all cultivable land and to all the trees of the world." So, Dr. Wheeler was bound by ties of love to all the books in libraries and to all the people who might read them. And who will prune his trees for him when he is gone?

❧ VIII ❧

We Have Been True to You, Melvil Dewey, after Our Fashion

Where did the trouble start? With Melvil Dewey. All professions tend to glorify their founders and to hand down to succeeding generations principles and traditions that have gathered around them. There is Hippocrates, the Greek physician who is known as the father of medicine; Socrates, the great teacher; St. Augustine, a man of God; Cicero, the lawyer; and Melvil Dewey, the librarian and founder of the American Library Association.

Melvil Dewey was a genius who made a great contribution to libraries of the world when he showed us how to catalog, classify, and arrange printed matter so that information in books would be in order on the shelves and available to all. It seems ungrateful to ask for more but I believe we might not be in trouble today if this ingenious man had not stopped with organizing knowledge but had been equally concerned with getting the ideas and the culture in books into the minds of the people.

I doubt that Melvil Dewey was worried about the cultural poverty of the masses of people, for among his many activities he founded the Lake Placid Club and helped set up its charter, barring entrance to all Negroes, Jews, and tuberculars. As a result, when the New York Library Association a year or so ago decided to honor our founder and hold their annual meeting at his shrine, the Lake Placid Club, they had

---

This chapter was added in the 1974 edition. *Ed.*

to abandon the idea, for many librarians were Jewish, many were black, and those living in New York City were probably tubercular.

Dewey and the cofounders of ALA did not put great emphasis on the promotion of reading nor have many of their successors. Indeed, it is difficult to find in library literature where reading for any other reason than to find information is stressed. From the date of the establishment of the profession, a library has been thought of as a suitably housed collection of books and materials classified and organized by subject, indexed in a catalog, and administered by a staff trained in research who could be consulted if necessary and who checked the books in and out. This conception has come down almost intact to this day and has been developed into a highly efficient system that has afforded citizens of all ages and classes a free, reliable source of information for practically every need. This is, of course, a great boon to American society. And yet, ever since libraries were founded, the general public has cherished the idea that one goes to the library for a "good" book, meaning a book to enjoy. This idea still prevails, for a survey made by the University of Maryland library school found that half the patrons of the Baltimore-Washington Metropolitan District came to the library simply for a "good" book to read.

The book has been beloved over the world down through the ages as a symbol of wisdom and enrichment. People attribute to the printed word a kind of magic so potent that they throw what seem to them evil books into the fire to break their spells. For the reader, the book is escape when the world crowds in; it is courage and inspiration and vision; it is an extension and enrichment of one's limited experience. It is loved for these reasons rather than for the information it contains. We value the dictionary, the history of art, the scientific treatise, but we love with a burning passion *Romeo and Juliet,* Homer's *Odyssey,* and *Anna Karenina.*

As long as there have been libraries, people have thought of librarians as book lovers and have hoped if they walked into a library that they would find professionals who would introduce them to congenial and inspiring authors and share with them the joy of reading. Librarians in general have played along with this idealized image of the library and librarians. And they have taken to themselves status in the community as the book's ambassadors when, in fact, most of them do very little reading and are in reality technicians who know the mechanical processes of making books and the information in them available but are no more concerned for enlarging the vision of the masses than was Melvil Dewey.

The librarian is not so in love with what is inside books as the system under which they are organized. Above all else, he loves the catalog. He is obsessed with it and wants everybody in the United States to share with him the joy of mastering it. If we were half as excited about good reading, we could save the nation. When the school or public librarian speaks to a class of youngsters, he usually chooses the catalog and its workings as his subject. The students may not wish to hear about it but he tells them anyway. But the real fun comes when the youngster comes to the library and asks for help. That's when we really have the teenager over a barrel. The procedure is to smile sweetly and say, "Look it up in the catalog." Though our social life is meager and love may have passed us by, we still have the power to make the youngster pull out a drawer, write down a number, and then try to find the book on the shelf.

Though manipulating the system to retrieve information is our main concern, we do include in the book collection fiction and belles-lettres—but we play them down. We are careful in our circulation reports to list fiction and nonfiction separately so we can prove to the city fathers and everyone else, including other librarians, that we are doing serious business and are not encouraging people to waste time reading stories. It seems more professional to put up a display entitled "Know Your State!" rather than "History with a Novel Twist" or "Profiles in Courage," which would combine fiction and nonfiction.

We feel as modern as tomorrow because we have added to the system all the newest technological gadgets: microfilm, teletype, computers, cassettes, films, and so forth, but we still do not know what is inside the books nor how to make them meaningful to readers. We are more concerned for the system than for people and their pressing problems. Our books could throw light on the serious and portentous social problems of the nation if they were read, but we do not bestir ourselves to read them, much less persuade other people to read them. We are better known to the public for our bad manners than for graciousness.

While the bad image writers give us is appalling, even more distressing is the fact that the public in general never feels the authors have misrepresented us. The librarian in Brooklyn who never cared enough about Betty Smith to even look at her; the pinch-nosed librarian who kept the good books from the young people and reveled in gossip in *The Sound and the Fury;* Saroyan's librarian who bawled out Ulysses and his little friend for handling books they could not read; and the unspeakable librarian in Memphis who browbeat and degraded young Richard Wright, forcing him to lie and cheat in order to borrow a book from her white library.[1] And recently in poking fun at a California town where amazing things happened, a television talk-show host brought a laugh when he said the town idiot was the librarian. The new president of Johns Hopkins University said a college president has to generate an image that can engender confidence in the institution, be the kind of personality that makes people feel good about the university.

This is the kind of image we librarians, from directors to assistants, need to generate.

We have been true to you, Melvil Dewey, right down the line from ALA to our library schools, our administrators, and our individual staff members. Let's take them in order.

Like Gulliver, ALA is so tied down by its thousands of Lilliputian details of organization and so geared to the informational approach to librarianship that it has little time or interest in setting the pace or assuming the leadership that would influence the people of America to read and think and understand in these perilous times. Long ago ALA should have established a program on TV where books would be dramatized by highly qualified professionals as the BBC is doing currently. And now that the BBC is sending people flocking into libraries for the *Forsyte Saga* and books about Elizabeth I, Henry VIII, and Cousin Bette, why are these shows sponsored only by the Ford Foundation, Mobil Oil, and Xerox? Could not the nation's libraries have been mentioned as cosponsors? Did anyone at ALA care enough about the promotion of reading to investigate the matter? And if the BBC discontinues its dramatizations in the future, is it likely that ALA will some day institute such programs with the help of foundations and commercial sponsors? Not unless the promotion of reading attains a higher priority than ever before.

When the younger librarians set up the Social Responsibilities Round Table, it sounded hopeful but it never seemed to connect with books and reading. As I understand it, these librarians wanted libraries to take stands on social issues. As an individual, I belong to the League of Women Voters, Nader's organization, Common Cause, and the American Civil Liberties Union because I wish to stand with these people on social issues. As a librarian, I have fought the same battle with books. There are on our shelves thousands of books that fight against prejudice, overpopulation, inhuman prisons, injustice, mistreatment of children, and all the other evils of our society. If we librarians feel social responsibility, books are our weapons. Our social obligation is to read these books and see that society reads them. This is far more difficult than carrying banners and taking institutional stands on such causes as Gay Liberation.

Probably ALA is not entirely responsible, but it is interesting to note that workshops listed periodically in *American Libraries* are largely centered on technical processes and bibliographical matters. It seems fair to say that ALA in spirit and practice perpetuates Dewey's old idea of libraries with the addition of new gadgets.

Dewey's idea of the library is also perpetuated by library schools where the students are trained in the Dewey tradition rather than being prepared to meet this new day with its needs and challenges. Look at the curriculum of the modern library school: Descriptive Cataloging, Subject Cataloging and Classification, Advanced Classification, Indexing and Abstracting, Automation of Library Services, Reference and Bibliography, Advanced Reference and Bibliography, Government Documents, Research, Administration, Principles of Book Selection, one or two electives on materials for children, and, rarely, a course called "Materials for Adolescents." Not one course on how to work on the floor of the library with people, no attempt to encourage individual growth and self-development and certainly no wide reading of books. Should not every library school offer courses on making use of radio and TV? Should there not be a course in public speaking that would train the student to speak effectively of books in public? Where are the courses in public relations and methods of penetrating the community and selling the idea of reading? Why not a course in the teaching of remedial reading so disadvantaged adults might one day become our readers? Should not every library school in a city have a project operating on the streets, experimenting with ways of reaching the disadvantaged, with library students on its staff under the supervision of a creative expert? Some of the teachers in library schools who have not worked in a public library in twenty-five years have no conception of today's library patrons, of the difficulties to be met, and the needs to be filled. Kenneth Harrison, a British librarian who visited some thirteen American library schools, writes, "Is it really all that unreasonable that we practicing librarians should ask the deans and faculties to produce people well equipped to deal with readers on the library floor and not just Johnny-heads-in-the-air? Of course we want vision and thoughtfulness, but we want these qualities combined with know-how and practical approach. But on the subject of vision . . . it certainly is a commodity in short supply at the moment. But I am hopeful that the output of the library schools will provide us with more librarians of vision, for 'where there is no vision,' the people will perish."

In the six or so library schools where I have taught, many of the students who were attracted to librarianship because they loved books and people are appalled at the aridity of the courses. Recently the head of a library school and I were discussing the recent project where library school students were sent to ALA at the expense of a firm interested in libraries. The head of the school remarked, "When the students came back, they all reported the same old thing—how dissatisfied students from all the schools were with their courses." A few months back, I had a friendly but vociferous argument with the head of another library school. I pointed out to him with my usual tact that his curriculum was lopsided with not enough recognition for the promotion of reading. He came at me full force, and in about the tenth round, when we were both hanging on the ropes, he said he had two questions to ask me: 1) If he agreed to include courses on the promotion of reading, where did I think he would find teachers? 2) He had been visiting public libraries and had found them by and large pretty dismal and administered by librarians with squinted vision. If he trained assistants to be dynamic readers' advisors, what did I think would happen to them under these administrators? He won the match by a K.O. for I could answer neither question. I could not think of a public library in the entire United States that had sold books and reading to an entire community and endeared itself to its people as Joe Wheeler sold the Enoch Pratt Free Library to Baltimore. How few public libraries are administered by men or women with vision who develop and inspire their staffs to serve people as he did. Often in my classes I have had students with charm, dedication, a love of books and people, and high intelligence. I write of such a student, "This girl should go far if she comes under inspired supervision." I despair when I think how slim the chances are that such will be the case.

And this brings us to administrators. While there are some excellent administrators who are widely read, creative, and determined to make books meaningful to their communities, too many public librarians define their jobs as making Dewey's system work. The emphasis is on the system rather than the people of the community. As long as the staff is on duty in the building, the books in order on the shelves, questions are being answered, and no one is complaining to the mayor, the administrator often feels his job is being done. He feels he has provided a well-rounded book collection and if people want to read the books, they can come and get them. Besides, the staff is too busy with housekeeping matters and the daily routines to be out of the building talking to people about books, appearing on TV, or distributing booklists and paperback books. Though service clubs or individuals might subsidize billboards or newspaper ads, he thinks it might be difficult to undertake. It may be as easy for the administrator to think up reasons for not rendering service beyond the call of duty to the public as it will be for the taxpayer to think up reasons for not straining himself to meet the librarian's budget requests.

But the most serious criticism of the administration and the public library is that, like Rip Van Winkle, they are stuck fast in yesterday. By and large, we have always laid out our buildings, selected our books, and allocated out staff for the middle-aged, middle class as we do today. Statistics tell us that by the end of the 1970s, over 50 per cent of the people in the United States will be under twenty-five. Yet most administrators either ignore work with young adults or, if they find it has been set up, boot it out, complimenting themselves all the while that the library "treats young people just like they do adults." This means ignoring them completely unless they ask for information. If YA work has not been abandoned and the administrator is a flaming liberal, one staff member is entitled the young adult librarian while all the rest of the staff are designated adult librarians. Go in any library and four out of five of the patrons will probably be teenagers; but four out of five of the staff will be adult librarians who are made to feel there is more status in serving adults even if they are not alive to be served. Should the administrator be realistic enough to establish YA work and provide young adult librarians who distinguish themselves as readers' advisors, these YA librarians will be promoted to be branch librarians, for if an assistant distinguishes himself as a readers' advisor, he reaches a dead end in his specialty. The only way up is in administering the system. Influencing young people to read and think has a limited future in the public library.

As for changing library schools and administrators, it is like an irresistible force meeting an immovable object. The administrator says he could never promote reading with the technically trained graduates of library schools and the library schools say if they produced readers' advisors, administrators would not employ them for they are looking for people with technical training. So library schools will continue to produce technicians—just what administrators want.

In the past the librarian was considered one of the community's important citizens. By and large, he was permitted to run the public library about as he saw fit, but not anymore. In these times of crises, where money is in very short supply, the librarian seated in his office administering a genteel staff of mechanics may become as extinct as the great auk. The public library of the future could be one large computer with answers to questions—presided over by a few computer stuffers.

If the public library is to survive, it will have to demonstrate that it makes a difference in the quality of life in the community. People must regard their libraries as oases in these critical times where an inspired, widely read staff permeates the community to introduce people— through books—to ideas, concern for society, inspiration, and delight. It is not enough that Melvil Dewey put the books in order on the shelves. We must take them down, read them, and give them to the people.

APPENDIX A

The Tool Shed

While chapters in the body of this book deal with the aims and goals of work with young adults, this appendix contains tools, i.e., instructions, lists, and suggestions designed to give public and school librarians new to YA work, and possibly future library-school teachers, practical pointers for promoting reading among adolescents.

BOOK SELECTION

The best books for young adults are the books that most truly interpret to them the process of living.* Since the adolescent clientele of the school and public libraries ranges from the most deprived and apathetic to the most fortunate and accelerated, it is necessary to use a sliding scale in selecting the best books for the various readers to be served. However, there are yardsticks for measuring creative writing that are as applicable to book selection for young adults as for adults.

Fiction should conform to the following principles:

1. *It should interpret life truly.*

The story should not be sensational, exaggerated, prettied up, or distorted. A realistic picture of the adult world, even if frankly written, may not be as harmful as books that make life seem too easy and too

---

*Appendix B reflects the selection policies of the Enoch Pratt Library when Edwards was the Coordinator of Work with Young Adults. *Ed.*

happy, and so do not prepare young people to understand the problems of maturity. The best books do not end like fairy tales, where after
all dragons are slain the handsome hero and beautiful heroine marry
and live happily ever after. People are neither all good nor all bad. Most
problems are not easy to solve. In well-written books people may suffer
intensely at times and sorrow and despair are mingled with triumph
and joy. If one looks about him at the people he knows, he will see few
perfectly happy, healthy, well-adjusted individuals. He will see injustice prevail on occasion and the innocent suffering for the guilty. He
may see fairly ordinary people rise to great heights of nobility and the
superintendent of the Sunday school embezzling the bank's funds. In
other words, life is complex and the writer who makes it appear too pat
or too ugly or too beautiful—the writer who oversimplifies—is probably not painting a true picture.

Caution: Librarians who select books for young adults must guard
with equal care against mistaking realistic writing for cheapness and
cheap writing for realism.

2. *The characters should be real and vital.*

They should react to situations in the story as they would in real life.
In many of the best novels the events related work a change in a
character over a long period of time and after much soul-searching.
Willie Keith in *The Caine Mutiny* [Wouk, 1954] changed from a mama's
boy to a man after months aboard an old minesweeper in the Pacific
during World War II. It took considerable time for Anna Karenina to
change from a brilliant figure in Russian society to a despairing suicide.
Willa Cather's Antonia became a fulfilled woman after a long, lonely
childhood and youth. All these transformations are credible. Too sudden a change is no more convincing in a novel than it is in real life.
Characters in books should react very much like their counterparts in
real life who share a similar heredity and environment. In this connection it might be said that novels of plot written with the idea of
spinning a good yarn are welcome entertainment and diversion as long
as their characters react as normal human beings. But the best novels
do more than recount events; they show how these events change the
characters. Young people prefer novels with sound characters developed from action and dialogue rather than from long explanatory
passages.

3. *Selection should be based on awareness of the world today, an understanding of modern youth, and common sense.*

Books containing realistic passages, whether they be creative works of fiction or factual nonfiction should be included in young-adult collections if the dominant theme of the book contributes to an understanding of life and if the questionable passages contribute to the development of the theme or the portrayal of character. When A. B. Guthrie wrote his magnificent *The Big Sky*, which had been researched carefully and was wonderfully true to life, there was fear that innocent teenagers might realize that this untamed mountain man shacked up with his beloved Teale Eye without hunting up a minister on the vast empty plains; that the baby was blind because of his past indiscretions; that he killed his best friend in a jealous rage. So the publishers brought out a cleaned-up edition for young people. *The Cruel Sea* suffered the same fate and was redone without the women and sex, carrying on its jacket the blessing of a highly placed English divine. If these two fine books in their original form are too hot for the timid librarian to handle, he does not have to purchase them. But it is not fair to the youngsters to make these virile books neuter. Let's not drape the nude Greek statues in the park. I am amazed that many school libraries in Guthrie's native state do not stock his distinguished novels.

Young people today, exposed as they are to the mass media and sophisticated as they are in their personal associations, are not likely to be upset by frank writing. When a character in a book uses "objectionable" language, the reader or reviewer should ask himself, "Is this what that character would say under the circumstances? Do I understand the character and the story better for the language used and the situations depicted? Does the book ring true?" If the answer to these questions is "Yes," there is no reason to condemn the book. It is the responsibility of librarians to show young people how to read such books with understanding rather than to deprive adolescents of them. It is easier to underestimate than to overestimate the ability of teenagers to understand books written for adults. Time spent hunting objectionable words and making lists of books to ban might be employed to better advantage in searching for books to enrich and delight young readers. And let us bear in mind Mayor Jimmy Walker's observation that "no girl was ever ruined by a book."

4. *Dull, didactic books, no matter how informative or how lofty the author's intentions, should be excluded from recreational collections for young adults.*

5. *Books written with a bias intended to persuade the reader of a religious or political point of view are out of place in recreational collections in public and school libraries.*

6. Moralistic writing that seeks to drive home a lesson should be passed over in favor of more subtle stories.

Some teenage novels do give youngsters sound advice but in an entertaining way. What is referred to here is the dull book concerned more with sin than good sense.

7. Interpretive writing that depicts the human heart is more useful in stimulating thinking and developing understanding than is factual information on the same subject, though both types of writing may be useful.

As has been said, pamphlets and books proving scientifically that all races are fundamentally the same are not as effective as novels and biographies that cause the reader to identify with the people of other races. Of course, young people with a scientific bent may prefer to read pure science and they should be encouraged to seek out bibliographies and refer to the catalog.

8. Titles that seem adequate but are no better than books on the same subject already in stock should be rejected unless the demand for that type of book exceeds the supply.

9. Books that present any racial or national group in a derogatory manner, that consistently use objectionable nicknames for ethnic groups or races, that perpetuate stereotyped racial characteristics and ideas, are not acceptable.

10. Fiction written especially for the teenager does not need to be judged by the standards set up for adult novels.

As I have said, teenage books that teach the apathetic the love of reading, that satisfy the younger adolescent's emotional and psychological needs and throw light on his problems, are tools that the skillful librarian uses to develop readers. They are acceptable if the characters, dialogue, problems, and situations are credible, if there is a sound code of behavior and morals, if they are in good taste and reasonably well written.

In a sports story, for instance, the reader usually wants an accurate play-by-play account of the crucial part of the game plus the reasoning that leads the hero to make the plays he does. In addition to action there must be suspense, drive, and purpose—the outcome must matter a great deal to the reader as well as the players.

11. Style that distinguishes a book as literature is very rare. Though it is to be cherished when found, it is not essential.

It is difficult to transmit to young people an appreciation of style for it is an elusive concept to grasp. Few adults appreciate style in many fields of art; many people have no comprehension of it at all. In many American homes the pictures on the walls portray a little golden-haired girl and her Collie dog or the old mill wheel. The most raucous music depicting the self unbuttoned appeals to more people than Beethoven's symphonies. Many of us with two college degrees cannot detect style in modern art or poetry. If we belabor the point of appreciating literary style, we may confuse young people unnecessarily. If we recommend only the best-written books and look down on those they can enjoy, we may undermine their pleasure in reading. Besides, it is far more important to awaken in young people a social consciousness than to insist that they appreciate style. *Black Like Me* is more meaningful for most of them than a novel by Thackeray.

The experienced reviewer has a kind of built-in Geiger counter that ticks loudly when his eye passes over writing of exceptional quality. The story may be as tough as Hemingway's *The Killers,* as polished as Cather's *Death Comes for the Archbishop,* or as gay [carefree] as Marquis' *Archy and Mehitabel* [1950]—but the originality, truth, and grace of the writing will, as Clifton Fadiman put it, set bells ringing inside the sensitive reader.

12. *The principles and standards of book selection should determine the books to be included in the collection rather than one's individual taste or pressure from citizens, however well meaning.*

In any given year one may not find five novels that pass all the tests cited above. One judges books as he does people by weighing faults against virtues. He decides in the end whether a book is worth buying despite its faults or is unacceptable despite its virtues—after reading the entire book, not after passing judgment on a few passages read out of context. One must be sure his conclusions are based on sound reasoning uninfluenced by personal feelings. Even so, no one's judgment is infallible.

Points to Be Considered in Judging Nonfiction

1. *The date of publication is especially important for history, travel, vocational, and similar books.*

Even in sports the rules change and once-famous players are forgotten. In certain fields of science a book three years old may contain unreliable statements and should be discarded.

2. How much of an authority is the author?

Diet and psychiatry are but two fields about which misleading information is published.

3. What is the author's point of view?

Race relations, civil rights, juvenile delinquency, and the draft can be approached from various angles.

4. Has the book vitality?

Many books pass all the other tests but become a drug on the market because they fail to interest the reader.

5. As was said of fiction, titles that seem adequate but are no better than those already in stock should be rejected unless there is a need for more books on the subject.

Various authors may write a biography of the same person, but two biographies of any individual are usually quite enough. It is easy to overstock on such subjects as ballet, insects, the North Pole, or other subjects that are of interest to only a very few readers. On the other hand, we should watch for books on subjects that might give our readers a new interest.

6. A quick evaluation:

In *Living with Books* [1935], from which many of these principles were borrowed, Helen Haines says that one can evaluate nonfiction quickly by noting the following: publisher, title page, introduction, chapter headings, readability. The first and last chapters often epitomize the purpose of the book. Read a controversial chapter. Note the style and references to sources of information. Test the index. The usefulness of a nonfiction title decreases if there is no index.

Some school library supervisors have set up ten tests of sound book-selection practice. Some of these were covered above, but they are listed here again:

1. Do you *read*—widely, regularly, critically?

2. Do you keep a running file of order cards based on your own reading, suggestions from teachers and students, and needs uncovered by use of the library?

3. Do you check books by reading reviews in accepted sources?

4. Is there a written statement of book-selection policy for your school?

5. Do you apply well-defined criteria for the book that you choose?

6. Do you select books in relation to a well-thought-out plan for the development of the total collection?

7. Do you consider school needs and pupil interests and abilities when choosing books?

8. Do you encourage wide participation in book selection?

9. Do you examine books before buying them whenever possible?

10. Do you compare related books to see which is preferable?

In *Books, Young People and Reading Guidance* [G. R. Hanna and M. K. McAllister, 1960], Hanna discusses book selection and sums up the matter by saying, "The librarian seeks to provide the most useful and at the same time, the most satisfying books at the highest literary level compatible with usefulness."

Book selection should be position rather than negative. The librarian who works with teenagers is more obligated to stimulate thinking and hand on our cultural heritage than to protect young people from life's realities. The book that leads a teenager from consideration of himself to concern for all men should be made not only available, but interesting to adolescents by being shelved in inviting collections and vitalized by outgoing librarians.

BOOK LISTS

A book list should be so designed that anyone who picks it up will be impelled to open it and see what is inside. Some librarians today are designing stunning lists for young adults, but not all. The best ones have such illustrations as a long, wicked-looking red car, a trumpet player, a reproduction of a clever drawing by a professional artist— whatever fits a vital subject and appeals to today's teenagers. The worst ones feature a teenage boy and girl looking as if they had just come from a meeting of the Youth for Clean Living Club. They are often seated, reading a book together, though the more daring depict the couple seated, leaning back to back and reading their separate books. A variation on this is the "upward and onward" theme—the climb up the mountain, the boy reaching down to give the girl a hand while clutching his book.

The same principles for illustrations and captions given in the section on displays hold good here. However, if the cut used on the cover is self-explanatory, a caption is not needed. For instance, a book list on the brotherhood of man has been put out with nothing on the cover but the reproduction of a *New Yorker* cartoon showing a hippie carrying a sign with the inscription "Dig Thy Neighbor." It is necessary to get permission from the publisher to use a cut from copyrighted material. This is, as a rule, not difficult to obtain. Since posters are not published, permission to enlarge a cut from published material and use it on a poster is not necessary.*

Most effective lists feature one subject, but there is more need for general lists than for general displays. Vacation reading lists distributed through the schools at the end of the school year are an excellent way of contacting the teenagers of a community. For either the public or school library, attractive lists will help establish good public relations and advertise the library as well as promote reading.

A school library might put out numerous bookmarks throughout the school year, tying the book to the school's activities. When the school play is given, bookmarks could be distributed featuring the cast of characters on one side and plays, biographies, and stagecraft on the other. For each of the school sports the bookmark might feature the season's schedule on one side and sports books on the other. Dances, a special speaker, assembly programs, and other activities could be tied to books in the library in this way. A library club could be responsible for this activity.

Unless lists are published in quantities over ten thousand, they can be produced very attractively and fairly inexpensively on a multilith machine. Either colored or white paper can be used; the color of the paper, the color of the ink, the format of the lists, the illustration on the cover, and the caption should all be in harmony.

Once the list has been printed, one should make it available in quantity and create a demand for it instead of storing the supply in a cupboard and handing the lists out gingerly. Lists should be put out where people can pick them up in the branches of a city system. They should be handed out on classroom visits, at book fairs, at teenage club meetings—wherever they would be welcomed. Then if requests for books on the list pour in, extra copies of the titles in demand can be ordered.

---

*The author is interpreting the fair use principle that guides the use of published materials broadly. These views are not supported wholly by the publisher. While the intent in this example is not commercial, each case must be weighed individually and against all aspects of the fair use principle. *Ed.*

ANNOTATION WRITING

If we design a list so attractive that anyone who sees it will pick it up, it is important that he not put it down when he reads the annotations or because there are no annotations. Simply listing authors and titles under various headings is better than nothing but it does not give the reader any indication of which titles would appeal to him and which would bore or baffle him. Below are sample annotations taken from published lists for young adults that illustrate the difference between a merely adequate annotation (a) and one written with art (b).

The King Must Die   Mary Renault

(a) The Theseus legend is vividly and dramatically retold in this story.

(b) Theseus steps from the realm of legend to enter the bull ring, thread the labyrinth with its minotaur, win Ariadne, and challenge the matriarchy of his day.

Johnny Tremain   Esther Forbes

(a) When an injury to his hand changed the life of a silversmith's apprentice, he found his own role to play in the beginnings of the American Revolution.

(b) Struggling Johnny Tremain, having lost his trade and birthright, finds himself involved in mysterious tea parties, firebrand politics, and secret meetings with Paul Revere, Sam Adams, and John Hancock.

Brave New World   Aldous Huxley

(a) In a highly satirical vein, Huxley pictures Utopia, scientific and industrialized. His predictions are bitter and forceful.

(b) In a world where science has solved all mankind's problems—where there is no pain, hunger, suffering, or freedom (none is needed)—one test-tube baby has dangerous thoughts about freedom and individuality.

Annotation writing is an art. Here are a few pointers, some of which were originally stated by Helen Haines in *Living with Books* and still hold true:

1. In most lists for young adults, an annotation should not run over about thirty-five words.

2. Try to write the annotation in one sentence, as two or more tend to give a jerky rather than a flowing rhythm.

3. Avoid too many adjectives. Instead of saying the story is interesting or delightful or exciting, use nouns and verbs to tell what was interesting or delightful or exciting.

4. The active voice is better than the passive.

5. The best annotations for young adults get moving with the first words. Somebody should be doing something, if possible.

6. Direct action can be varied with a statement that catches the attention. (See annotation (b) for *Brave New World*.)

7. Do not give the story away.

8. Do not overrecommend the book.

9. Include statements that place the book in its proper time and place.

10. After copy for a list is completed, read the annotations aloud. Awkward expressions, too frequent use of the same word, and other inelegancies can be avoided this way.

11. Only occasionally begin annotations with *A* and *The*.

12. Never use the word *you*. This word is overly familiar and gives an annotation a hortatory, saving-the-reader-for-democracy tone that is highly objectionable. All annotations should be written as if for adults, without condescension or a patronizing tone.

13. Do not repeat the title or any information it gives.

The librarian's annotation tells:

1. What the book is about and how it ends
2. The setting and period covered
3. Literary qualities
4. Usefulness
5. Limitations
6. To whom it will appeal
7. How it compares with other books in the field

The necessary bibliographic information should appear under the author and title at the head of the card. The annotation need not be confined to one sentence but should be written in a flowing style and should not exceed about fifty words, as longer annotations necessitate two review cards and crowd library files. One should keep in mind that this is not so much a literary exercise as a buying guide to tell a librarian whose funds are probably low whether or not the book reviewed will be a good investment.

BOOK TALKS

The objectives of giving book talks to teenagers are:
1. To sell the idea of reading for pleasure
2. To introduce new ideas and new fields of reading
3. To develop appreciation of style and character portrayal
4. To lift the level of reading by introducing the best books the audience can read with pleasure
5. To humanize books, the library, and the librarian

Anyone without an emotional problem or a speech difficulty can talk about books effectively if he wants to badly enough, if he is enthusiastic about books and wishes to share his pleasure in them, and if he is well prepared.

There are various ways of giving book talks and any speaker can measure the effectiveness of his method by the number of young people who come to the library to borrow the books spoken about.

One method of preparing a talk is to select a dramatic incident from a book about which one is enthusiastic. The incident should have plot and continuity enough to hold an audience, and preferably, should not occur at the end of the book. Introduce the characters and tell only enough of the story leading up to the incident selected to make the talk intelligible. If the incident to be related is in the first person, it can be changed to the third or left as it is written and introduced by some such remark as, "This is the way Jane Eyre tells what happened." The typed copy of the talk should run approximately four and a half pages, double-spaced, as a general rule. Read the prepared talk aloud for its sound and style. Do not point out lessons or use a hortatory tone. Do not end with "If you want to know what happened, read the book" or leave the audience dangling. Challenge an accelerated class at times by telling them the book to be presented demands thought and concentration.

Whether one memorizes a talk or not, he should type it as it is intended to be given. There are two reasons for this: (1) If the talk is given some months later, one will not have to reread the book but merely the typed talk. (2) Over the years one can build up an extensive repertoire of successful talks to be given to new classes. As books go out of print or lose their appeal, book talks based on them should be discarded for it is important that the books talked about be available and have strong appeal to the current generation.

Few people speak well extemporaneously. Words do not come to them quickly enough and they seem disorganized, halting, and self-conscious. By reading over a typed talk many times, a speaker can be sure of the order of events to be related and appropriate words will come to him easily. Since the author's language usually has a fluidity few amateurs can attain, it is well to use his words as much as possible, supplying needed interpolation and cutting as necessary. After many presentations of the talk the speaker will unconsciously have memorized it just as he did "America" by singing it over several times. The sooner he memorizes the talk, the smoother his presentation will be.

The Technique of Delivery

1. Do not begin to speak until the audience is ready to listen. Wait for attention with good humor. Create a favorable impression of yourself quickly and unobtrusively without a hostile stare or a rap for order.

2. State clearly the author and title of the book. In addition, if possible, distribute a list of titles to be presented in either thumbnail sketches or book talks. The list might be captioned "Speaking of Books," and if long, broken up into interest sections such as: "To Keep You Up at Night," "For the Nonconformist," "Geared to a Man's Taste," "For the Female of the Species," "Current Happenings."

3. Be sure everyone in the room can hear all that is said.

4. Bring the story to life so vividly that the speaker disappears and only the story lives. Any gesture or tone that enhances the story is right; anything that calls attention to the speaker is wrong. Almost any planned gesture is a mistake.

5. Change the pace of speaking to suit the tempo of the story.

6. Vary the tone. For excitement a low tone is best—a tense whisper is more effective than a yell.

7. For emphasis the pause is essential. For example, "He looked down the well and saw [pause, take a breath through the mouth, expanding the diaphragm] a *hand* sticking out of the water."

8. When two characters are conversing look to the right for one, to the left for the other, and throughout the talk keep them in the same relative positions. When Jane Eyre speaks to Mr. Rochester

she should look directly into his eyes, not out the window. Since he is taller than she, she will look up a bit. Mr. Rochester, who is standing opposite her, will look to the left if she looked to the right and will look down a bit, directly into her eyes but not at the floor, when he is talking to her. Between their remarks the speaker looks at the audience for "he said" or "she replied," as these words are not part of the conversation between the two main characters.

9. Stand firmly without rocking. Never back off from an audience unless you wish to indicate fear or hesitancy.

10. *Never* apologize to the audience for yourself. If you were able to drag yourself to the platform or into the classroom, make a final effort and look glad to be there.

11. Do not read to an audience if it can be avoided. The minute you take your eyes from them you decrease the intensity of their attention. Even a talk on poetry is a hundred times more effective if memorized and recited with one's eyes on the audience. Always look at the audience.

12. Do not indulge in nervous gestures. How many librarians have straightened out paper clips as they spoke! Keep your hands out of the picture unless they are helping to tell the story.

13. Do not pretend to have read books you have not read.

14. The face should reflect the feelings of the speaker. An expressionless face cuts the audience off from sharing with the speaker the emotions generated by the book. The eyes, face, and hands make the difference between a tape recording and a book talk.

15. Undue emphasis on *a* and *the* make a talk sound memorized. These articles are pronounced with the sound of the short *u* and elided into the next word, i.e., "uboy," "thusong."

16. The feet can indicate a change of scene or the passing of time. As one recounts the events of an exciting battle at night, he stands with feet normally close together with his weight on the ball of one foot. As the last bomb drops and the battle ends, the speaker stops speaking, relaxes, moves his free foot to the side, and shifts his weight to it. Not until the other foot comes to rest in its normal new position does the speaker begin to tell what happened the next morning. Thus the audience has a chance to shift to a new place and time.

17. Watch for boredom. If you selected a love story and chairs are beginning to squeak and there is some coughing, make a quick

change. Do not scold the audience or let them know you realize all is not going well. Say something like "Well, to make a long story short, she broke up with the city boy and married her cousin's friend. But let me tell you about Douglas Bader, the legless aviator in the R.A.F."

18. If it is possible to record a talk on a tape recorder and hear it played back, one can see where a change of tempo, a shorter or longer pause, or more variation in tone would improve delivery.

19. The public librarian visiting the school should speak in the library if possible and make the fullest use of the books in it, assembling the books to be talked about and allowing time for the students to check them out. Whether the talks are made by the school or the public librarian, it is often a good idea to stop talking ten minutes before the end of the period and encourage browsing.

20. A book talk is more effective when given to small rather than large groups. An audience of one class numbering around thirty is a group with which one can usually establish the good rapport more likely to lead to reading.

Remember, the librarian who gives books talks is not on trial as a performer but as a promotor of reading and his effectiveness should be judged by the amount of reading done as a result of his talks.

Book talks to classes or groups are effective in themselves but a class visit to the library can be something special if the librarian selects a subject or a theme and introduces it by making use of realia, music, posters, or films. From people living in the community, from travel agencies, consulates, teachers, and the teenagers themselves, one may borrow interesting collections, art objects, jewelry, costumes of other countries and other times. Artistic displays, a book talk, and a film in conjunction with the introduction of books on the subject can make a class visit to the library a memorable experience.

BOOK DISCUSSIONS

Whoever undertakes to lead a book discussion has homework to do. He must read the book to be discussed carefully, noting passages that throw light on the author's purpose or show motivation of character or express a point of view that seems important. In his mind there should be a clear idea of the book's theme. What is the author saying about his main character or characters? How good is the writing? Is the book really true to life? What are its limitations? Professional reviewers often point out interesting matters for consideration that may not occur to the discussion leader. If the book is not new, outstanding critics may have written essays about it. After thorough preparation one should formulate three or four questions likely to provoke thought and bring out differences of opinion.

If one is leading a group discussion with teenagers, the ice can be broken by asking first, "If you had this book under your arm and a friend asked you what it was about, how would you tell him without being long-winded and tiresome and without giving away the ending?" Three or four might have a try at this. If the book under discussion were Maugham's *Of Human Bondage* and no really inspired answer were forthcoming, the leader might suggest that it is the story of a fellow with a clubfoot trying to find out what he wanted to be and do who got hung up with the wrong girl.

Some provocative questions likely to lead to a spirited discussion might be: "Why did Philip Carey stay with Mildred so long when he knew she was wicked and cruel?" "If you were a psychiatrist and had Philip on the couch, what would you say was bugging him?" "How would you predict his future? Will he be happy or not? Why?" "Was Philip in any way a typical young man?"

Often by playing devil's advocate the leader can so provoke people who had intended to sit and listen that they will plunge into the discussion. He should not overplay this role but should generate an air of excitement about the book and inject enough humor to amuse the audience when the argument becomes tense. In the end he should attempt to make a summary statement about the book on which all can agree, but if there is a sharp difference of opinion, he should sum up both sides, bringing in the opinion of professional critics as well as his own. He should, however, assure the audience that his opinion carries no more weight than anyone else's. The leader's role is to provoke thought and discussion and not to settle the matter once and for all.

The same technique can be used with a class of library-school students. This is also a good way to teach the application of the principles of book selection. If from one to three students report on a title read and discuss it in this way with the instructors and if the discussion is lively, many others will feel compelled to read the book and "get with it."

DISPLAYS

Every year when autumn leaves fall, out come the posters featuring autumn leaves in school and public libraries over the country. The poster is usually entitled "Fall Reading." As cold weather sets in "Fall

Reading" is changed to "Winter Reading," illustrated with a picture of someone in an armchair in front of a fireplace reading while snow falls outside. "Spring Reading" usually features a row of paper jonquils, while "Keep Cool with a Book" shows a girl reading in a hammock with a cool drink within reach. These displays save a lot of shelving, as almost any book can be tossed in the collection beneath the poster, but they are corny and ineffective. They do no more than brighten up some corner a bit and call attention to reading. The young person who sees them in the library gets no message.

Displays are more effective if they feature a single concrete idea under such captions as "Damsels in Distress" (Gothic novels); "Music and All That Jazz"; "Growing Up Black"; "Laugh-In"; "Profiles in Courage"; "How Do I Love Thee." Whatever the subject for display, it is quite important that it be relevant to the teenager's world. Books on the subject should be directly under the poster, and if possible, lists related to the subject should accompany the display and be made available in quantity.

There should be an illustration that will catch attention and work with a striking caption to sell an idea. One strong illustration is better than two or three; don't gild the lily with a lot of little doodads that may be clever but clutter up the display and divert attention from the subject presented. Avoid the hortatory upward-and-onward tone in both caption and illustration as well as the use of the word *you*. A clever cartoon that elicits a laugh can drive home a point more effectively than a heavy-handed effort to be instructive. Two examples come to mind. A cartoon from the *Saturday Review* featured a kangaroo mother carrying quite a sizable offspring in her pouch and saying to him, "Don't you think it's about time you got yourself a job?" The Pratt Library used this on a list entitled "From High School to a Career." Another from the same magazine showed a caveman sitting, waiting his turn outside the Patent Office, clutching a wheel. This illustrated a list called "Science in Fact and Fiction." Cartoons in such magazines as the *Saturday Review of Literature* and *The New Yorker*, collections of commercial art, a book of designs, a clever ad, and various other sources can supply many ideas. When possible, cut out an illustration that looks promising and file it for future reference. Otherwise make a note describing the cut and indicating where it is located and include the note in the file of illustrations to be used for displays. This saves endless searching later and makes it possible to plan a plentiful supply of posters as they are needed. In selecting the cuts keep in mind that simple line drawings are easier to reproduce than complicated illustrations or halftones.

By removing one shelf from a section of shelves, a perfect location that has the effect of a stage can be provided for a display. If the poster to be used does not completely fill the rear space, cover the space with colorful pasteboard that complements the design of the poster and then attach the poster to this background. Amateurish lettering can spoil an otherwise artistic display—use the different types of ready-made letters that are available.

Displays should be changed often. If one plans six months ahead and prepares the posters likely to be useful, he will be able to introduce a variety of books to many readers. If only a very few books are borrowed a week after the display is put up, the librarian should be skeptical of its effectiveness. If the books are still there after two weeks, take the display down. For that matter, even a good display can be replaced in two or three weeks. There is no point in displaying books already in great demand, such as teenage romances, as the supply of titles will soon be exhausted and no one will have received a new idea for reading or stimulation to broaden his horizon.

If one is searching for inspiration for a new display, it is a good idea to find a telling illustration first, then plan a display around it. Otherwise one may select a subject, civil rights, for instance, and have to search for days before finding a cut that is not preachy or dull. It is better to keep ideas you wish to promote in the back of your head and collect appropriate cuts over a period of time, filing them to be used as needed.

Be sure there are readable books available in sufficient quantity on the topic to be featured if the promotion of recreational reading is the purpose of the display. There is not a large enough supply of books about Hawaii or the South Pole or motorcycles to justify a display of recreational reading on these subjects. Do not crowd such a display with books of information that the librarian himself would not care to read. Do not include classics just because they are classics. What high-school boy wants to read *Captains Courageous* [Kipling, 1897]? And many of them can get along without *Two Years Before the Mast* [Dana, 1840]. In this connection, do not use the displays to circulate books that just sit on the shelves. Young people must come to feel that if a book is on display, it must be good. Otherwise we will slow down the development of the reader by losing his confidence in our recommendations.

The school librarian would do well to ask his principal at the beginning of the school year to assign to the library a talented art student who will be given a school letter at the end of the year for service to the library. This student might be treated as a specialist and assigned only art work. The librarian should feel responsible for subjects for display, illustrations, and captions, while the student will do the actual preparation. Student suggestions should be welcome but the librarian must see that the posters have tone and quality, and if possible, a new twist rather than a cliché-ridden approach.

The display should amuse or pique the curiosity of the observer who, moving in for a closer look, will find his hand on a book ready to be borrowed.

PAPERBACKS

When paperbacks first appeared they were, as a rule, pulps. The more innocuous were set in the Wild West and were trite and sensational. The cruder titles emphasized crime and sex, depicting on their covers women in some stage of undress or in intimate scenes with virile, handsome men—as someone has said, there was a pretty girl on the jacket and no jacket on the pretty girl. How publishers discovered there was more money to be made by turning to better literature jacketed with better taste is not known, but they did change. Could it be possible that publishers improved the tone of their covers because in those days, when a parent's disapproval carried some weight, they did not wish to stir up parental opposition to their youngsters purchasing these books? Some people are not fully aware of the change in both quality and appearance of paperbacks and still feel that readers of taste avoid these upstarts of the publishing world and read only hard-cover books. This point of view represents the horse-and-buggy stage of reading promotion and is a thoughtless refusal to use one of the librarian's most effective weapons against reluctance to read. If one looks through *Paperbacks in Print,* he will find an abundance of enriching reading, much of it to be had for less than one dollar per volume. Hundreds of the titles are on standard lists for young adults.

There are psychological reasons not clearly understood for the surprising appeal of paperbacks. It may be their size—they are so easy to carry about. People may think a book in paperback is an abridgement that will take less time to read than the hard-cover version. In a few cases this is true, but by and large the paperback publisher has bought the copyright from the original publisher and reprinted the book in toto without margins. Whatever the reasons, it is a known fact that people generally will read a book in paperback that they have passed over in hard cover. Such an excellent book as *Act One* may sit indefinitely on the shelves in hard cover to be snatched up and read as a paperback.

Teenagers are especially enthusiastic over paperback books. Macy's department store in New York City made the pockets of blue jeans

---

The section "Paperbacks" is more interesting for its view of the paperback novel in 1974 than for instructions on the use of paperbacks by librarians and teachers today. Nevertheless, for people generally interested in the evolution of books, these comments should prove enlightening. *Ed.*

larger to fit paperbacks, yet some librarians argue that they cannot fit paperbacks into their budget because they wear out so fast. A strong case can be made for the opposite point of view. Paperbacks are not expensive until they are cataloged and processed. Librarians have a consuming passion to do things to books. (It has been said that we do everything to a book but read it.) If they purchase a paperback, it seems to them unthinkable not to classify it, catalog it, provide it with a catalog card, make a shelf list card, file the cards, and stamp the secret code on a certain page. Then when the book is withdrawn they do it all over again, but backwards as in the TV ad where the tired woman's nerves unravel like a rope until she takes Anacin and the rope rewinds itself. Certainly this process is essential for books in hard cover and for the more expensive, original paperbacks but it does not pay off for a recreational collection. If there is already a card in the catalog for Smith's *A Tree Grows in Brooklyn* in hard cover, why not purchase additional copies in paperback, paste a book pocket with a book card in each, and call it square? At the Pratt Library the library stamp and the agency number are the only preparations applied. All paperbacks are checked on the electric charging machines with a dummy card marked *one miscellaneous charge,* and if the book is not returned, no messenger is sent. It has even been argued that it is cheaper for the library to give paperbacks away and let people return them if they wish rather than to circulate them in the regular way.

By the time we do all the things we can do to a paperback, we run the price up about $1.50 per copy, according to ALA figures. If we lose one of the books that was not cataloged, we will have lost about sixty cents. Had we cataloged the book, we would have lost $2.10. Of course, if the paperback is the only edition of a title, there is need for a card in the catalog to indicate the holding.

Let's look at it this way, *To Kill a Mockingbird* in hard cover originally cost $4.95. The paperback cost sixty cents. From its first publication this novel was in great demand. Everyone was talking about it, and then a forthcoming movie was announced. Not only was the book popular, but it was also just what we had been looking for to depict the needless cruelty of prejudice. Any library concerned for young people and the public weal would have bought one copy of the book for teenagers. This first copy would have been in hard cover. When it became evident that one copy would circulate to only about thirteen readers in a year (if the loan period were four weeks and each reader kept the book for the time allowed), some duplication should have seemed essential. Another copy in hard cover processed for $1.50 would have cost $6.45 and would have supplied thirteen more readers. The same investment would have bought ten paperbacks with enough left over for ten cards and pockets and would have given 130 more teenagers the opportunity to read a moving novel of social significance when they wanted to read it. A delay of a year diminishes the desire to read any book. If we believe reading is enriching, the number of people we can reach with a meaningful book is important. For most books in heavy demand it would seem a good idea to purchase one title in hard cover and as many paperback duplicates as funds will allow.

If fifty circulations is the life expectancy of a hard-cover title of *To Kill a Mockingbird* and we pay $6.45 to get the book on the shelves, the cost per circulation is thirteen cents. If we pay sixty cents for the paperback and get only five circulations from it, the cost is twelve cents per circulation—that is, if we can free ourselves from the compulsion to process the paperback. Of course, many paperbacks circulate more than five times. Some librarians are enthusiastic about special jackets and reinforced covers for paperbacks. If the cost of the materials and time spent do more for the cause of reading than would a duplicate copy, it would seem justifiable, but the librarian should be sure that more important projects are not sacrificed in this use of time.

When a paperback book falls apart, if we have done nothing more than stamp the library's name on it and put a card and pocket in the back, all we have to do is toss the book into the wastebasket—there is no catalog card to pull, no shelf list to change. If any records of holdings are necessary, they can be made on p-slips with tallies and kept in a desk drawer. We worry over theft and loss, but as was said above, a sixty-cent loss is not so painful as a $6.50 loss. Actually we lose far more hard-cover titles than any of us wish to admit.

Libraries should do more advertising. TV properly utilized on a professional level could send prospective readers rushing to libraries. Why do we never see ads about libraries and books in newspapers or billboards advertising the public library? The paperback book is a form of reading promotion and pays its way as such, in addition to supplying reading material. However, the effectiveness of paperbacks is lost without the proper means of calling them to the reader's attention. Packed in shelves with only their spines showing, they do not catch the eye of the prospective reader.

In a collection for young adults paperbacks are best displayed on a revolving rack. Airports, bus stations, and newsstands realize people have a psychological urge to keep turning a rack to see what is displayed in each section. It is essential that paperbacks be placed so their covers catch the eye. In most libraries space is at a premium and there is no room for elegant stationary racks to be placed against the wall. The revolving rack should contain titles of a recreational nature only. Paperbacks on serious scientific theories, the development of the drama, the history of civilization, and so forth, should be processed as much as necessary and shelved with hard-cover books on the same subject. In fields of science where expensive books become obsolete in three or so years, it would save money to buy the books in paperback and shelve them with books in the same field, that is, if the paperback comes on the market in time to be useful. It might also be a good idea to use paperbacks to feel out demand in fields where we hope the students may be interested but have reason to doubt they will be.

There are machines on the market that dispense paperbacks for sale, but some of the companies selling the machines control book selection, making the machines impractical for young-adult and school librarians. If a suitable machine is purchased, it should not take the place of the rack which offers books free to all readers. The machine is for the convenience of those who cannot get a book from the library in time for an assignment because undue pressure has been put on its stock, and for those who wish to build up their personal libraries.

Paperbacks are here to stay. They are the most effective method of reading promotion since Gutenberg, and any librarian working with teenagers is not doing his best for them if he does not make use of them.

THOUGHTS BENEATH A BO TREE
(*Especially for School Librarians*)

Encyclopedias say that when My Lord Buddha sought to gain insight into life's meanings, he meditated in solitude under a Bo tree and experienced a spiritual awakening known as "the enlightment." Anyone planning to be a school librarian might do well to find a Bo tree and sit in meditation under its branches until he experienced "the enlightenment" on his life's vocation. He might ask himself what he hoped to accomplish as a high-school librarian and how he would set about to attain his goals.

Under the Bo tree the future librarian would decide that in whatever position he found himself, he would make his library the "Big L" in the thoughts of the student body and faculty of his high school. He would resolve never to appear as a frustrated, defeated librarian, making do with leavings and eliciting pity or sinking into anonymity. Whatever was blocking him, he would eventually remove by one means or another to ensure that the school was served as it should be served. He would resolve never to lose his temper or raise his voice or be short with any student. Above all, he would plan to read and read and read. He would keep his sense of humor functioning and stand before students and faculty as their friendly, capable readers' advisor, as well as the information resource of the school. He would not seek popularity and love, but rather respect as a person and a librarian.

Early in his first year at the school he would ask for a conference with the principal to which he would go armed with a book-selection policy he had written out. This policy would state clearly what he hoped to do for the school, his standards for book selection, his procedure for handling complaints, and his general thoughts on the administration of the library. By asking the principal to read the policy carefully to see if they could agree on it, he might go a long way in educating an indifferent principal on the role of the library in the school. After the principal agreed to the policy, the librarian should ask if he might present it to the faculty.

At the faculty meeting the librarian should appear smartly dressed, rested, and full of vitality and should use the occasion to present the book-selection policy—this time by discussing it rather than reading it, explaining how he hoped to serve the school, paying special attention to book selection and the problem of censorship, demonstrating what could be accomplished by book talks to classes, visits of classes to the library for a period, and the atmosphere of warm cordiality he hoped to maintain in the library. This would also be the time to ask for continual suggestions and advice from the faculty.

Thereafter he would make it his business to convince each member of the faculty that it would be to his advantage to make constant use of the library for himself and his classes. How many high-school librarians bemoan the indifference of faculty members in general to the library while pointing with pride to the few teachers who come in every morning to read the daily paper or chat. A resourceful librarian can "sell" the idea of using the library. A faculty indifferent to the library often reflects an inadequate librarian. Too often a teacher has no reason to feel the librarian is interested in his field or can tell him anything about it he does not already know. He is honestly not convinced that consulting the librarian would be fruitful. It is up to the librarian to give such a teacher a different point of view.

A friendly little gesture sometimes wins over a faculty member—asking advice, or when an interesting new book comes in, sending it to the teacher to review or just to enjoy. But the most effective way of gaining respect and cooperation is a demonstration of knowledge and ability. In the field of reading promotion one way of doing this is to invite a class to visit the library during a period either for an introduction to collateral reading for a unit to be studied or for recreational reading. Using realia, music, book lists, a bang-up book talk, and a film, the librarian can bring books and the library alive for the students and convince the teacher that the librarian can enrich the teaching of his subject.

The librarian sitting under the Bo tree would resolve not to appear shy and self-conscious. If the P.T.A. asked him to address their organization, he would jump at the chance and give them a thundering good talk on what the library was doing to enrich their children, possibly ending with an introduction of the student aides and a demonstration of their performance in the service of the library. The aides might even hand out bookmarks they had helped prepare featuring books for parents to read or suggestions for Christmas or graduation gifts. If the P.T.A. does not ask the librarian to talk, the librarian should volunteer.

If the librarian is not included on committees to plan units of study or to revise the curriculum, the explanation could be poor public relations. Possibly he has not convinced department heads that with his knowledge of books and students, he is essential to such a committee. And speaking of public relations, why are so many groups of library aides made up of the school's "lost dogs"? Too often the desk is manned by overly effeminate boys, bossy little girls, and "eager beavers." It seem that those who can are members of other school activities; those who can't are library aides. This may be good therapy but it is poor public relations. Certainly the librarian should take his share of the unattractive youngsters but it would be well to give the impression that poised, popular, creative young people wish to be attached to the library.

The librarian should have a conference with the principal before the aides are appointed. He should lay before the principal a plan to make the library doubly effective that would require truly outstanding student aides. The plan might include:

1. A library club where books are discussed and aides are taught to give book talks. From this training, qualified student speakers could go through the school, visiting classes to introduce books and selling the idea of reading for pleasure.

2. A regular column in the school paper advertising new books in the library.

3. Designing, reproducing, and keeping on hand a supply of bookmarks that would advertise the library and correlate reading and the school's activities, as was discussed in the section "Book Lists" above.

4. Planning and putting on a school assembly.

5. A book-reviewing, mimeographed periodical by and for teenagers on the order of *You're the Critic* described in the body of the book.

6. A P.T.A. program.

7. Keeping a paperback book rack stocked with up-to-date titles approved for young adults, from which books will circulate to all.

8. Buying a machine to dispense paperback books and putting students in charge of its operation and the handling of monies involved. If the machine is out of the question, other arrangements could be made for the sale of books which could be handled by the student aides.

9. A poll of the student body to determine the ten most popular books.

10. A faculty meeting in the library early in the year where the aides and the librarian would "model" the new books by parading them down a runway and remarking on them in the manner of a Dior fashion show.

If such a program were presented to teenagers with personality and creativity, it is quite likely they would want to have a part in it. These young people could make the library the dynamo of the school, and think what it would do for the students themselves.

Under the Bo tree the librarian should attempt to work out some way of getting cards held for nonpayment of fines back into the hands of their owners, for the students most in need of books and reading are the very ones whose cards are usually in the drawer at the desk. A librarian in a Baltimore high school in a deprived community gave all the cards back, canceling the fines. Then he set a fruit jar on his desk labeled "Conscience Money," meaning "Pay what you feel you can." The students evidently interpreted this to mean "If you feel guilty about something, a contribution would help." Whatever the explanation, he collected more money by fruit jar than he had by fines and everyone kept his card. He even invited the boys and girls to meet each other in the library during their lunch hours, and in the process of hosting the social hour sent most of his guests out with books. The conventional librarian who followed him almost lost her mind. Eventually she had better order and fewer readers.

The librarian should resolve that lessons given in the use of the catalog should not be the heart and soul of the library program—the only contact some students have with the library. Instead the student should remember the library for the books and films presented with such enthusiasm that he had fallen under their spell.

The librarian should work out the best possible relationship with the principal of the school. In the matter of book selection it is to be hoped that the supervising librarian for a large system would be in charge, but if the principal has the authority to make final decisions on the purchase and circulation of books for the school, the librarian should pray that he will have a first-hand knowledge of books and modern standards of selection and the moral courage to stand firm in a crisis. A prayer for a faculty with the same point of view might be in order.

If the faculty and principal should be overly conservative and unaware of standard practices, the librarian should work tactfully to bring them to a more liberal point of view. If the librarian were considering a frank, realistic new book for purchase, was convinced it belonged in the library, and has found support for it in standard tools, he should ask the principal to read it before he adds it to the collection. If he agrees the librarian might add the book, the librarian would look to him for support if complaints were made. But if the principal failed to stand firm and yielding to pressure, demanded that the librarian remove criticized books, the librarian should resign for every book the librarian removes proves him either incompetent for having added the book or a coward for removing it. Self-respect is in the balance. It is a good idea to nail down the new job before resigning, nor should one leave without quietly explaining to the principal why it was impossible to work under him any longer.

Another thought resulting from meditation under the Bo tree would be the importance of cooperating with the public library. All too often both public and school librarians have allowed petty jealousy of their individual territories to take precedence over the enrichment of the students. If public and school librarians joined forces and worked effectively together, they could triple or quadruple the results they accomplish working separately. Public librarians are sometimes indifferent and when they approach the schools are not well enough prepared. School librarians are inclined to consider the public librarian's visits an invasion of their territory. The public librarian who gives book talks in the schools should encourage the use of the school library and the circulation of its books, mentioning the public library as a second source. The school librarian should encourage the students to join the public library and to make use of its facilities. The two institutions should work hand in glove to develop each student to his full potential as a reader.

Finally, on graduation night, as each student walks across the stage the librarian should ask himself, "What contribution did I make to this student? Have I enlarged his vision and taught him the joy of reading? Have I made books so meaningful to him that he will read all his life, or have I just furnished him with information for assignments?"

FILMS AND OTHER MEDIA

Anyone who has seen such films as *Two Men and a Wardrobe, The Occurrence at Owl Creek Bridge, Phoebe,* and *The Hand* knows that films have a great contribution to make to the enrichment, understanding, and delight of young adults.

In any book on library work with young adults there should be a discussion of films, records, and other media for they have become an important and meaningful part of the modern library's plans for the teenager. However, someone else will have to write of these wonderful new media since they reached their present high level of development after my retirement from the Pratt Library. Furthermore, I wish to stand primarily on my advocacy of the book.

READING LIST

This list of books for young adults is really a suggested list for the beginning librarian to read in order that he may feel some assurance as he works with readers of varying age and ability. It is not inclusive, nor is it a list for all time, since many of the books will suffer the fate of Ozymandias. No two librarians would make identical lists, but each of these books has something to say to teenagers, and if given the right reader, will enrich and delight him.

A. For Younger Readers

Anonymous	*Go Ask Alice*
Arundel	*The Longest Weekend*
Bonham	*Durango Street*
Cavanna	*Almost Like Sisters*
Colman	*Bride at Eighteen*
Craig	*It Could Happen to Anyone*
Decker	*Switch Hitter*
Felsen	*Crash Club*
Gilbreth	*Cheaper by the Dozen*
Hinton	*The Outsiders*

Hunt	*Up a Road Slowly*
Hunter	*Soul Brothers and Sister Lou*
Mathis	*Teacup Full of Roses*
Norton (Andre)	Any title
Petry	*Tituba of Salem Village*
Stolz	*Pray Love, Remember*
Werbsa	*The Dream Watcher*
Wolff	*A Crack in the Sidewalk*
Zindel	*My Darling, My Hamburger*
Zindel	*The Pigman*

B. Useful Titles for Transferring the Reader to Adult Books

Asimov	*Fantastic Voyage*
Brontë	*Jane Eyre*
Clarke	*2001: A Space Odyssey*
Du Maurier	*Rebecca*
Frank	*Diary of a Young Girl*
Freedman	*Mrs. Mike*
Graham	*Dove*
Green	*I Never Promised You a Rose Garden*
Griffin	*Black Like Me*
Gunther	*Death Be Not Proud*
Head	*Mr. & Mrs. Bo Jo Jones*
Heyerdahl	*Kon-Tiki*
Hilton	*Lost Horizon*
Hitchcock	*Stories for Late at Night*
Holt	*Mistress of Mellyn*
Lane	*Let the Hurricane Roar*
Mitchell	*Gone with the Wind*
Nathan	*Portrait of Jennie*
Smith	*Joy in the Morning*
Thane	*Tryst*
Trahey	*Life with Mother Superior*
Weastheimer	*My Sweet Charlie*

C. Adult Titles for Good Readers

Angelou	*I Know Why the Caged Bird Sings*
Borland	*When the Legends Die*
Braithwaite	*To Sir, with Love*
Brown	*Bury My Heart at Wounded Knee*
Brown	*Manchild in the Promised Land*

Buck	*The Good Earth*
Cleaver	*Soul On Ice*
Dunning, ed.	*Reflections on a Gift of Watermelon Pickles*
Gaines	*The Autobiography of Miss Jane Pittman*
Golding	*Lord of the Flies*
Guthrie	*The Big Sky*
Hart	*Act One*
Kaufman	*Up the Down Staircase*
Knowles	*A Separate Peace*
Lee	*To Kill a Mockingbird*
Little	*The Autobiography of Malcolm X*
Massie	*Nicholas and Alexandra*
Parks	*A Choice of Weapons*
Paton	*Cry the Beloved Country*
Remarque	*All Quiet on the Western Front*
Rosten	*The Education of Hyman Kaplan*
Salinger	*The Catcher in the Rye*
Segal	*Love Story*
Seton	*Katherine*
Smith	*A Tree Grows in Brooklyn*
Wouk	*The Caine Mutiny*
Wright	*Black Boy*

D. Advanced Reading

Baldwin	*Go Tell It on the Mountain*
Camus	*The Plague*
Dostoevski	*Crime and Punishment*
Dreiser	*An American Tragedy*
Faulkner	*The Sound and the Fury*
Fitzgerald	*The Great Gatsby*
Hemingway	*A Farewell to Arms*
Huxley	*Brave New World*
Joyce	*Portrait of the Artist as a Young Man*
Kafka	*The Trial*
Koestler	*Darkness at Noon*
Malamud	*The Fixer*
Maugham	*Of Human Bondage*
Orwell	*1984*
Renault	*The King Must Die*
Solzhenitsyn	*One Day in the Life of Ivan Denisovitch*
Steinbeck	*The Grapes of Wrath*
Steinbeck	*Of Mice and Men*

Styron   *The Confessions of Nat Turner*
Tolstoy   *Anna Karenina*
Tolstoy   *War and Peace*

A BIBLIOGRAPHY FOR THE LIBRARIAN
WORKING WITH TEENAGERS

[*See* Appendix C for a bibliography for librarians who work with young adults, prepared by Betty Carter for this edition.]

APPENDIX B

Selection Policies for Books for Young Adults

Note: For the latest information about handling complaints about literature for young adults, *see* the Young Adult Library Services Association's *Hit List for Young Adults 2: Frequently Challenged Books* (Chicago: American Library Association, 2002).

It is the aim of this library's service to young adults to help them through books to find self-realization, to live in their communities as citizens of this democracy, and to be at home in the world. This aim is constantly kept in mind when books are selected for the young adult collections throughout the system, and each book purchased fits into this plan. The Book Selection Policies for young adult work in this library are based on the following principles:

1. That the young adult collections should be composed of books that widen the boundaries of adolescents' thinking, that enrich their life, and help them fulfill their recreational and emotional needs. Materials to help an adolescent prepare school assignments are in the reference and general adult collections rather than the young adult collections. However, school demands are considered if the books requested are both of a recreational nature and in the field of special interest to teenagers, such as World War I, popular science, etc.

2. That while our aims are clearly stated, the rules for selection cannot be written out ahead of time except in general terms, for each book must be considered separately. In other words, books have both faults and virtues, and if the virtues far overbalance a fault, a book may be included. With this in mind, the so called "touchy" areas in book

This statement of policies was prepared by Margaret Edwards for Enoch Pratt Free Library in 1962. *Ed.*

selection for teenagers are handled as follows: (a) The use of profanity or of frankness in dealing with sex may be deplorable, but when a book opens a clearer vision of life, develops understanding of other people, or breaks down intolerance, these virtues must be weighed against the possible harm to be done by some regrettable word or passage in the book, particularly where taste rather than morals is offended. (b) Simple books of sex information for teenagers belong on the open shelves of young adult collections. It seems important that young adults gain sound information since they are sure to gain information of some kind on the subject. If the books are treated as are interesting books on other subjects, much can be done to give teenagers a healthful attitude toward sex. (c) Religious books of an obviously denominational nature whose primary purpose is to present one sect as superior to another are not purchased for young adult collections, nor are books that belittle any faith. Only well-written books that make no attempt to sway the emotions of the adolescent toward or against any one faith should be included in special collections for young adults.

3. That all types of readers must be considered in setting up a book collection. Simple teenage stories of boy-girl relationships teach young and reluctant readers a love of reading—the first step in the development of any reader. At the other end of the scale is the older, better reader, often the superior student, who is forming his own philosophy and wishes to read adult titles that throw a clear light on the process of living. As the young adult collection serves primarily as an introduction to adult reading, in this library the majority of titles purchased are duplicates of adult books. However, this collection also includes titles written specifically for "teenagers" which are not bought in adult departments. When new titles of this type appear, if there is any question of the age level to which they will appeal, the Coordinators of Work with Children and Young Adults usually agree arbitrarily to place them in one department or the other. Only outstanding titles of books in unusual demand are placed in both the children's and young adult collections.

4. All fiction is read before purchase; also nonfiction titles of biography, travel, humor, drama, etc. Factual books, such as vocational books or those on sport techniques are examined closely. If adult titles recommended for "Y" purchase are not in the Central adult collection, the subject department head concerned is consulted, since the adult department must purchase the first copy of the title or *agree to its addition in the "Y" collection only.* In case of difference of opinion, the Assistant Director or Director is consulted. This applies only to adult titles. Books written specifically for young adults may be purchased even though not in the adult subject department collections.

5. That the young adult librarians working in committees should, after a period of training, be responsible for the selection of new books, but that any book selected may be challenged by any of the young adult librarians at any time, when the book will be reconsidered by the entire group. Though, as a rule, the young adult librarians read the controversial books under consideration and decide by vote in their regular monthly meeting whether to accept or reject these titles, it is the Coordinator of Work with Young Adults who has the final responsibility for and the final authority in the selection of books for young adult collections, subject to the ultimate responsibility of the Director.

6. That when the demand for books on any subject has been fairly met, new books in the field may be rejected, for no other reason except that a wiser use can be made of the book fund. At all times, a new book must be measured against other books available to determine what purchase seems wisest in view of our needs and the funds on hand.

7. That the young adult collection at Central should contain a copy of any book bought for young adults anywhere else in the system, but each branch collection should be made up of the books best suited to the community of young adults it serves.

APPENDIX C

A Bibliography
for the Librarian
Working with Young Adults
by Betty Carter

LIBRARY SERVICE TO YOUNG ADULTS

American Association of School Librarians and the Association for Educational Communications and Technology. 1998. *Information power: Building partnerships for learning.* Chicago: American Library Association.

American Association of School Librarians and the Public Education Network. 2001. *The information-powered school.* Chicago: American Library Association.

Bodart, Joni Richards, ed. 1980. *Booktalk!* New York: H. W. Wilson.

———. 1985. *Booktalk! 2.* New York: H. W. Wilson.

———. 1988. *Booktalk! 3.* New York: H. W. Wilson.

———. 1992. *Booktalk! 4.* New York: H. W. Wilson.

———. 1996. *Booktalking the award winners: Young adult retrospective volume.* New York: H. W. Wilson.

———. 1998. *Booktalking the award winners 4.* New York: H. W. Wilson.

Browman, Jennifer. 2001. *Booktalking that works.* New York: Neal-Schuman.

Editor's note: The genesis for this list comes from Patty Campbell's list in the 1994 edition of *The Fair Garden and the Swarm of Beasts.* I have eliminated a few books and added others.

Chelton, Mary K. 1994. *Excellence in library services to young adults: The nation's top programs.* Chicago: American Library Association.

———. 1997. *Excellence in library services to young adults: The nation's top programs.* 2d ed. Chicago: American Library Association.

———. 2000. *Excellence in library services to young adults: The nation's top programs.* 3d ed. Chicago: American Library Association.

Jones, Patrick. 1998. *Connecting young adults and libraries: A how-to-do-it manual.* 2d ed. New York: Neal-Schuman.

Jones, Patrick, and Joel Shoemaker. 2001. *Do it right! Best practices for serving young adults in school and public libraries.* New York: Neal-Schuman.

Kan, Katharine L. 1998. *Sizzling summer reading programs for young adults.* Chicago: American Library Association.

Knowles, Elizabeth, and Martha Smit. 2001. *Reading rules! Motivating teens to read.* Littleton, Colo.: Libraries Unlimited.

Latrobe, Kathy, and Mildred Knight Laughlin. 1989. *Readers theatre for young adults.* Littleton, Colo.: Libraries Unlimited.

Mondowney, Jo Ann G. 2001. *Hold them in your heart: Successful strategies for library services to at-risk teens.* New York: Neal-Schuman.

Rochman, Hazel. 1987. *Tales of love and terror: Booktalking the classics, old and new.* Chicago: American Library Association.

Scales, Pat R. 2001. *Teaching banned books: Twelve guides for young readers.* Chicago: American Library Association.

School Library Journal's best: A reader for children's, young adult, and school librarians. 1997. Edited by Lillian Gerhardt, Marilyn L. Miller, and Thomas W. Downen. New York: Neal-Schuman.

Talk it up! Book discussion programs for young people. 1999. Edited by Ann Brouse. Albany: New York Library Association.

Vaillancort, Renée. 2002. *Managing young adult services: A self-help manual.* New York: Neal-Schuman.

The VOYA reader. 1990. Edited by Dorothy Broderick. Lanham, Md.: Scarecrow.

The VOYA reader 2. 1998. Edited by Mary K. Chelton and Dorothy Broderick. Lanham, Md.: Scarecrow.

Wilson-Lingbloom, Evie. 1994. *Hangin' out at Rocky Creek: A melodrama in basic young adult services in public libraries.* Lanham, Md.: Scarecrow.

YALSA Professional Development Center—<http://www.ala.org/yalsa/profdev/>

YALSA-BK. Send a message to listproc@ala.org. Leave the subject line blank. For the message type "Subscribe YALSA-bk first name last name."

Young Adult Library Services Association. 1995. *Youth participation in school and public libraries: It works.* Chicago: American Library Association.

———. 2000. *Bare bones young adult services: Tips for public library generalists,* by Renée Vaillancort. Chicago: American Library Association.

———. 2002. *New directions for library service to young adults.* With Patrick Jones and edited by Linda Waddle. Chicago: American Library Association.

YOUNG ADULT LITERATURE AND READING—BACKGROUND

Aronson, Marc. 2001. *Exploding the myths: The truth about teenagers and their reading.* Lanham, Md.: Scarecrow.

Carlsen, G. Robert, and Ann Sherrill. 1988. *Voices of readers: How we come to love books.* Urbana, Ill.: National Council of Teachers of English.

Cart, Michael. 1996. *From romance to realism: Fifty years of growth and change in young adult literature.* New York: HarperCollins.

Carter, Betty, and Richard F. Abrahamson. 1990. *Nonfiction for young adults: From delight to wisdom.* Phoenix: Oryx.

deVos, Gail, and Anna E. Altmann. 1999. *New tales for old: Folktales as literary fictions for young adults.* Englewood, Colo.: Libraries Unlimited.

Donelson, Kenneth L., and Alleen Pace Nilsen. 2001. *Literature for today's young adults.* 6th ed. New York: Scott Foresman.

Dresang, Eliza. 1999. *Radical change: Books for youth in a digital age.* New York: H. W. Wilson.

Krashen, Stephen. 1993. *The power of reading: Insights from the research.* Littleton, Colo.: Libraries Unlimited.

Lukens, Rebecca J., and Ruth K. J. Cline. 1995. *A critical handbook of literature for young adults.* New York: HarperCollins.

Manguel, Alberto. 1996. *A history of reading.* New York: Viking Penguin.

Moore, John Noell. 1997. *Interpreting young adult literature: Literary theory in the secondary classroom.* Portsmouth, N.H.: Heinemann.

Nimon, Maureen, and John Foster. 1997. *The adolescent novel: Australian perspectives*. Wagga Wagga, N.S.W.: Centre for Information Studies.

Two decades of the ALAN Review. 1999. Edited by Patricia P. Kelly and Robert C. Small. Urbana, Ill.: National Council of Teachers of English.

YOUNG ADULT LITERATURE— COLLECTION ASSESSMENT AND LISTS

Ammon, Bette D., and Gale W. Sherman. 1998. *More rip-roaring reads for reluctant teen readers*. Englewood, Colo.: Libraries Unlimited.

Bodart, Joni Richards. 2000. *The world's best thin books: What to read when your book report is due tomorrow*. Rev. ed. Lanham, Md.: Scarecrow.

———. 2002. Radical Reads: *101 YA novels on the edge*. Lanham, Md.: Scarecrow.

Books for the teen age. Annual. New York: New York Public Library.

Books for you: A booklist for senior high school students. 2001. Edited by Kylene Beers and Teri Lesesne. Urbana, Ill.: National Council of Teachers of English.

The Coretta Scott King awards book: 1970–1999. 1999. Edited by Henrietta M. Smith. Chicago: American Library Association.

Fonseca, Anthony, and June Michele Pulliam. 1999. *Hooked on horror: A guide to reading interests in horror fiction*. Englewood, Colo.: Libraries Unlimited.

Gillespie, John T. 2000. *Best books for young teen readers*. Englewood, Colo.: Libraries Unlimited.

Gillespie, John T., and Ralph J. Folcarelli. 1998. *Guides to collection development for children and young adults*. Englewood, Colo.: Libraries Unlimited.

Herald, Diana Tixier. 1997. *Teen genreflecting*. Englewood, Colo.: Libraries Unlimited.

———. 1999. *Fluent in fantasy*. Englewood, Colo.: Libraries Unlimited.

Holley, Pam Spencer. 2002. *What do young adults read next? Vol. 4*. Detroit: Gale.

Kunzel, Bonnie, and Suzanne Manczuk. 2001. *First contact: A reader's selection of science fiction and fantasy*. Lanham, Md.: Scarecrow.

MacRae, Cathi Dunn. 1998. *Presenting young adult fantasy fiction*. New York: Twayne.

Middle and junior high school catalog. 8th ed. 2001. New York: H. W. Wilson.

Monseau, Virginia R. 2000. *Reading their world: The young adult novel in the classroom.* Portsmouth, N.H.: Heinemann.

Rochman, Hazel. 1993. *Against borders: Promoting books for a multicultural world.* Chicago: American Library Association.

Schon, Isabel. 2000. *Recommended books in Spanish for children and young adults: 1996–1999.* Lanham, Md.: Scarecrow.

Senior high school library catalog. 16th ed. 2002. New York: H. W. Wilson.

Smith, Karen Patricia. 1994. *African-American voices in young adult literature: Tradition, transition, transformation.* Lanham, Md.: Scarecrow.

Spencer, Pam. 1994. *What do young adults read next? Vol. 1.* Detroit: Gale.

———. 1997. *What do young adults read next? Vol. 2.* Detroit: Gale.

———. 1999. *What do young adults read next? Vol. 3.* Detroit: Gale.

Young Adult Library Services Association. 1994. *Best books for young adults: The history, the selections, the romance.* By Betty Carter. Chicago: American Library Association.

———. 2000. *Best books for young adults.* 2d ed. With Betty Carter, Sally Estes, and Linda Waddle. Chicago: American Library Association.

———. 1996. *Hit list: Frequently challenged young adult books, with Merri Monks.* Chicago: American Library Association.

———. 2002. *Hit list for young adults 2: Frequently challenged books, with Teri Lesesne and Rosemary Chance.* Chicago: American Library Association.

———. 1996. *Outstanding books for the college bound, with Marjorie Lewis.* Chicago: American Library Association.

Zitlow, Connie S. 2002. *Lost masterworks of young adult literature.* Lanham, Md.: Scarecrow.

YOUNG ADULT LITERATURE—ANNUAL AWARDS AND LISTS

Individual Book Awards

Coretta Scott King Award—<http://www.alaorg/srrt/csking/index. html>

Michael L. Printz Award—<http://www.ala.org/yalsa/printz/ index.html>

National Book Awards for Books for Young People—<http://209.67. 253.214/nbf/docs/nba01_final_young.html>

Body of Work Awards

Margaret A. Edwards (MAE) Award—<http://www.ala.org/yalsa/ edwards/index.html>

Annual Book Lists

ALEX Awards—<http://www.ala.org/yalsa/booklists/alex/>

Best Books for Young Adults—<http://www.ala.org/yalsa/booklists/ bbya/>

Booklist Editors' Choices: Adult Books for Young Adults. Appears every January in *Booklist*. <http://www.ala.org/booklist/v98/ edch-ya.html>

Booklist Editors' Choices: Books for Youth: Older Readers. Appears every January in *Booklist*. <http:www.ala.org/booklist/v98/edch-yo.html1#older>

Bulletin Blue Ribbons. Appears every January in *The Bulletin for the Center of Children's Books*. <http://www.lis.uiuc.edu/puboff/ bccb/blue01/html>

Horn Book Fanfare. Appears every January/February in *The Horn Book*. <http://www.hbook.com/fanfare02.shtml>

Quick Picks for Reluctant Young Adult Readers—<http://www.ala. org/yalsa/booklists/quickpicks>

SLJ's Best Books. Appears every December in *School Library Journal*. <http://www.slj.com>

SLJ's Best Books: Adult Books for Young Adults. Appears every December in *School Library Journal*. <http://www.slj.com>

Young Adults' Choices. Appears every October in *Journal of Adolescent & Adult Literacy*. <http://www.reading.org/choices/yac2002. html>

YOUNG ADULT LITERATURE—BIBLIOGRAPHICAL RESOURCES

Ashbranner, Brent K. 1990. *The times of my life: A memoir*. New York: Dutton.

Authors and artists for young adults. 1989. Edited by Agnes Garrett and Helga P. McCue. Vol. 1– . Detroit: Gale.

Bishop, Rudine Sims. 1991. *Presenting Walter Dean Myers*. New York: Twayne.

Bloom, Susan P., and Catheryn M. Mercier. 1991. *Presenting Zibby O'Neal*. New York: Twayne.

———. 1997. *Presenting Avi*. New York: Twayne.

Brown, Joanne. 1998. *Presenting Kathryn Lasky*. New York: Twayne.

Campbell, Patty. 1989. *Presenting Robert Cormier*. New York: Twayne.

Cart, Michael. 1995. *Presenting Robert Lipsyte*. New York: Twayne.

Children's Literature Web Guide—<http://www.ucalgary.ca/~dk brown/authors.html>

Copeland, Jeffrey S. 1993. *Speaking of poets: Interviews with poets who write for children and young adults*. Urbana, Ill.: National Council of Teachers of English.

———. 1995. *Speaking of poets 2: More interviews with poets who write for children and young adults*. Urbana, Ill.: National Council of Teachers of English.

Crowe, Chris. 1999. *Presenting Mildred Taylor*. New York: Twayne.

Daly, Jay. 1989. *Presenting S. E. Hinton*. New York: Twayne.

Davis, James E., and Hazel K. Davis. 1992. *Presenting William Sleator*. New York: Twayne.

Davis, Terry. 1997. *Presenting Chris Crutcher*. New York: Twayne.

Day, Frances Ann. 1997. *Latina and Latino voices in literature for children and young adults*. Portsmouth, N.H.: Heinemann.

Duncan, Lois. 1982. *Chapters: My growth as a writer*. Boston: Little, Brown.

Forman, Jack Jacob. 1988. *Presenting Paul Zindel*. New York: Twayne.

Gallo, Donald R. 1989. *Presenting Richard Peck*. New York: Twayne.

Hipple, Ted. 1990. *Presenting Sue Ellen Bridgers*. New York: Twyane.

Hogan, Walter. 2001. *The agony and the eggplant: Daniel Pinkwater's heroic struggles in the name of YA literature*. Lanham, Md.: Scarecrow.

Jones, Patrick. 1998. *What's so scary about R. L. Stine?* Lanham, Md.: Scarecrow.

Kerr, M. E. 1983. *Me, me, me, me, me: Not a novel*. New York: HarperCollins.

Krull, Kathleen. 1995. *Presenting Paula Danziger*. New York: Twayne.

McGlinn, Jeanne M. 2000. *Ann Rinaldi: Historian and storyteller*. Lanham, Md.: Scarecrow.

McKissack, Patricia C., and Frederick L. McKissack. 1999. *Young, black, and determined: A biography of Lorraine Hansberry.* New York: Holiday House.

Meltzer, Milton. 1988. *Starting from home.* New York: Viking.

Mohr, Nicholasa. 1994. *Growing up inside the sanctuary of my imagination.* New York: Messner.

Myers, Walter Dean. 2001. *Bad boy: A memoir.* New York: Harper-Collins.

Naylor, Phyllis Reynolds. 2001. *How I came to be a writer.* Rev. ed. New York: Aladdin.

Nilsen, Aileen Pace. 1987. *Presenting M. E. Kerr.* New York: Twayne.

Nixon, Joan Lowery. 2002. *The making of a writer.* New York: Delacorte.

Norris, Jerrie. 1988. *Presenting Rosa Guy.* New York: Twayne.

Paulsen, Gary. 2001. *Guts: The true stories behind Hatchet and the Brian books.* New York: Delacorte.

Peck, Richard. 1991. *Anonymously yours.* New York: Messner.

Phy, Allene Stuart. 1988. *Presenting Norma Klein.* New York: Twayne.

Poe, Elizabeth. 1998. *Presenting Barbara Wersba.* New York: Twayne.

Reed, Arthea J. 1996. *Presenting Harry Mazer.* New York: Twayne.

———. 2000. *Norma Fox Mazer: A writer's world.* Lanham, Md.: Scarecrow.

Reid, Suzanne Elizabeth. 1997. *Presenting Ursula K. Le Guin.* New York: Twayne.

Salvner, Gary M. 1996. *Presenting Gary Paulsen.* New York: Twayne.

Speaking for ourselves: Autobiographical sketches by notable authors of books for young adults. 1990. Edited and compiled by Donald R. Gallo. Urbana, Ill.: National Council of Teachers of English.

Speaking for ourselves, too: More autobiographical sketches by notable authors of books for young adults. 1993. Edited and compiled by Donald R. Gallo. Urbana, Ill.: National Council of Teachers of English.

Spinelli, Jerry. 1999. *Knots in my yo-yo string: The autobiography of a kid.* New York: Knopf.

Stan, Susan. 1996. *Presenting Lynn Hall.* New York: Twayne.

Twentieth century young adult writers. 1994. Edited by Laura Standley Berger. Detroit: St. James.

Uchida, Yoshiko. 1991. *The invisible thread: An autobiography.* New York: Messner.

Weirdt, Maryann N. 1990. *Presenting Judy Blume*. New York: Twayne.

When I was your age: Original stories of growing up. 1996. Edited by Amy Ehrlich. Cambridge, Mass.: Candlewick.

When I was your age 2: Original stories of growing up. 1999. Edited by Amy Ehrlich. Cambridge, Mass.: Candlewick.

Writers for young adults: Supplement. 2000. Edited by Ted Hipple. New York: Scribner.

Writers for young adults: Vol. 1–3. 1999. Edited by Ted Hipple. New York: Scribner.

Yep, Laurence. 1991. *The lost garden*. New York: Messner.

Zindel, Paul. 1992. *The Pigman and me*. New York: HarperCollins.

PROFESSIONAL AND REVIEW MAGAZINES

ALAN Review. Urbana, Ill: National Council of Teachers of English. <http://www.thinkworks.info/alan/home/article.php?sid=4>

Appraisal: Science Books for Young People. Boston: Northeastern University. <http://www.appraisal.neu.edu>

Book Report. Worthington, Ohio: Linworth. <http://www.linworth.com/bookreport/html>

Booklist. Chicago: American Library Association. <http://www.ala.org/Booklist>

Bulletin of the Center for Children's Books. Chicago: University of Chicago. <http://www.lis.uiuc.edu/puboff/bccb>

English Journal. Urbana, Ill.: National Council of Teachers of English. <http://www.ncte.org/ej/toc/EJ0916TOC.shtml>

The Horn Book. Boston: Horn Book. <http://www.hbook.com>

The Horn Book Guide. Boston: Horn Book. <http://www.hbook.com> for print subscription. <http://www.hornbookguide.com> for online subscriptions.

Journal of Adolescent & Adult Literacy. Newark, Del.: International Reading Association. <http://www.reading.org/publications/jaal>

Kliatt Young Adult Paperback Guide. Newton, Mass.: Kliatt.

Knowledge Quest. Chicago: American Library Association/American Association of School Librarians. <http://www.ala.org/aasl/kqweb/index.html>

School Library Journal. New York: Bowker. <http://www.sljreviews news.com/index.asp?publication=slj>

School Library Media Research. Chicago: American Library Association/American Association of School Librarians. <http://www.ala.org/aasl/SLMR/index.html>

Signal. Newark, Del.: International Reading Association. <http://www.reading.org/dir/sig/signetal.html>

Teacher Librarian. Toronto, Ont.: Rockland. <http://www.teacherli brarian.com/index.html>

Voice of Youth Advocates. Lanham, Md.: Scarecrow. <hitp://www. voya. com>

Voices from the Middle. Urbana, Ill.: National Council of Teachers of English. <http://www.ncte.org/vm/VM0094TOC.shtml>

YAttitudes. Chicago: Young Adult Library Services Association. <http: // members.ala.org/yalsa/>

JOURNAL ARTICLES AND BOOKS BY MARGARET EDWARDS

Alexander, Margaret (maiden name)

1938.   Introducing books to young readers. *ALA Bulletin* 32 (1 October): 685–690.

1939. How to read and like it: A discussion of the poorer reader. *Pennsylvania Library and Museum Notes* 17 (July): 2–6.

1941. Promotion of recreational reading for young people. *Pennsylvania Library and Museum Notes* 18 (April): 11–71.

1943. Wisdom crying in the streets. *Library Journal* 68 (May): 347–349.

1944. Adventures with a book wagon. *Illinois Libraries* 26 (April): 132–137.

Edwards, Margaret Alexander

1948. Introducing books to young readers. In ALA, Libraries for Children and Young People Division, Post-War Planning Committee, *The public library plans for the teen age*. Chicago: American Library Association, 57–62.

1948. The librarian and the united nations youth. *Top of the News* 4 (September): 14–17.

1951. Future with young people. *Iowa Library Quarterly* 16 (April): 131–138.

Service to young adults at the Enoch Pratt Free Library. *Indiana Librarian* 10 (September): 56–59; *Library Journal* 82 (15 September 1957): 2170.

1955. Service for the adolescent. *Top of the News* 12 (December): 35–37.

1956. Many a thousand brick. *Library Journal* 81 (15 May): 1282–1285.

1956. A little learnin'; satin gowns in Childress, Texas. *ALA Bulletin* 50 (June): 379–386.

1958. Mrs. Grundy go home. *Wilson Library Bulletin* 33 (December): 304–305.

1960. Introducing young people to a life-long pleasure. *Library Journal* 83 (15 January): 218–221.

1960. Open wonderful new worlds. *Wilson Library Bulletin* 34 (March): 494–495.

1960. It all started with Prometheus. *California Librarian* 21 (April): 93–96.

1960. Book selection for young adults. *School Library Association, California Bulletin* (May): 9–11.

1960. Time when it's best to read and let read. *Wilson Library Bulletin* 35 (September): 43–45.

1961. [Review of] ALA, AASL. Discussion guide for use with the standards. *School Library Journal* 10 (January): 44–45.

1961. For auld lang syne, my dears. *Maryland Libraries* 27 (winter): 11–13.

1961. In the opinion of teenagers. *Top of the News* 18 (December 1961): 57–60; (March 1962): 72; (October 1962): 67–68.

1963. How to give a book talk. *Ohio Library Association Bulletin* 33 (April): 21–23.

1963. The librarian, the teen-ager and the book. *Florida Libraries* 14 (June): 11–13.

1964. Taming the young barbarian. *Library Journal* 89 (15 April): 1819–1821.

1964. Art of librarianship. *Southeastern Librarian* 15 (summer): 114–119.

1964. Book is to read. *Idaho Librarian* 16 (July): 97–103.

1965. Time and season for the better reader. *Top of the News* 21 (April): 229–235.

1965. The fair garden and the swarm of beasts. *Library Journal* (1 September): 3379–3383.

1965. A long way to Tipperary. In *The library reaches out: Reports on library service and community relations,* edited by K. M Colpan and E. Castagna. Dobbs Ferry, N.Y.: Oceana, 135–161.

1967. City kid and the library. *Top of the News* 24 (November): 62–71.

1968. Urban library and the adolescent. *Library Quarterly* 38 (January): 70–77.

1969. *The fair garden and the swarm of beasts: The library and the young adult.* New York: Hawthorn.

1970. YA: The library bastard. *Utah Libraries* 12 (spring): 32–43.

1970. Ladder to lean on the sky. *Catholic Library World* 42 (November): 161–167.

1970. Youth, books, and guidance. *North Carolina Libraries* 28 (winter): 8–14.

1971. No barefeet. In *Survival Kit.* Chicago: American Library Association.

1971. Where's Nicholas Vedder? *Canadian Library Journal* 28 (September): 371–373.

1971. I once did see Joe Wheeler plain. *Junior Library History* 6 (October): 291–302.

1974. *The fair garden and the swarm of beasts: The library and the young adult.* 2d ed. New York: Hawthorne.

1974. Public library and young adults: A viewpoint. In *Educating the library user,* edited by J. Lubans. New York: Bowker, 56–58.

1974. Reason to read. *Canadian Library Journal* 31 (August): 307–308.

1994. *The fair garden and the swarm of beasts: The library and the young adult.* Foreword by Patty Campbell. Chicago: American Library Association.

JOURNAL ARTICLES AND BOOKS ABOUT MARGARET ALEXANDER EDWARDS

Biographical Listings and Obituaries

American Library Association. 1988. *ALA yearbook of library and information services 1989: A review of library events, 1988.* Vol. 14. Chicago: American Library Association.

A biographical directory of librarians in the United States and Canada. 5th ed. 1970. Edited by Lee Ash. Chicago: American Library Association.

Who's who in library service. 3d ed. 1955. Edited by Dorothy Ethlyn Coe. New York: Grolier Society.

Who's who in library service. 4th ed. 1966. Edited by Lee Ash. Hamden, Conn.: Shoe String.

Books and Journal Articles about Margaret Edwards

Atkinson, Joan. 1986. Pioneers in public library services to young adults. *Top of the News* 43 (fall): 27–44.

Braverman, Miriam. 1979. *Youth, society and the public library.* Chicago: American Library Association, 179–241.

Breen, Robert G. Library loss, farm's gain. 1962. *The Sun* (17 September): 11.

Campbell, Patty. 1994. Foreword to *The fair garden and the swarm of beasts: The library and the young adult.* By Margaret A. Edwards. Chicago: American Library Association.

———. 1994. Reconsidering Margaret Edwards: The relevance of *The Fair Garden* for the nineties. *Wilson Library Bulletin* 68 (October): 35–38.

———. 1998. *Two pioneers of young adult services.* Lanham, Md.: Scarecrow.

Carter, Betty. 1992. Who is Margaret Edwards and what is this award being given in her honor? *ALAN Review* 19 (spring): 45–48.

———. 1998. Margaret Alexander Edwards: Reaching out to young adult librarians. *Journal of Youth Services in Libraries* 11 (winter): 175–180.

Chelton, Mary K. 1987. Margaret Edwards: An interview. *Voice of Youth Advocates* 10 (August/September): 112–113.

Hannigan, Jane A. 1996. A feminist analysis of the voices for advocacy in young adult services. *Library Trends* 44 (spring): 851–874.

Hearne, Betsy, and Christine Jenkins. 1999. Sacred texts: What our foremothers left us in the way of psalms, proverbs, precepts, and practices." *The Horn Book* 75 (September/October): 536–558.

Rosenkoetter, Susan. 1966. A bio-bibliography of Margaret Alexander Edwards. Master's thesis, University of Denver.

The Alex Awards:
Introduction and List

by Betty Carter

Reflecting both the teenagers she served and the times in which she worked, Margaret Edwards championed adult books for young adults. She worked with older adolescents and visited high schools, which, during her tenure at Enoch Pratt, were typically configured as grades ten through twelve. Then, as well as today, much of what these older students read was adult fare. Edwards believed that as teenagers moved toward adulthood, their reading should progress from juvenile to adult offerings: "The librarian should know his readers and books well enough to be able to introduce readable, appealing adult titles at the propitious time and see that the young reader gradually moves into adult reading with all the enthusiasm he once had for teenage stories" (Edwards 1994, 63).

Edwards was not alone in her commitment to adult books for young adults. Winifred B. Jackson, chair of the 1948 Booklist Committee for the American Library Association (a precursor to today's Best Books for Young Adults [BBYA] Committee), shares comments from Jane Roos, then president of the Young People's Reading

Roundtable: "It seems to me that the easier part of the work [book selection for young adults] is selecting titles from the juvenile lists. We need to select from the adult books for our readers, those that are beyond the children's reading level" (Jackson 1948, 5).

As a member of Jackson's 1948 committee, Edwards concurred that selection should concentrate on adult books. One reason for this focus was Edwards's fear that some librarians might not order adult titles, especially those with elements of controversy, without tacit approval from the American Library Association (ALA). She wrote, "The high school librarians of Baltimore are listing such titles as *Gentleman's Agreement* and *Chequer Board* without dissent from anyone. . . . In these days when our very existence is threatened by narrow mental outlooks it seems to me it is high time to cease withholding valuable novels from people because of a frank sex passage or two that after all have little new to tell them" (Jackson 1948, 5–6). Edwards's influence must have swayed the committee, for, as Jackson states in her recommendations concerning the charge of the committee, "Forward-looking librarians in small towns and high school libraries need the sanction of A.L.A. for such books as *Chequer Board* and *Gentleman's Agreement*. It should be the function of the Booklist Committee to point the way" (Jackson 1948, 6).

And point the way it did. Until 1973, books appearing on BBYA lists were typically those released by adult divisions of publishing houses. After the groundbreaking success of S. E. Hinton's *The Outsiders* and Paul Zindel's *The Pigman* in the late 1960s (both of which failed to make BBYA lists, presumably because they originated in juvenile divisions), young adult publishing grew dramatically. Sophisticated young adult books, such as Barbara Wersba's *Run Softly, Go Fast*, which slipped on the 1970 BBYA list, helped define this infant field as one worthy of respect and, consequently, as a genre with outstanding components deserving representation on any recommended reading list.

That representation grew over the years, and by 1980 only 20 percent of the BBYA list consisted of adult books (Young Adult Library Services Association 1994, 39). Numbers of adult books increased during that decade, possibly because of the influence on BBYA of members such as Michael Printz, who constantly reminded the committee to search adult publishing for "stretch" books that would challenge older teens. Such titles were difficult to locate, hard to obtain, long to read, and being edged out by a renaissance in young adult publishing that introduced more and more books aimed at sixteen- and seventeen-year-olds. By the 1990s BBYA lists again became more reflective of fine books originally published for young adults than of corresponding fare published primarily for an adult audience.

Even today, with so many outstanding books published in young adult divisions, librarians cannot ignore adult books. As young adults are trying to become more adultlike, they naturally turn to books read by an older audience. Often teenagers begin their forays into adult books with best-sellers, such as Sebastian Junger's *The Perfect Storm*, Rick Bragg's *All Over But the Shoutin'*, or Kent Haruf's *Plainsong*. Older young adults are ready for books that concentrate more on theme than character or plot, and adult books such as Danzy Senna's *Caucasia* or Dawn Turner Thrice's *Only Twice I've Wished for Heaven* fill this niche. Young adult readers of nonfiction typically must turn to the adult shelves when looking for books. As editor Marc Aronson said during a 1999 telephone interview, "While we publish many books for older teens, nonfiction books for the same audience are pushed way in the back." There's also an issue for genre readers, especially those drawn to science fiction and fantasy. Certainly books published in juvenile houses and recognized by BBYA committees, such as Philip Pullman's *The Golden Compass* and J. K. Rowling's *Harry Potter and the Sorcerer's Stone*, have found legions of young adult readers, but avid fans usually move to adult fiction early in the junior high years. In short, many adult books speak to and challenge young adults, but the recognition of such was, in 1997, not systematic within the Young Adult Library Services Division.

Before she died, in 1988, Margaret Edwards established a trust that would "be used to experiment with ways of effectively promoting the reading of young adults and of inspiring young adult librarians to realize the importance of reading and to perfect themselves as readers' advisors" (Edwards 1994, xxiii). The trust has funded many local projects, such as Baltimore's annual Books for the Beast conference as well as the 1994 and 2002 editions of *The Fair Garden and the Swarm of Beasts*. In addition, three times the trust has conferred recognition grants on libraries with outstanding programs for young adults and sponsored three publications detailing that work, the first, second, and third editions of *Excellence in Library Services to Young Adults* (Chelton 1994, 1997, 2000).

In 1997 the trustees awarded the Young Adult Library Services Association (YALSA) a grant for a five-year project, called the Adult Books for Young Adults Project, that would highlight the role of adult books in young adults' reading lives, making it again "possible to expand programs bringing young adults and their literature together in a way that is consonant with Edwards's pioneering interests" (Taylor 1997). Truly a reflection of who Margaret Alexander Edwards was and what she stood for, this grant was used to fund the costs for a series of programs focusing on "Teen Readers and Adult Books" from 1998 to 2002. Held during the annual ALA conference, these programs featured librarians, scholars, authors, and editors covering topics from writing to selecting to marketing to readers' advisory. (The first program included a lecture by Richard F. Abrahamson that provided background and rationale for the five-year program and is reproduced in appendix E.) Deborah Taylor sums up this part of the project in ALA's June 1997 press release: "The librarians who work with today's young adults know that many of them prefer to read books written for adults, yet publishers of adult books and bookstores don't aggressively market to teens. This grant gives YALSA the opportunity to reexamine and revitalize the use of adult books with teenagers" (American Library Association 1997).

Beyond knowing how to use books, Margaret Edwards was about books: about reading books, about recommending books, about discussing books. And so was the YALSA Adults Book for Young Adults Task Force, which created an annual "top ten" list of recommended adult books for young adults. For five years, this annual list was featured in concert with a program as committee members booktalked the year's winners. Michael Cart, 1997 YALSA president, spoke of the importance of both the list and the program: "At a time when young adult literature is in jeopardy, the Edwards grant is truly significant not only in recognizing the importance of adult literature for young adults, but also by elevating its stature as a viable body of literature" (Cart, 1997).

In an inspired partnership, YALSA worked with *Booklist*, ALA's official review journal, to create the top ten list, which was renamed the Alex Awards in honor of Margaret Alexander Edwards, known as Alex by her friends. Bill Ott, editor and publisher of *Booklist*, shared his enthusiasm: "We're excited to work with YALSA in this new project that will increase the visibility and importance of using adult books with young adults" (Ott 1997). And YALSA was equally excited to tap into *Booklist*'s solid reputation for highlighting adult books for young adults. Starting with Barbara Duree's tenure as Young People's Books editor in 1953, the *Booklist* youth editors, like Edwards and Jackson and Roos, mentioned above, have made cross-recommendations of adult titles a priority. Every issue recommends adult books suitable for young adults by noting titles with general young adult interest, a limited teenage audience, or particular curriculum value. In addition, an April edition of *Booklist* prints the annual Alex Awards to coincide with National Library Week. A listing of the first five years of Alex winners follows this introduction. Both future and past lists can be found at <http:// www.ala.org/yalsa/booklists/alex/index.html>.

The Teen Readers and Adult Books project, as funded by the Margaret A. Edwards trust, has run its five years. This project leaves five outstanding programs focusing on adult books, a strong list of fifty adult books that should appeal to young adults, and a permanent place in the ALA awards for the continuance of the Alex Awards. The *Journal of Youth Services in Libraries* celebrated the centennial of Margaret Edwards's birth with a special section in 2002 ("Celebrating the Centennial of Margaret Alexander Edwards's Birth 2002"). An annual committee within the Young Adult Library Services Association will select these ten books. When discussing the concept with the original task force, Deborah Taylor said to think about looking for the next *To Kill a Mockingbird* (Taylor 1997). The criteria reflect that standard. Fiction and nonfiction books eligible for the Alex Award must be published the previous calendar year, be marketed primarily to adults, be well written and highly readable, and have strong potential for teen appeal (Alex Awards).

Librarians today work in different circumstances and with different tools than did Margaret Edwards. Contemporary young adult literature offers its intended audience thousands of sophisticated and mature books. But adult works still have a special niche in the reading lives of teenagers. Librarians must search out the best from each publishing venue and be sure these books get to the young adults they serve. Despite the decades that separate our work from Edwards's, the responsibility of bringing adult books and young adults together remains an indispensable obligation. That's the tradition Margaret Edwards instituted. The Alex Awards continue it.

Works Cited

Alex Awards. June 2002. <http://www.ala.org/yalsa/booklists/alex/index.html>

Alex Awards: Background and Criteria. <http://www.ala.org/yalsa/yalsainfo/alexinfo.html>

American Library Association. 1997. YALSA receives $25,000 grant from the Margaret Alexander Edwards Trust. Chicago: The Association. Press release.

Aronson, Marc. 1999. Telephone interview with Betty Carter, 18 October.

Bragg, Rick. 1997. *All over but the shoutin'*. New York: Pantheon.

Cart, Michael. 1997. Telephone interview with Betty Carter, 21 July.

Celebrating the centennial of Margaret Alexander Edwards's birth. Special section. 2002. *Journal of Youth Services in Libraries* 15 (summer): 44–54.

Chelton, Mary K., ed. 1994. *Excellence in library services to young adults: The nation's top programs*. Chicago: American Library Association.

———. 1997. *Excellence in library services to young adults: The nation's top programs.* 2d ed. Chicago: American Library Association.

———. 2000. *Excellence in library services to young adults: The nation's top programs.* 3d ed. Chicago: American Library Association.

Edwards, Margaret. 1994. *The fair garden and the swarm of beasts: The library and the young adult.* Chicago: American Library Association.

Haruf, Kent. 1999. *Plainsong.* New York: Knopf.

Hinton, S. E. 1967. *The outsiders.* New York: Viking.

Hobson, Laura Z. 1947. *Gentleman's agreement.* New York: Simon & Schuster.

Jackson, Winifred B. 1948. Selecting adult books for young adults. *Top of the News* 31 (December): 5–6.

Junger, Sebastian. 1997. *The perfect storm: A true story of men against the sea.* New York: Norton.

Lee, Harper. 1960. *To kill a mockingbird.* Philadelphia: Lippincott.

Ott, Bill. 1997. Telephone interview with Betty Carter, 21 July.

Pullman, Philip. 1997. *The golden compass.* New York: Knopf.

Rowling, J. K. 1999. *Harry Potter and the sorcerer's stone.* New York: Scholastic/Arthur Levine.

Senna, Danzy. 1998. *Caucasia.* New York: Putnam/Riverhead.

Shute, Nevil. 1947. *The chequer board.* New York: Morrow.

Taylor, Deborah. 1997. Telephone interview with Betty Carter, 21 July.

Thrice, Dawn Turner. 1997. *Only twice I've wished for heaven.* New York: Crown.

Wersba, Barbara. 1970. *Run softly, go fast.* New York: Atheneum.

Young Adult Library Services Association. 1994. *Best books for young adults: The history, the selections, the romance.* By Betty Carter. Chicago: American Library Association.

Zindel, Paul. 1968. *The Pigman.* New York: Harper & Row.

TEEN READERS AND ADULT BOOKS— A WINNING COMBINATION

The Alex Awards—1998 to 2002

Caroline Alexander   Knopf, 1998
The Endurance: Shackleton's Legendary Antarctic Expedition

The photos will grab teens first: a three-masted wooden vessel broken and splintered; rugged ice-encrusted faces of the ship's crew;

fields of ice stretching into infinity. The Imperial Transatlantic Expedition, Sir Ernest Shackleton's daring but ill-fated attempt to cross the South Pole, comes to life in pictures taken by one of the crew and in the words of the men who lived the extraordinary Antarctic adventure. It's an exhilarating account of one of the greatest episodes in the history of polar exploration and one of history's all-time great survival stories.

David Bearshears   Simon & Schuster, 1999
High Exposure

Admittedly stubborn and driven, Bearshears recounts his life story—recollections of his abusive father and tumultuous childhood; his discovery and dedication to mountain climbing, which he has always equated with humankind's belief in hope; and his entry into filmmaking. His account of his 1996 Everest IMAX Filming Expedition, during which he and his crew sought to rescue survivors and reclaim the bodies of the people caught in the well-publicized Everest calamity, is a natural link to Jon Krakauer's 1998 Alex winner, *Into Thin Air*. The danger, the audacity, the adventure will keep teens enthralled and send them to the shelves to find similar titles.

David Bodanis   Simon & Schuster, 1997
The Secret Family: Twenty-four Hours inside the Mysterious Worlds of Our Minds and Bodies

With surprises and information on every page, Bodanis's book peels back the layers of our minds and bodies to reveal a churning world of tiny, invisible components, living and inanimate, in ourselves and in our surroundings, that silently and secretly affect us. By following the activities of a family—mom, dad, baby, young son, and teenage daughter—through a typical day from breakfast to bedtime, he makes readers active partners in a mysterious and fascinating science adventure. If teens are shocked to discover there's embalming fluid on postage stamps, just wait till they find out what's floating around the local mall.

James Finney Boylan   Warner, 1998
Getting In

Boylan takes wicked aim at the college mystique, bringing together three adults and four high school seniors for a whirlwind tour of swanky eastern colleges that turns into a journey of self-discovery none of them will ever forget. Long-kept secrets, betrayals, and complex relationships between teens and between teens and their parents mark this raucous, sexy, and also moving novel that gives new meaning to going off to college and coming of age.

James Bradley, Ron Powers   Bantam, 2000
Flags of Our Fathers

Bradley had a vested interest in finding out about the six men who were immortalized by the famous flag raising on Iwo Jima in 1945. His father was one of them, though he rarely spoke of the event. Determined to learn more, Bradley investigated. His powerful, straightforward account, written with Ron Powers, brings to light what he discovered—not only about his father and the other celebrated soldiers, a few barely out of their teens, but also about the battle itself and its effects on those who fought.

Gillian Bradshaw   Tor/Forge, 2000
The Sand Reckoner

Sand was best for calculations. When Archimedes wrote on his cloak, he upset his sister. But no one remained angry at this distracted young man for long, not when they learned he was a genius who could make weaponry that might keep Roman soldiers at bay. Invoking her background in history and the classics, Bradshaw extrapolates an episode in the life of one of the greatest mathematicians and engineers of antiquity, mixing it with a story about a Roman slave in the midst of the enemy. There's romance, war, and history of the ancient world, all tightly wrapped in a vivid sense of the joy derived from human invention.

Rick Bragg   Pantheon, 1997
All Over But the Shoutin'

Bragg, a Pulitzer Prize–winning correspondent, didn't start out to be a writer. In fact, he sort of fell into it. He recalls this personal journey in a rags-to-riches memoir that begins in 1959 in Alabama, where "white people had it hard and black people had it harder than that, because what are the table scraps of nothing?" In vivid prose, by turns comic and affecting, he recalls growing up white and poor in the South; his difficult relationship with his abusive, alcoholic father; and his love for his courageous mother, who raised him and taught him what really mattered.

Geraldine Brooks   Viking, 2001
Year of Wonders: A Novel of the Plague

A year after the plague strikes her village, Anna reflects on how the townsfolk handled their minister's request to remain in town to prevent the illness from spreading. Faith, then healing herbs and potions keep everyone going—until doubt creeps in, and witch-hunting, greed, and madness take over the villagers' lives.

Orson Scott Card   Tor, 1999
Ender's Shadow

Call it a parallel novel; call it a companion. Call it sf; call it adventure. No matter what it's called, this exciting novel, by the author of the very popular *Ender's Game* (1985), is what Card's readers have been waiting for. Bean, an orphan living on the streets, finds himself plucked from desperate straits and placed in Battle School, where his tactical skills earn him respect and a role with Ender Wiggin in battle. Wiggin's world is recognizable, but Bean's voice and character make this return to it extraordinarily fresh. This is a sure bet for *Ender's Game*'s many teen fans, but it also stands very well alone.

Rebecca Carroll   Crown, 1997
Sugar in the Raw: Voices of Young Black Girls in America

Carroll captures the voices of the next generation of African American women in this vibrant collection of interviews. Teenagers will hear themselves plainly and powerfully echoed in the honest, unfiltered words of fifteen young black women, who range in age from eleven to twenty. From a variety of backgrounds and in very different ways, they speak candidly about their personal lives, their race, their gender, and their futures as black women. A paperback format and a winning cover add to the YA appeal.

Tracy Chevalier   Plume, 2000
The Girl with the Pearl Earring

Dutch painter Vermeer's portrait of a girl with a pearl earring is a quiet, radiant tribute to an unnamed girl. In Chevalier's imaginative, elegant novel, the lovely young woman is given a name, Griet; an age, sixteen; and a job, servant in the household of the painter himself, a household full of secrets and prejudice. The result is a richly envisioned coming-of-age story that will sweep teens back in time to a place so vivid it seems a character in itself.

Breena Clarke   Little, Brown, 1999
River Cross My Heart

Strong-willed Alice Bynam is convinced that by moving to Georgetown, her family will have more economic and educational opportunity. That's true, but "whites still rule the roost" in the 1920s, and they've barred ten-year-old Johnnie Mae and her friends from swimming in a local pool. When Johnnie Mae opts for the river, instead, her younger sister, Clara, drowns, leaving her family and community behind to struggle with the personal loss and the legacy of racial injustice.

Esme Codell   Algonquin, 1999
Educating Esme

Fifth-grader Melanie instinctively knows what Codell finds out when she begins as a twenty-four-year-old first-year teacher in an inner-city Chicago school: "You got to know everything." And that doesn't mean just what the textbooks say. As Codell gamely reveals in her forthright diary entries, it means fighting lazy teachers and unsupportive administrators; it means dealing with violence and racism; it means marshaling energy, imagination, and wit enough to ensure her students the best possible education. Teens who have been through "the system" can't help but recognize the landscape.

Larry Colton   Warner, 2000
Counting Coup

Colton, a former professional baseball player turned journalist, spent fifteen months on the Crow Reservation in Montana to observe Hardin High School's girls' basketball team. One player stood out: Sharon LaForge, a talented but troubled teenager. As her story deepened and unfolded, so did Colton's understanding of the conditions on the reservation as they affected the players' lives and aspirations. His involving account of what he saw and what he learned is a realistic yet inspirational view of contemporary "young people of the Plains."

Karin Cook   Pantheon, 1997
What Girls Learn

This poignant, honest novel calls up themes that teenagers will easily recognize from reading young adult books—family relationships, sibling rivalry, the death of a parent. In fact, this reads as if it were written just for teens. With a fine ear for dialogue and a firm grasp on the concerns of adolescent girls, Cook tells the story of two sisters—Tilden, quiet and good; Elizabeth, the family rebel—and their relationship with their beloved mother, Frances. When Frances marries Nick, the girls must adjust; when Frances is diagnosed with breast cancer, the girls' lives change in ways they never expected.

Andie Dominick   Scribner, 1998
Needles

"I know about needles. My sister leaves them everywhere." So begins this absorbing memoir of a growing up marked not by illegal drugs, but by diabetes. In graceful yet unsparing prose, Dominick recalls the exacting routines, the doctors, the hospitals, and the struggle for normalcy that shaped her older sister's life and later ruled her own. Although a candid record of the ravages of illness on family and self, Dominick's story is also an inspirational account of hope and courage.

William Doyle   Doubleday, 2001
An American Insurrection: The Battle of Oxford, Mississippi, 1962

When James Meredith became the first black man to enter the University of Mississippi, he "forced America to face the contradiction of second-class citizenship for multitudes of its black citizens, not with speeches, boycotts, or sit-ins, but on a battlefield." Doyle takes teens to two of those battlefields: a cerebral one, where Meredith, President John Kennedy, and Governor Ross Barnett grapple over politics; and a physical one, where federal troops and local mobs converge on the university campus.

David Anthony Durham   Doubleday, 2001
Gabriel's Story

Upset when he has to leave Baltimore to join his mother and her new husband on a Kansas farm, fifteen-year-old African American Gabriel and his new friend, James, run away from their homes to join a group of mostly white cowboys herding cattle to Texas. Too late, they realize that their cowboy comrades are their worst enemies. A graphic, richly poetic view of frontier life during Reconstruction.

Barbara Ehrenreich   Holt/Metropolitan, 2001
Nickel and Dimed: On (Not) Getting By in Boom-Time America

To find out if individuals can survive on the "wages available to the unskilled," journalist Ehrenreich spent twelve months working at a variety of minimum-wage jobs. Her experiences offer a gritty glimpse into the world of day-to-day work, a stark picture of living from hand to mouth, and a personal perspective on the politics of welfare.

Leif Enger   Atlantic Monthly, 2001
Peace like a River

Set in a quiet 1960s Minnesota community, this magical debut novel centers around eleven-year-old asthmatic Reuben Land and his family—his father, his brother, and his precocious younger sister. Life turns upside down when Davy, Reuben's older brother, kills two intruders who plan to harm the family. After Davy breaks out of jail, the Lands leave their home and set out to find him.

Jonathan Scott Fugua   Bancroft, 1999
Reappearance of Sam Webber

There's a strong sense of place in this ultimately warm, reassuring novel set in a poor, racially tense Baltimore neighborhood. Sam Webber doesn't like his new home, a smelly apartment light-years away from the middle-class area where he spent his first eleven years. Since his father's disappearance, he's felt responsible for protecting his mother, but he's so sad and scared he can't even help himself: druggies and muggers patrol the streets; bullies hound him in school. His only friend is the school's black janitor, who turns out to need Sam as much as Sam needs him. Themes of racism, urban violence, depression, and family structure threaded through the story make the book effective for discussion as well as for independent reading.

Neil Gaiman   Avon, 1999
Stardust

Many teens will already know Gaiman from *Neverwhere* (1997) and his Sandman graphic novels. In this book, which makes fantasy accessible to a wide audience, seventeen-year-old Tristran Thorn pledges to fetch for his beloved a star that has fallen on the far side of the wall that marks the edge of the village where he lives. His quest takes him into the land of Fairie, where nothing along the way is really what it seems. Fantasy fans will see in this the work of many of their favorite writers; teens new to the genre will have a fine first reading experience; all will be charmed by the warmth and creativity of Gaiman's wonderful combination of comedy, romance, and energetic adventure.

John Gilstrap   Warner, 1998
At All Costs

That federal agents happened to be looking for someone else didn't matter once they learned that Jake and his wife, Carolyn, were on their Ten Most Wanted List. By that time, though, the Donovans, with their thirteen-year-old son, were already on the run and committed to proving that the sixteen people whose lives they were accused of taking were viciously murdered by someone else. Gilstrap, the author of *Nathan's Run* (1995), combines his expertise as an explosives safety expert with political dirty dealing and breakneck pacing to produce a terrific nail-biter that will leave teens clamoring for more.

Linda Greenlaw   Hyperion, 1999
The Hungry Ocean

Greenlaw, the captain of the *Hanna Boden*, sister ship to the *Andrea*

Gail, whose loss was portrayed in the 1998 Alex winner *The Perfect Storm,* by Sebastian Junger, tells a different but equally fascinating story of life at sea. Hers is a record of a typical month-long sword-fishing trip—the backbreaking work, the danger, the uncertainty of the weather, and the thrill of a gritty job that makes the sea a home. "Writing has proven to be hard work, often painful," she says. "I can honestly say I'd rather be fishing."

Pete Hamill   Little, Brown, 1997
Snow in August

A piece of history comes to life for young adults in a vivid novel about prejudice, love, courage, and miracles. Eleven-year-old Michael Devlin lives with his widowed mother in a working-class neighborhood in 1940s Brooklyn, in the shadow of Ebbet's Field. The last thing he expects to find is a friend in Rabbi Judah Hirsch, a refugee from Prague, who trades wonderful stories from Jewish folklore for lessons in English and American culture, especially the sport of baseball. When religious prejudice rears its ugly head, Michael's real world and Hirsch's fantastical one fold together in a powerful, unexpected way.

Elva Trevino Hart   Bilingual Press, 1999
Barefoot Heart

"My whole childhood, I never had a bed," begins Hart's bittersweet recollections about growing up one of six children in a migrant family that made the circuit from Texas to Minnesota each year. Her stories about her family, especially her stern but caring father, and about breaking away only to return home, show the moving struggle of an immigrant population, as well as the universal personal struggle of finding, then acknowledging, oneself.

Kent Haruf   Knopf, 1999
Plainsong

They were always connected—in the way people in small towns are: the elderly McPheron brothers, unschooled but wise in other ways; high school teacher Tom Guthrie and his mischievous sons, Bobby and Ike; and Victoria Roubideaux, seventeen and pregnant, with nowhere to go. In this plainspoken yet graceful story that is at once complex and elemental, Haruf deftly brings his characters together, slowly turning them into a family ready to face private fears with a renewed sense of hope, connection, and joy.

June Jordan   Basic, 2000
Soldier: A Poet's Childhood

A poet and professor of African American studies, Jordan turns her eyes inward yet again, this time on her own history, in a haunting coming-of-age memoir of the first twelve years of her life. Writing in the flowing language of a prose poem, she recalls being caught in a cultural disconnect, a black child in a white world, and draws a vivid portrait of her father, alternately brutal and caring, who became the biggest influence in her life. His demands, which she usually accepted without question, like a "little soldier," coupled with his desire for her success, made her strong.

Sebastian Junger   Norton, 1997
The Perfect Storm: A True Story of Men against the Sea

In 1991, as Halloween nears, a cold front moves south from Canada, a hurricane swirls over Bermuda, and an intense storm builds over the Great Lakes. These forces converge to create the cruelest holiday trick of all, a 100-year tempest that catches the North Atlantic fishing fleet off guard and unprotected. Readers weigh anchor with sailors struggling against the elements; they follow meteorologists, who watch helplessly as the storm builds; and, by helicopter and boat, they navigate 100-foot seas and 120-mph winds to attempt rescue against harrowing odds.

Jesse Lee Kercheval   Algonquin, 1998
Space

In a memoir so beautifully and seamlessly written that teens will think it is fiction, Kercheval tells her own story, beginning when, at age ten, she moved with her family to a home in Cocoa, Florida, in view of Cape Kennedy. Set against the promise implicit in the launching of Apollo, her touching recollection of her youth and teenage years—her strange, unhappy parents; her difficulties fitting into a new school; and her first love—speaks to universal concerns about growing up and resurrects a pivotal episode of American history and culture for a new generation.

Steve Kluger   Avon/Bard, 1998
Last Days of Summer

"Dear Mr. Banks, I am a 12-year-old boy and I am dying of an incurable disease," begins the first of many letters sent by determined, perfectly healthy Joey Margolis to tough-talking, loose-cannon Charlie Banks, rookie third basemen for the New York Giants. Filled with energy, heart, and laugh-out-loud humor, this poignant epistolary novel looks at loneliness, friendship, and love in a way that both transfixes and transcends its 1940s setting.

Jon Krakauer   Villard, 1997
Into Thin Air: A Personal Account of the Mt. Everest Disaster

Only a handful of people have stood atop Everest. Krakauer is one of them, but the story he tells here is not of glorious triumph.

Rather, it is a true account of survival and death that will grab YA readers from the very first page. Krakauer had a front-row seat to the headline-making 1996 climbing disaster that resulted in the deaths of five people, and his account of the unfolding tragedy, filled with keenly observed details, is not only a transfixing drama, but also an inquiry into survivor guilt and the outer limits of human strength and responsibility.

Kobie Kruger   Ballantine, 2001
The Wilderness Family: At Home with Africa's Wildlife

Kruger eagerly embraced her husband's assignment to a remote ranger station in South Africa, where her life revolved around temperamental hippos, rambunctious badgers, and three beautiful, willful daughters. What she didn't count on was the starving lion cub that her husband brought home.

Juliet Marillier   Tor, 2000
Daughter of the Forest

The first book in the Sevenwaters fantasy trilogy sets a high standard for those to follow. Beginning with the bewitchingly romantic jacket, the novel plunges readers into a world of fairy tales and magic. Marillier's fresh, richly embellished telling centers on a Celtic myth in which the youngest of seven children (and the only girl) must restore her loving brothers, who have been turned into swans. To do so she has to weave them each a shirt from a blistering plant that tears her skin to shreds.

Donna Morrissey   Houghton/Mariner, 2001
Kit's Law

Kit lives in a ramshackle cottage with her mentally challenged mother, Josie, the town tramp, and her loving, protective grandmother, Lizzy. When Lizzy dies, Kit fights to keep her mother out of an asylum, but Josie's wild ways make it difficult. Speculations about the identity of Kit's father and Kit's first love add more texture to this earthy but charming first novel, which is set in Newfoundland.

Mel Odom   Tor, 2001
The Rover

Four-feet-tall Wick, Third Level Librarian in the Vault of All Known Knowledge, is an imaginative Halfer who longs for the drama he reads about in books. He finally gets a chance to experience adventure when he's kidnaped by pirates, sold into slavery, rescued by thieves, and sent to rob a tomb. Lighthearted, exuberant, and fun.

Nathaniel Philbrick   Viking, 2000
In the Heart of the Sea: The Tragedy of the Whaleship Essex

It's the story Melville drew on for *Moby Dick:* an enormous whale bent on the destruction of the whaling ship that is chasing it. But Philbrick delves much deeper into the actual history of the nineteenth-century ship, the *Essex*, and the twenty sailors aboard, many of whom died when the vessel was tragically sunk. The details about the whaling industry in Nantucket and how oil was extracted from the huge creatures are fascinating, as are the facts and speculation about the physical and psychological ramifications the disaster had on the crew. It's a riveting tale of struggle, heroics, and cowardice, vividly told.

Connie Porter   Houghton, 1999
Imani All Mine

This deceptively simple, first-person novel takes readers into the heart and mind of fifteen-year-old Tasha, whose love for her baby, Imani, is as strong as her fear of the rapist who fathered the child. In the stark language of a tough urban neighborhood, Tasha comes alive on the page as she struggles to reconcile her love and hope for her daughter with the violence that resulted in Imani's conception. A sad though ultimately hopeful novel, compelling from its very first page.

Kim Stanley Robinson   Bantam, 1998
Antarctica

The popular author of the Mars trilogy takes readers on a journey to a place with an equally inhospitable climate, bringing along a disparate group of characters with vastly different agendas for the frozen continent. Teens who like multilayered sf will be as pleased with the vivid blend of fact and fiction Robinson uses to depict the stark landscape as they are by the story's diverse cast and its gradually widening circle of intrigue.

Esmeralda Santiago   Perseus/Merloyd Lawrence, 1998
Almost a Woman

The author of *When I Was Puerto Rican* (1993) continues to limn her past, this time focusing on her adolescence and young womanhood. In a patchwork of memories, she recalls her guilty longing to escape the Brooklyn barrio, where she lived with her mother and large, extended family, and what she finds (including an affair with an older man) when she leaves. The mixture of regret, joy, and confusion is unmistakable in this portrait of a daughter growing up in two cultures.

Danzy Senna   Putnam/Riverhead, 1998
Caucasia

Questions about integration, intermarriage, identity, and the status of mixed-race children bubble beneath the surface of this dramatically rich, heartrending novel set in the 1970s. When her white mother, a civil rights activist, goes into hiding, Birdie, the lighter-skinned of two daughters, goes with her. The traumatic leave-taking not only separates Birdie from her beloved older sister, but also loosens her grasp on her mixed-race heritage, a legacy that turns out to be increasingly important to her as she enters her teens.

Ben Sherwood   Bantam, 2000
The Man Who Ate the 747

There's humor and sweet romance in this novel set in small-town America, but what teens will probably like best is the story's quirky backdrop. Nebraska farmer Wally Chubb is ingesting an airplane— a 747, which he is methodically grinding into a paste and using like ketchup on his food. Even J. J. Smith, Keeper of the Records for *The Book of Records*, thinks the feat is astounding—even more so when he discovers that Wally has no interest in breaking records. Wally is doing everything for love.

Robert Silverberg   Tor; dist. by St. Martin's, 1998
Legends: Stories by the Masters of Modern Fantasy

It reads like an honor roll of sf/fantasy writers: Orson Scott Card, Ursula Le Guin, Anne McCaffrey, Robert Jordan, Stephen King, and more. With editor Silverberg carefully supplying background, eleven stellar genre writers reenter the universes they so lovingly created in series: McCaffrey returns to Pern, Silverberg writes again about Valentine as king, Roland the Gunslinger continues his journey toward the Dark Tower. Series fans won't be disappointed in the least, and the novellas provide teens who don't know the earlier books with a wonderful preview of what's in store.

Darin Strauss   Dutton, 2000
Chang and Eng

Little is known about the famous conjoined brothers, Chang and Eng, from Thailand, who came to the United States as exploited sideshow celebrities. But in this remarkable novel, narrated by Eng, Strauss tells the brothers' stories, both as individuals and as one. As their history as performers, farmers, husbands, and fathers smoothly unfurls, teen readers will come to understand the true nature of the twins' unbreakable bonds.

Velma Maia Thomas   Crown, 1997
Lest We Forget: The Passage from Africa to Slavery and Emancipation

In a cleverly designed interactive book, the creator of the Black Holocaust Exhibit relates "the pain of my people." Her simple yet descriptive words tell the story of slavery and the struggle for freedom—from the African villages to the boats, from the plantations to the end of the Civil War and "Jubilee," the day of freedom. Letters and newspaper clippings personalize the story, and reproductions of documents, meant to be pulled from envelopes and pouches attached to the pages, bring the past directly into the present.

Dawn Turner Trice   Crown, 1997
Only Twice I've Wished for Heaven

Eleven-year-old Tempest doesn't like her new home in Lakeland, a planned community for African Americans. Most of her school classmates are boring, and their prissy airs anger and puzzle her. What saves her is a friendship with troubled Valerie, an outsider like herself, and the secret trips she makes each day to Miss Jonetta's liquor store on fascinating Thirty-fifth Street, where she discovers great courage and caring—and terrible secrets about the world of grown-ups and about her best friend.

Vineeta Vijayaraghavan   Soho, 2001
Motherland

Fifteen-year-old Maya must reconcile her Indian heritage with her life as a modern American teen when she goes to spend the summer with her grandmother in India. An accident and an unexpected illness are the catalysts for the revelation of a family secret that gives Maya a profoundly different view of her mother—and ultimately herself.

Rebecca Walker   Putnam/Riverhead, 2001
Black, White, and Jewish: Autobiography of a Shifting Self

Born in 1969 to civil rights activists who defied convention, Walker was a "movement child." But when the movement changed course, and her white father and black mother divorced, Walker found herself without an identity—a misfit: too black for some; not black enough for others. A poignant, sometimes angry recollection about racism, growing up, growing away, and finding oneself.

Alan Watt   Little, Brown, 2000
Diamond Dogs

A father-son relationship is at the heart of this contemporary novel, which is as hard hitting in language and physical description as in the turbulent emotions it explores. Like his abusive, demanding father, seventeen-year-old Neil is an angry bully, who usually diffuses his temper on the football field. One evening, while driving drunk, he hits and kills a pedestrian and hides the body in the trunk of his father's car. When Neil's father, the sheriff, chooses to ignore the crime, the father and son are forced to acknowledge the secret that has been tearing them apart for years. Tense drama and a powerful portrayal of a classic YA theme are expressed in a thoroughly authentic teen voice.

Connie Willis   Bantam, 1997
To Say Nothing of the Dog; or, How We Found the Bishop's Bird Stump at Last

Part time travel, part mystery, part comedy of errors, this clever fantasy has lots to offer YAs, not the least of which is a chance to sink deeply into a piece of history they won't know much about. The year is 2057, and rich Lady Schrapnell has promised to finance Oxford University's time-travel project if she's assisted in her endeavors to rebuild Coventry Cathedral, which was destroyed by the Nazis in 1940. The grueling search for church artifacts has given time-traveler Ned Henry an advanced case of time lag. But it isn't rest he gets when he's sent back to the year 1888; it's another time-traveler's mistake that he must help correct before it alters the entire course of history.

Bibliographic information in this listing reflects each title's publisher and date of publication.

APPENDIX E

Back to the Future with Adult Books for the Teenage Reader

by Richard F. Abrahamson

Let me begin by thanking the Edwards Adult Books for Young Adults Lecture Committee for inviting me here today. Thanks also to Linda Waddle and the staff at YALSA for their good work. Most importantly, my special appreciation goes to the Trustees of the Margaret Alexander Edwards Trust for sponsoring this event and my congratulations to them as we all celebrate the tenth anniversary of the Trust and its good works.

What a daunting assignment you have given me—a lecture on the subject of adult books for adolescent readers. A daunting task all right, but what a wonderful journey you sent me on. I intend to take you on that journey this afternoon. Right off I'd like to say that what I hope this first lecture will do, at least in part, is take us back in time to look at where we have been on this subject. After that I'll offer some current insights and findings and end by pointing to the future and where we might wish to go, and so my title, "Back to the Future with Adult Books for the Teenage Reader."

Richard F. Abrahamson is professor of literature for children and young adults in the College of Education at the University of Houston.

Editor's note: This speech was presented at "Teen Readers and Adult Books: A Winning Combination," ALA Annual Conference, Washington, D.C., June 28, 1998, as part of the Adult Books for Young Adults Project supported by the Margaret Alexander Edwards Trust. Originally published in the *Journal of Youth Services in Libraries* 11, no. 4 (1998): 378–387.

It is my hope that over the next five years you will hear from speakers with very different backgrounds. I worry all the time that all we do is talk to each other. That is, librarians talk only to other librarians, English teachers talk only to other English teachers, reading teachers only to reading teachers. We read only the journals in our fields, if that, and though we might all share the same goal of getting books and teens together, we simply do not know the good work, scholarship, and books in each other's areas. With that in mind, let me say up front that I stand before you as someone trained as an English educator and reading teacher.

I made the trek from the woods of Maine to Iowa City and the University of Iowa because of Bob Carlsen's *Books and the Teenage Reader* (1967). I started teaching high school in the northern woods of Maine armed with an M.A. in English, a thesis on Steinbeck, and the certain knowledge that high school seniors would sign up in droves for my senior seminar on Chaucer. The first book I was told to teach sophomores was Joseph Conrad's *Heart of Darkness*. Imagine my sense of panic when I went to the local pharmacy (there was no bookstore) to try to buy a copy of the Monarch or Cliff Notes for Conrad's book and found out they didn't sell them. For several weeks I stumbled my way through teaching that book. The students didn't like it, and neither did I. I was too new a teacher to know that this was the wrong book for the wrong students at the wrong time. I muddled through with more confidence than my students because left for me in the file drawer of my teacher desk was the 100-item multiple-choice test on Conrad's novel published by a company in Iowa. Those first few weeks teaching I bluffed my students, and they bluffed me.

One weekend I stopped at the University of Maine bookstore and happened to pick up a copy of *Books and the Teenage Reader*. I read it with the excitement of a desperate English teacher who feared he had chosen the wrong profession. In the book someone spoke to me for the first time about adolescents as real people with specific reading interests. They weren't just empty vessels to be filled. Here was new information for me about Robert Havighurst and developmental tasks, subliterature, adolescent literature, and adult books for teenage readers. I ordered some young adult novels from one of the teen book clubs, put Conrad and his friends on the shelf, and started teaching with books that the class agreed on. It was exciting. Students perked up, read more, discussed more, and I knew I'd chosen the right profession.

My B.A. in English from William and Mary and my M.A. in English from the University of Maine hadn't taught me anything about teaching English to adolescents. I just needed to know more. A couple of telephone calls to Iowa, and I was enrolled in Carlsen's correspondence course on adolescent literature. I was hooked from the first assignment of writing my reading autobiography to submitting the fifty book cards. Toward the end of that course, Bob wrote something on one of my papers asking if I'd ever thought about a doctorate. Three months later my wife and I rolled into Iowa City in a Volkswagen packed with everything we owned. It is fair to say I went to Iowa because of Bob, *Books and the Teenage Reader*, and adolescent literature. He did for me what his teacher, Dora V. Smith, did for him: he was my mentor and my inspiration.

So in 1975 I found myself at the University of Iowa studying with Carlsen. In the world of English education, Bob Carlsen was/is Margaret Edwards—taskmaster, mentor, writer of wonderful articles about books and young adult readers, and author of one of the most important books in the field, *Books and the Teenage Reader*. Bob had received his degree at the University of Minnesota studying with the legendary English educator Dora V. Smith. It was Dora V. who in the 1930s separated children's literature from adolescent literature and taught the first university course on adolescent literature. Listen as Carlsen describes her course:

> She began with examining subliterature (she called it trash): the comics, juvenile series books, sentimental romances, and adventure stories. Then she moved on to teenage books, including animal stories. Next came adult books that teenagers might read. Finally there were discussions of books of poetry and biography (Carlsen 1984, 28).

Notice that even in that first university course ever taught on young adult literature, adult books adolescents would read were a part of the curriculum.

Back in Iowa in the 1970s I learned from Carlsen about the work of Margaret Edwards. While I don't pretend to speak for Edwards, I suspect these two trailblazers had great respect for each other's work. I know Carlsen respected Edwards because he wrote an article titled "What Beginning English Teachers Need to Know about Adolescent Literature" (Carlsen 1979). In it he writes about Edwards and the 300 books that were required reading for all her YA specialists, and in this article he follows with his own list of books beginning English teachers need to know.

There is something else that Edwards and Carlsen had in common—a belief in the importance of promoting free reading for teenagers. In Margaret Edwards's will she writes that the money in her trust may be spent "for the purpose of promoting the free reading of teenagers and young adults" (*Margaret Alexander Edwards Trust: The Lady, the Librarian, and Her Legacy* 1991). One of Carlsen's greatest legacies to the English teaching profession was the establishment of free reading classes in secondary schools: a curriculum innovation that flourished during the 1970s in high schools across the country. Although free reading meant slightly different things to Edwards and Carlsen, both affirmed the value of adolescent readers selecting books on their own.

Carlsen's ideas about free reading were based on the pioneering work of an important English educator named Lou L. LaBrant. Although Dr. LaBrant did not invent free reading, she is the person who popularized it and carried out some of the most quoted research on the effectiveness of the approach. LaBrant started with a group of tenth-graders at the Ohio State University Lab School. Their literature program was free reading. They read what they wanted. LaBrant continued teaching these same students as they moved through grades eleven and twelve. Throughout, the free reading literature program was used. Employing a careful system of record keeping, she showed very clearly that these students read more books than they would have in a more structured, traditional literature program (LaBrant 1936).

What makes LaBrant's work especially impressive is that she kept track of these students long after they graduated from high school. She interviewed them years later, and her findings were published in "The Guinea Pigs after Twenty Years" (1961). There were two very impressive findings. First, she found that her guinea pigs, as adults, did markedly more reading than most other groups of adults examined. That is, free reading helped to create active, adult readers. Her second finding, perhaps more important, was that her grown students expressed a strong concern for, and were active participants in, the development of their children's reading habits. The "guinea pigs," as adults, read to and with their children, took trips to the library, and encouraged their children to pick books that keyed into their individual interests. The concern for the child's attitude toward books and reading was not just the province of the mothers responding to LaBrant's study. As the researcher writes, "In general, it may be said that all of the thirteen fathers seemed to accept responsibility for reading habits as a part of family living" (LaBrant 1961, 156).

Please note that free reading as LaBrant and Carlsen saw it is not Sustained Silent Reading (SSR) or Drop Everything and Read (DEAR). This is an English class where students select books, discuss those books with a teacher, and those teachers then provide reading guidance and suggestions for the next book to read. Such free reading classes flourished in the University of Iowa Lab School and became part of the English curriculum in schools around the country. Not surprisingly, several of Carlsen's doctoral students kept track of what these high school sophomore, juniors, and seniors read. One researcher analyzed eighteen semesters of reading records and found that the teens in this Iowa Lab School program read " largely popular adult books" (Means 1976, 148).

This realization that older teenagers were selecting, reading, and enjoying adult books sent Carlsen and his doctoral students on to a new project. Beginning in the early 1970s, and lasting eighteen years, Carlsen and his research team published an annual list called the "Iowa Books for Young Adults List" that was published in *English Journal* and distributed around the country. Carlsen wished to find out "what new books will appeal to young adults who have outgrown most of the so-called adolescent novels" (Fair 1990, 10).

To find out what older teens preferred reading, he sent graduate students into free reading classes in Iowa, Illinois, and Texas armed with copies of new books sent by publishers. The new books were left in the classrooms for students to read, and each adolescent reader was asked to fill out a critique card after he or she had finished a book. Every few weeks graduate assistants returned to confer with the teens, trade out the old books for new ones, and record further teen responses. The most popular books read by these fifteen- to nineteen-year-olds became the yearly "Iowa Books for Young Adults List." For almost two decades this project provided teachers and librarians with a list of popular new books for older adolescents. In 1990 a doctoral student decided to look at the 3,492 student response cards that helped form the Iowa lists from 1982 to 1989 to see what she could discover about the reading interests of older teens. Elizabeth Fair found that over the eight-year period studied, young adults chose contemporary realism, mystery, and nonfiction as the most popular kinds of books. Adolescent literature did find its way onto the lists mingling with adult titles: Chris Crutcher's *Running Loose* (1983) and *Crazy Horse Electric Game* (1987), Susan Beth Pfeffer's *The Year without Michael* (1987), Richard Peck's *Remembering the Good Times* (1985) but also his adult book *Family of Women* (1983), and, of course, Stephen King, from *Pet Sematary* (1983) to *It* (1986) (Fair 1990).

It is, however, in the area of nonfiction where we see adult books predominate. Teenagers chose adult biographies of famous people and autobiographies and biographies of athletes: books about Michael Jordan, John McEnroe, and Bear Bryant. Priscilla Presley's *Elvis and Me* (1985) was the most popular nonfiction book for girls, while boys chose Warner Fussell, Rick Wolf, and Brian Zernik's *Baseball . . . A Laughing Matter* (1987), which is a compendium of quotes and jokes about baseball including, of course, Yogi Berra sayings such as, "If the people don't want to come out to the park, nobody's going to stop 'em" (Fair 1990, 113).

My point in this look back at history is to demonstrate that for decades the best thinkers in the field of library work, English education,
and reading have seen the role adult books play in the reading lives of
young adults. I would suggest to you, however, that we have forgotten these lessons from the past or at least not paid much attention to
them for some time now. And with that, let's move to the present.

There are lists of reasons why many of us who work in the field of
teen reading don't spend as much time as we should talking about
adult books. The first is, we can't get our hands on review copies.
When Betty Carter and I were editing *Books for You* (1988), the senior
high book list published by the National Council of Teachers of
English (NCTE), we had to beg publishers to send us review copies of
adult books. It seemed that the folks in the juvenile division of marketing never talked to their counterparts in the adult division, and so
we relied on fine librarians like Linda Waddle, who had access to adult
books in her library. It is never easy and constantly frustrating even for
important committees within ALA to get the adult books.

But there is a second and more important reason why I don't spend
as much time as I should discussing adult books for teens with the
teachers I speak to and work with. It is because for too many years
English teachers have put overly difficult adult books in the hands of
young adults and wondered why they didn't enjoy reading. And
worse, once we picked the adult books we wanted to teach, we never
changed them. I offer the following as evidence.

Arthur N. Applebee conducted a national survey to find out what
were the most frequently required book-length works in English
classes grades nine to twelve. They are *Romeo and Juliet, Macbeth,
Huckleberry Finn, Julius Caesar, To Kill a Mockingbird*, and *The Scarlet
Letter*. He compared his new survey with one done in 1963. The only
real changes that took place were that in 1963 *Macbeth* was on top
instead of *Romeo and Juliet*, and since 1963 we've pretty much dropped
Silas Marner. The bottom line is really no change in thirty-plus years
(Applebee 1993).

Couple those findings with the fact that the wonderful free reading
classes history tells us were so powerful have all but disappeared from
the high school English and reading programs and you get some sense
of why there is hesitation to talk about adult books. It is a hard enough
sell to get even a few YA books into classrooms. If we truly cared about
creating lifetime readers, we wouldn't be talking about either young
adult books or adult books; we'd be discussing the need to use both.

If we want librarians and teachers to be talking about both young
adult books and adult books for teens, those of us educating the new
crop of librarians and teachers and teaching courses in Literature for

the Adolescent need to be sure we include assignments that get our students reading adult books as part of the course. We are not doing that as well as we should be. Consider this.

Recently a doctoral student at the University of Tennessee surveyed eighty-seven professors of young adult literature nationwide. She asked us if we used core books in our courses—that is, certain titles that everyone in class would read and discuss. More than half of the professors responded that they did use core books. The most common core books required were Lois Lowry's *The Giver,* Robert Cormier's *The Chocolate War,* Katherine Paterson's *Jacob Have I Loved,* S. E. Hinton's *The Outsiders,* and Walter Dean Myers's *Fallen Angels.* On the list of the most required novels you won't find an adult book. While it is certainly true that we may simply talk about adult books and not require a core title, it suggests to me that our courses need to be doing more in the area of adult books for teen readers (Comer 1997).

Now, before we get to the future, I'd like to share with you some new research Betty Carter and I have been working on. Unfortunately, Carlsen's Iowa Books for Young Adults Project ended shortly after his retirement about a decade ago. The closest thing we have to that list now is the International Reading Association's (IRA) annual "Young Adults' Choices" list. Each year students in grades seven through twelve, in four different locations around the country, read new books submitted by the publishers and vote for their favorites. The most popular thirty titles or so appear each year in the November issue of IRA's *Journal of Adolescent & Adult Literacy.* It differs from the Iowa poll because grades seven through twelve are surveyed, not just older teens. Further, adult books are typically not titles publishers send. Still, analysis of the nonfiction titles selected as young adult favorites over last four years does tell us some interesting things borne out by years of the Iowa project.

When Carter and I analyzed the nonfiction titles that appeared on "Young Adults' Choices" lists from 1994 to 1997, we found the following:

1. Only three names appear twice as authors of popular nonfiction—Janet Bode, Michael Ford, and Albert Marrin.

2. Biography is, by far, the most favored type of nonfiction selected.

3. Following biography, the most preferred form of nonfiction was the interview.

Let's look at biography first. The analysis of eight years of the "Iowa Books for Young Adults List" showed that older teens wanted to read sports and celebrity biographies (Fair 1990). The same findings surface in our analysis of "Young Adults' Choices," with one addition. Today's young adults also want to read biographies of important historical figures. Biographies of Jackie Robinson, Deion Sanders, Tyrone Bogues, and Michael Jordan share the popularity stage with Lucille Ball, Rosa Parks, Malcolm X, Ulysses S. Grant, and Robert E. Lee.

Lovers of nonfiction for adolescents know the good work of Janet Bode and her ability to interview teens and let them tell their own stories as they do in *Heartbreak and Roses: Real Life Stories of Troubled Love* (1994). Equally popular with teens was her earlier book *Death Is Hard to Live With: Teenagers Talk about How They Cope with Loss* (1993). Michael Thomas Ford tapped a similar reading hot spot with *The Voices of AIDS* (1995), mingling interviews with facts about the AIDS virus. What becomes clear here is that young adults are interested in true stories of real people facing trying circumstances.

I wrote the initial guidelines for the Young Adults' Choices Project and think it provides all of us with some good information about what new books are popular with a national sampling of adolescents each year. Two points bother me, though. Because it embraces all students in grades seven through twelve, it doesn't allow us to tease out the favored titles of older students in grades eleven and twelve. Moreover, because publishers seldom send adult books, we can't get a handle on what adult titles older readers might choose if given a chance. These concerns led me to one last list.

Every few weeks the *Chronicle of Higher Education* publishes a list of the best-selling books in college bookstores. The list is called "What They Are Reading on College Campuses." Because the schools reporting have large undergraduate populations, it seems reasonable to conclude that these college best-sellers would tell us a good deal about the reading preferences of eighteen- to twenty-year-old readers. Yes, it is a slightly skewed population because these are the students admitted to college, but it does, I believe, give us some indication of what older teens are reading. Carter and I focused on the nonfiction books selected by college readers because that is the area, you remember, where the Iowa poll showed the greatest number of adult books being selected by teens.

On college campuses biography and celebrity books are high on the preference chart just as they were in IRA's "Young Adults' Choices" and before that on the "Iowa Books for Young Adults Lists." When we looked at four years of "What They Are Reading on College Campuses," we found college students selected these adult biographies, autobiographies, and celebrity books: Maya Angelou's *Heart of a Woman* (1997) and *Wouldn't Take Nothing for My Journey Now* (1993); Colin Powell's *My American Journey* (1995); Walter Cronkite's *A Reporter's Life* (1997); Andrew Morton's *Diana: Her True Story* (1997);

Breaking the Surface (1995), Greg Louganis's autobiography; Paul Reiser's *Couplehood* (1995); and Jerry Seinfeld's *Seinlanguage* (1995).

While IRA's "Young Adults' Choices" list found Bode's true stories of teens very popular, that reading preference continues with college students selecting Jack Canfield et al.'s *Chicken Soup for the Soul* (1993), *Chicken Soup for the Teenage Soul* (1997), and *Chicken Soup for the Woman's Soul* (1996). Older teens also want true stories of people living lives of action, adventure, and unusual human experiences. So, you will find on the college list both of Jon Krakauer's books *Into the Wild* (1996) and *Into Thin Air* (1997). Here is also Sebastian Junger's *The Perfect Storm* (1997) and Helen Prejean's *Dead Man Walking* (1996). *Into Thin Air* and *The Perfect Storm* are both popular titles with older young adults and provide proof that this year's committee selecting the Alex Awards knows much about the reading interests of adolescent readers.

As we finish this look at adult books for teen readers, we've visited the past to take a look at the research and pay homage to Margaret Edwards, Bob Carlsen, Dora V. Smith, and Lou L. LaBrant. We docked in the present to look at popular nonfiction in IRA's Young Adults' Choices Project and compared that with the adult nonfiction books students are selecting to read on college campuses. Fueled with that knowledge, let's blast into the future. Allow me to make some suggestions for things I hope we will do over the next five years that will serve to shine the light more intensely on the role of adult books in the literacy lives of young adults.

First, I'd love to see more articles in the professional journals of ALA, IRA, and NCTE focus on adult books and teen readers. It would be wonderful to see the same in *School Library Journal, VOYA, The Horn Book,* and others. These important publications inform the profession and serve to highlight significant issues. Such articles will, however, never see the light of day (even if the editors want them) if professionals like those of you in this room don't write them.

Second, those of us who teach young adult literature classes need to redouble our efforts to make adult books a part of our courses and focus the attention of the next generation of librarians and teachers on the role adult books play in the reading lives of older high school students.

Third, I believe that library clubs, teen advisory panels, and library reading groups in both school and public libraries are the places where free reading happens these days. So if we want today's teens to derive benefits Lou L. LaBrant and Bob Carlsen documented decades ago in their free reading classes for young adults, we need to celebrate the existing library reading groups, start new ones, and report the results at conferences and in newspaper, magazine, and journal articles.

Finally, to the members of YALSA and the trustees of the Margaret Edwards Trust, let me suggest something that would help both adolescents and those of us who work with them. I'd love to see the now defunct "Iowa Books for Young Adults List" be resurrected as the annual Edwards "Adult Books for Young Adults List." New review copies of adult books could be shared with library reading groups composed of high school juniors and seniors in four sites across the country. Over the course of a year students would read the books, discuss them, and select their favorites. The top twenty-five books from this national sampling would appear each year in *JOYS* and be made available from YALSA. Not only would it serve to highlight four exemplary library reading programs, but it would also provide all of us with an important yearly list. No one else is doing this. What a help it would be to teenagers, librarians, and teachers, to say nothing of how it would serve to continue the work Margaret Edwards started so many years ago.

Works Cited

Abrahamson, Richard F., and Betty Carter, eds. 1988. *Books for you: A booklist for senior high students, tenth edition.* Urbana, Ill.: National Council of Teachers of English.

Angelou, Maya. 1993. *Wouldn't take nothing for my journey now.* New York: Random House.

———. 1997. *Heart of a woman.* New York: Random House.

Applebee, Arthur N. 1993. *Literature in the secondary school: Studies of curriculum and instruction in the United States.* Urbana, Ill.: National Council of Teachers of English.

Bode, Janet. 1993. *Death is hard to live with: Teenagers talk about how they cope with loss.* New York: Delacorte.

———. 1994. *Heartbreak and roses: Real life stories of troubled love.* New York: Delacorte.

Canfield, Jack, and Mark Victor Hansen, comps. 1993. *Chicken soup for the soul.* Deerfield Beach, Fla.: Health Communications.

Canfield, Jack, Mark Victor Hansen, and Kimberly Kirberger, comps. 1997. *Chicken soup for the teenage soul.* Deerfield Beach, Fla.: Health Communications.

Canfield, Jack, Mark Victor Hansen, Jennifer Read Hawthorne, and Marci Shimoff, comps. 1996. *Chicken soup for the woman's soul.* Deerfield Beach, Fla.: Health Communications.

Carlsen, C. Robert. 1967. *Books and the teenage reader: A guide for teachers, librarians, and parents.* 2d rev. ed. 1980. New York: Harper & Row.

————. 1979. What beginning English teachers need to know about adolescent literature. *English Education* 10 (May): 195–202.

————. 1984. Teaching literature for the adolescent: A historical perspective. *English Journal* 73 (November): 28–30.

Comer, Melissa. 1997. The design and teaching techniques of YA literature courses—survey results. Personal correspondence with author—summary results sent to all survey participants.

Cormier, Robert. 1974. *The chocolate war.* New York: Pantheon.

Cronkite, Walter. 1997. *A reporter's life.* New York: Knopf.

Crutcher, Chris. 1983. *Running loose.* New York: Greenwillow.

————. 1987. *Crazy Horse electric game.* New York: Greenwillow.

Fair, Elizabeth Rhae. 1990. What young adults like to read: A comparison of Iowa Books for Young Adults data from 1982 to 1989 with other reading interest studies. Ph.D. diss., University of Iowa.

Ford, Michael Thomas. 1995. *The voices of AIDS.* New York: Morrow.

Fussell, Warner, with Rick Wolf and Brian Zernik. 1987. *Baseball . . . a laughing matter.* St. Louis, Mo.: Sporting News.

Hinton, S. E. 1967. *The outsiders.* New York: Viking.

Junger, Sebastian. 1997. *The perfect storm: A true story of men against the sea.* New York: Norton.

King, Stephen. 1983. *Pet sematary.* New York: Doubleday

————. 1986. *It.* New York: Viking.

Krakauer, Jon. 1996. *Into the wild.* New York: Villard.

————. 1997. *Into thin air: A personal account of the Mt. Everest disaster.* New York: Villard.

LaBrant, Lou L. 1936. *Au evaluation of the free reading in grades ten, eleven, and twelve.* Ohio State University Studies, Contributions in Education, No. 2. Columbus: Ohio State University Press.

————. 1961. The guinea pigs after twenty years. In *The use of communication media,* edited by Margaret Willis. Columbus: Ohio State University Press, 127–164.

Louganis, Greg, with Eric Marcus. 1995. *Breaking the surface.* New York: Random House.

Lowry, Lois. 1993. *The giver.* Boston: Houghton Mifflin.

Margaret Alexander Edwards Trust: The lady, the librarian, and her legacy [brochure]. 1991. Baltimore: Margaret Alexander Edwards Trust. unp.

Means, Harrison J. 1976. Nine years of individualized reading. *Journal of Reading* 20 (November): 144–149.

Morton, Andrew. 1997. *Diana: Her true story.* New York: Simon & Schuster.

Myers, Walter Dean. 1988. *Fallen angels.* New York: Scholastic.

Paterson, Katherine. 1980. *Jacob have I loved.* New York: Crowell.

Peck, Richard. 1983. *Family of women.* New York: Delacorte.

———. 1985. *Remembering the good times.* New York: Delacorte.

Pfeffer, Susan Beth. 1987. *The year without Michael.* New York: Bantam.

Powell, Colin, with J. Persico. 1995. *My American journey.* New York: Random House.

Prejean, Helen. 1996. *Dead man walking: An eyewitness account of the death penalty in the United States.* New York: Vintage.

Presley, Priscilla. 1985. *Elvis and me.* New York: Putnam.

Reiser, Paul. 1995. *Couplehood.* New York: Bantam.

Seinfeld, Jerry. 1995. *Seinlanguage.* New York: Bantam.

The Margaret A. Edwards (MAE) Award: Introduction and List

by Betty Carter

Since the 1930s a committee within the American Library Association (ALA) has been selecting books for teen readers. In 1966 this list received its present name, "Best Books for Young Adults" (BBYA), and its present charge: to select outstanding books of proven and potential worth for a young adult audience. As solid as these lists are, they nonetheless feature individual titles, and, although several authors have multiple entries, neither the annual BBYA list (Best Books for Young Adults 2002) nor the retrospective ones developed every five years, such as "Top 100 Choices for Teens" (2000), directly honor the authors who produce those works. Similarly, "Quick Picks," books recommended for the reluctant young adult reader, also compiled annually by a committee within the Young Adult Library Services Association (YALSA), cite individual titles (Quick Picks for the Reluctant Young Adult Reader 2002) but do not specifically recognize an author whose body of work speaks to young adults.

In an effort to acknowledge those authors who have, over time, made major contributions to young adults and their reading, Neil A. Perlman, the publisher of *School Library Journal (SLJ)*, in 1986 approached Lillian N. Gerhardt, then editor-in-chief, and asked her to develop such an award. Gerhardt decided that *SLJ* should not give the award but rather sponsor it, and she asked YASD (the Young Adult Services Division of ALA, presently known as YALSA) to develop criteria and to administer it. Thus, in 1986, the concept of the *School Library Journal* Young Adult Author Award/Selected and Administered by the American Library Association's Young Adult Services Division was born. YASD's then–Past President Joan Atkinson, Vice President/President Elect Vivian Wynn, and President Marian Hargrove worked with a special committee to develop the guidelines for this award. Their resulting charge states in the American Library Association's 1991/1992 *Handbook of Organization* that the award is to be given to a "living author or co-author whose book or books, over a

Members of the Margaret Alexander Edwards Trust joined YALSA President Bonnie Kunzel and Margaret A. Edwards 2002 Award winner Paul Zindel at the 2002 YALSA Awards Luncheon on June 15, 2002. From left: Julian Lapides, Trustee of the Margaret Alexander Edwards Trust; Bonnie Kunzel, YALSA President; Paul Zindel, MAE Award winner for 2002; Linda Lapides, Trustee; Ray Fry, Trustee; and Anna Curry, Trustee. The Trust was also there to celebrate the centennial of the birth of Margaret A. Edwards.

period of time, have been accepted by young people as an authentic voice that continues to illuminate their experiences and emotions, giving insight into their lives. The book or books should enable them to understand themselves, the world in which they live, and their relationship with others and with society" (American Library Association 1991/1992, 92).

In addition to these broad goals, the committee established specific criteria for selecting a recipient and the particular books for which that individual would be cited. According to YALSA's "Policies and Procedures for the Margaret A. Edwards Award," a selection committee will be formed and will serve for two consecutive years. When choosing an author and naming specific books honored in the award, the committee must consider these five criteria:

1. Does the book(s) help adolescents to become aware of themselves and to answer their questions about their role and importance in relationships, society, and in the world?
2. Is the book(s) of acceptable literary quality?
3. Does the book(s) satisfy the curiosity of young adults and yet help them thoughtfully to build a philosophy of life?
4. Is the book(s) currently popular with a wide range of young adults in the many different parts of the country?
5. Does the book(s) serve as a "window to the world" for young adults?

In addition, each book cited for the award must have been in print since the time of original publication and be at least five years old.

Two changes have evolved since the award was first established. First of all, the award was originally set up as biennial recognition; now it is given every year. Second, the name has been changed. Although the original title, the *School Library Journal* Young Adult Author Award/Selected and Administered by the American Library Association's Young Adult Services Division, clearly outlined both the sponsorship and administrative responsibilities, it was, as Gerhardt admitted in a June 1998 editorial, "a mouthful" (p. 4). In 1990 a YASD committee recommended the award be renamed the Margaret A. Edwards Award, or MAE Award, in honor of the woman who brought literature for young adults and young adult readers' advisory services to the attention of the library profession. That name stands today.

School Library Journal adds more than just its name as the sponsoring institution. The journal endows this award with a check to the author and annually highlights the author with an interview in its June publication. In June 1998 Gerhardt focused on the award by outlining its background and history in an issue that featured on the cover a commissioned oil portrait of S. E. Hinton, the first recipient (Gerhardt 1998, 4).

The criteria for this award honor Margaret A. Edwards's commitment to both teens and their reading material. They provide the same kind of national recognition to an author who speaks to young adults and who does so with lasting works. The following individuals, and the listed books, have received the Margaret A. Edwards Award.

References

American Library Association. 1991/1992. *Handbook of organization.* Chicago: American Library Association.

Best Books for Young Adults. 2002. <http://www.ala.org/yalsa/booklists/bbya>

Gerhardt, Lillian N. 1998. SLJ and YASD: The story of an award. *School Library Journal* 44 (June/July): 4.

100 Best Books for Teens. 2000. <http://www.ala.org/yalsa/booklists/bestofbest2000.html>

Quick Picks for the Reluctant Young Adult Reader. 2002. <http://www.ala.org/yalsa/booklists/quickpicks>

Young Adult Library Services Association. n.d. "Policies and Procedures for the Margaret A. Edwards Award." Chicago: American Library Association.

THE MARGARET A. EDWARDS AWARD WINNERS

1988   S. E. Hinton

The Outsiders. 1967. New York: Viking.

Since his parents' death, Ponyboy's brothers and their gang of friends have become his family. But when that family is caught in a web of violence, Ponyboy begins to understand what loyalty really means.

Rumble Fish. 1975. New York: Delacorte.

Brothers, caught in an environment of violence, are as incapable of changing their behavior as are the fighting fish that battle to their deaths.

Tex. 1979. New York: Delacorte.

The life of easygoing Tex is complicated by his older brother's serious outlook and the frequent absences of his father. Simply surviving becomes a real challenge.

That Was Then, This Is Now. 1971. New York: Viking.

In this sequel to *The Outsiders*, Bryon and Mark at sixteen are still inseparable, but Bryon is beginning to care about people while Mark continues to hot-wire cars, steal, and do things for kids.

1989   No award given

1990   Richard Peck

Are You in the House Alone? 1976. New York: Viking.

After receiving a series of threatening notes, Gail Osburne is raped by one of the richest and most popular boys in her school—but nobody believes her story.

Father Figure. 1978. New York: Viking.

The security that Jim Atwater finds in his role as surrogate father to his eight-year-old brother is threatened when, after their mother's suicide, the boys are packed off to spend the summer with their father, who long ago abandoned them.

The Ghost Belonged to Me. 1975. New York: Viking.

Peck mixes humor with the supernatural in this tale of Alexander Armsworth, who must make sense out of a strange figure—the ghost of Inez Dumaine.

Ghosts I Have Been. 1977. New York: Viking.

In a hilarious sequel to *The Ghost Belonged to Me*, Alexander Armsworth meets his match in Blossom Culp, whose wits and psychic powers save the day.

Remembering the Good Times. 1985. New York: Delacorte.

Meeting at a time of change in their lives, Kate, Buck, and Trav develop a special friendship—but even their mutual caring can't keep the gap from widening or aver the tragedy of Trav's suicide.

Secrets of the Shopping Mall. 1979. New York: Delacorte.

Little did Barnie and Teresa know that they wouldn't be the only runaways living in Paradise Park, a suburban shopping mall.

1991   *Robert Cormier*

After the First Death. 1979. New York: Pantheon.

Ben tries unsuccessfully to balance his father's betrayal and his own failure after a busload of children is hijacked by a group of ruthless terrorists.

The Chocolate War. 1974. New York: Pantheon.

"Sweets" abound at Trinity High while a schoolmaster feasts on his students' fear—a bitter story of one student's resistance and the high price he pays.

I Am the Cheese. 1977. New York: Knopf.

A victim of amnesia, and under the influence of drugs administered by mysterious and unidentified questioners, teenager Adam searches through haunting memories that must not be recalled or revealed if he is to survive.

1992   *Lois Duncan*

Chapters: My Growth as a Writer. 1982. Boston: Little, Brown.

Duncan tells about her need and desire to be a writer from the time she was ten years old; examples of her early writing are used to demonstrate how life becomes fiction and to show how her career develops.

I Know What You Did Last Summer. 1973. Boston: Little, Brown.

Last summer four teenagers were involved in a hit-and-run accident. This summer, they are the intended victims as someone is bent on revenge.

Killing Mr. Griffin. 1978. Boston: Little, Brown.

A group of high school students kidnaps a strict English teacher to get even with him—and what starts as a prank becomes a horror.

Ransom. 1966. New York: Doubleday.

When four teenagers are kidnapped, they learn that they must work together to win their freedom.

Summer of Fear. 1976. Boston: Little, Brown.

When she first comes to visit, Rachel's cousin Julia seems just a little strange. But, gradually, Rachel begins to suspect something sinister.

The Twisted Window. 1987. New York: Delacorte.

Handsome, charming, and good looking, Brad seems much more

sophisticated than the high school boys Tracy usually dates. She discovers that those good looks hide his plans for finding his sister. But is he rescuing or kidnapping her?

1993   M. E. Kerr

Dinky Hocker Shoots Smack. 1972. New York: Harper & Row.

Dinky's mother is so absorbed with helping drug addicts that she overlooks her own daughter's real needs.

Gentlehands. 1978. New York: Harper & Row.

Buddy's world is turned upside down when he falls in love and then, catastrophically, when he discovers that his refined and cultured grandfather is a notorious Nazi war criminal.

Me, Me, Me, Me, Me: Not a Novel. 1983. New York: Harper & Row/Charlotte Zolotow.

A series of autobiographical anecdotes from Kerr's youth relate to their use in her novels.

Night Kites. 1986. New York: Harper & Row.

Seventeen-year-old Jim's relationships with his family and friends change when his older brother reveals he has AIDS.

1994   Walter Dean Myers

Fallen Angels. 1988. New York: Scholastic.

Seventeen-year-old Richie Perry's stint in Vietnam brings home to him the agony and futility of war as he learns to kill and watches his comrades die.

Hoops. 1981. New York: Delacorte.

Lonnie and the rest of his Harlem ghetto basketball team learn the fine art of playing and winning like pros from Cal, who once was one.

Motown and Didi. 1984. New York: Viking.

Living in Harlem, Motown and Didi have their own ways to escape the harshness of their neighborhood. When they start falling in love, the question becomes, Can they survive together?

Scorpions. 1988. New York: Harper.

Jamal's ability to be a good student and to live up to his father's expectations is challenged by his role as a gang leader.

1995   Cynthia Voigt

Building Blocks. 1984. New York: Atheneum.

Braum has difficulties understanding his father. When he travels back to his father's childhood, however, he begins to see his dad in a new way.

Dicey's Song. 1982. New York: Atheneum.

In a sequel to *Homecoming,* Dicey discovers that just being safe is not enough to build a strong family.

Homecoming. 1981. New York: Atheneum.

Dicey realizes her mother has left for good. Now, she and her three siblings must find a place to call home.

Izzy Willy Nilly. 1986. New York: Atheneum.

Who are your real friends? Izzy struggles to rethink her friendships after losing a leg in a car crash.

Jackaroo. 1985. New York: Atheneum.

Legend tells of Jackaroo, who helped the kingdom in times of trouble. When Gwen finds a cape in an abandoned cabin, she wonders if it's time for Jackaroo's return.

The Runner. 1985. New York: Atheneum.

Bullet, a seventeen-year-old cross-country runner, finds that compromise is sometimes necessary if an athlete is going to be the best.

A Solitary Blue. 1983. New York: Atheneum.

Jeff Green's mother leaves home when he is only seven, and when she shows up in his life again, Jeff learns some hard lessons about loving and caring.

1996   Judy Blume

Forever. 1975. Scarsdale, N.Y.: Bradbury.

Kathy and Michael believe their love will last forever. But even after they express that love through a sexual relationship, Kathy begins to question the strength of that commitment.

1997   Gary Paulsen

Canyons. 1990. New York: Delacorte.

When Brennan finds the skull of an Apache Indian, the fates of both are mysteriously entwined.

The Crossing. 1987. New York: Orchard/Richard Jackson.

An alcoholic army sergeant and a homeless Mexican orphan come together in an unlikely friendship.

Dancing Carl. 1983. Scarsdale, N.Y.: Bradbury.

Carl comes to McKinley, Minnesota, in the winter, drunk and maybe crazy, but he soon holds the attention of the entire town with his power and strange dance.

Hatchet. 1987. New York: Viking.

On the way to visit his father, Brian's plane crashes, killing the pilot and leaving Brian as the only survivor. He must use all his strength and wits to hang on until help arrives.

Winter Room. 1989. New York: Orchard.

Seated around a cozy fire in "the winter room," Elton and his brother Wayne challenge the truth of Uncle David's almost mythological stories about death and survival during his earlier life in Norway.

Woodsong. 1990. New York: Bradbury.

Through his dogsledding adventures in the Minnesota wilderness, where there are wolves, deep snow, and minus-thirty-degree temperatures, the author comes to understand nature's ways and harrowing surprises.

1998   Madeleine L'Engle

Meet the Austins. New York: Vanguard, 1960; and *A Ring of Endless Light.* New York: Farrar, 1980.

Readers follow the Austin family through twenty years of love and loss.

A Swiftly Moving Planet. New York: Farrar, 1978.

Charles Wallace travels back in time to avoid a present-day calamity.

A Wrinkle in Time. New York: Ariel, 1962.

Charles Wallace Murry and his sister, Meg, save their scientist father by following the shortest distance between two points, which they discover is not a straight line, but, instead, a wrinkle.

1999   Anne McCaffrey

Dragonriders of Pern Series. *Dragonflight.* 1968. New York: Walker.

Lessa must rebuild Benden Weyr and impress the gold dragon Romota to save Pern.

Dragonquest. 1971. New York: Ballantine.

This second entry in the Pern Series follows the Holders and Craqthalls as they try to destroy thread at its source.

White Dragon. 1978. New York: Ballantine.

Jaxon and Ruth find out who they are when they discover Pern. In the process, they alter Pern's past.

The Harper Hall Trilogy. *Dragonsong.* New York: Atheneum, 1976; *Dragonsinger.* New York: Atheneum, 1977; and *Dragondrums.* New York: Atheneum, 1979.

These three books follow Menolly, a young girl living in Pern, who wants to become a harper but also has a talent for training fire-lizards.

The Ship Who Sang. 1969. New York: Walker.

Helen, born with a love of music, great intelligence, and multiple physical disabilities, must live in a capsule to eliminate her physical problems.

2000   Chris Crutcher

Athletic Shorts. 1991. New York: Greenwillow.

These tales of love, death, bigotry, and heroism are of real people with the courage to stand up to a world that often puts them down.

Chinese Handcuffs. 1989. New York: Greenwillow.

A winning triathlete's need to understand his older brother's suicide is complicated by memories and daring challenges.

The Crazy Horse Electric Game. 1987. New York: Greenwillow.

Star athlete Willie Weaver's crippling accident forces him to leave his family and friends to rebuild his shattered life.

Running Loose. 1983. New York: Greenwillow.

Louie takes a stand against his coach and playing dirty football, falls in love, and loses his girlfriend in a fatal accident—all in his senior year.

Staying Fat for Sarah Byrnes. 1993. New York: Greenwillow.

When the horrific truth about Sarah's past is revealed, only her true friend Eric ("Moby") Calhoun can help her come to terms with her family and plan for her future.

Stotan! 1986. New York: Greenwillow.

A high school coach invites four members of his swim team to a week of rigorous training that tests their moral fiber as well as their physical stamina.

2001   Robert Lipsyte

The Brave. 1992. New York: HarperCollins/Charlotte Zolotow.

Sonny Bear, half white and half Moscondaga Indian, wants to be a boxer but has difficulty controlling his anger until he meets Alfred Brooks, a New York City cop and former contender.

The Chief. 1993. New York: HarperCollins.

In this sequel to *The Brave,* Sonny is embroiled in a debate concerning the construction of a casino on the reservation.

The Contender. 1967. New York: Harper & Row.

Alfred Brooks doesn't know if he has what it takes to become a boxing champion. He does find out, however, he can be a champion in life if not in the ring.

One Fat Summer. 1977. New York: Harper & Row.

Overweight Bobby Marks confronts the ridicule of friends and sheds his excess pounds in a comical story of his last fat summer.

2002   Paul Zindel

The Effect of Gamma Rays on Man-in-the-Moon Marigolds: A Drama in Two Acts. 1971. Drawings by Doug Kingman. New York: Harper & Row.

An alcoholic mother stifles the lives of her two teenage daughters, one who is bordering on madness and the other who is a sensitive, loving person, in this prizewinning drama.

My Darling, My Hamburger. 1969. New York: Harper & Row.

Four high school seniors, used to dealing with the problems in their individual families, now face a different kind of problem: what to do with an unwanted pregnancy?

The Pigman. 1968. New York: Harper & Row.

John and Lorraine, alienated from their families and their peers, tell of their ill-fated relationship with a strange old man, Mr. Pignatti, whom they call the Pigman.

The Pigman and Me. 1993. New York: HarperCollins/Charlotte Zolotow.

Zindel recounts his bizarre adventures growing up on Staten Island, when his neighbor's father becomes his personal "pigman" and teaches him to cope with his rootless family.

The Pigman's Legacy. 1980. New York: Harper & Row.

John and Lorraine befriend an old man who is hiding from the IRS in the Pigman's house, and through the hilarious and poignant experiences they share with him, they discover the legacy of love that the Pigman left them.

Notes and References

Chapter I

1. Octavius Walton, *Whiter than Snow*. One of a series of religious tracts published at the turn of the century.

2. "If you have two loaves of bread, sell one and buy a hyacinth," saying attributed variously to Persian, Greek, or Chinese tradition. Yet another version appears in *Not by Bread Alone* by James Terry White (1907).

3. Rebecca Sophia Clarke (Sophie May, pseud.), *Little Prudy* (1909). One of a series that includes *Little Prudy's Dotty Dimple*, *Little Prudy's Sister Susie*, *Little Prudy's Cousin Grace*, etc.; Annie Fellows Johnston, *The Little Colonel* series (1901–1909); Harriet Milford Lothrop (Margaret Sidney, pseud.), *The Five Little Peppers* series (around 1880); Eleanor Porter, *Pollyanna* (1913); Lucy Maud Montgomery, *Anne of Green Gables* (1908).

4. Horatio Alger, *A Boy's Fortune*. One of a series of romantic fantasies (1869–1890) about the rise to fame and fortune of disadvantaged boys through hard work and pluck.

5. Mary Jane (Hawes) Holmes, Meadow Brook Farm series (late nineteenth century).

6. Hans and Fritz were characters in a long-lived and popular comic strip created by Rudolph Dirks beginning in 1897, titled "The Captain and the Kids" but better known as "The Katzenjammer Kids"; "Mutt and Jeff" was a comic strip drawn by Bud Fisher; Maggie and Jiggs were characters in a comic strip entitled "Bringing Up Father," created by George MacManus.

7. Klara Mundt (Louise Mulbach, pseud.), *Henry VIII and His Court* (1864).

8. "Are not two sparrows sold for a penny? And not one of them will fall to the ground without your Father's will." Matthew 10:29.

Chapter II

1. Maureen Daly, *Seventeenth Summer* (1942); "Ken McLaughlin": An exhaustive search by Los Angeles Public Library has failed to locate a source for this character; Jody Baxter, a character in *The Yearling* by Marjorie Kinnan Rawlings (1938); Holden Caulfield, a character in *Catcher in the Rye* by J. D. Salinger (1951); Dobie Gillis, a character in *The Many Loves of Dobie Gillis* by Max Shulman (1951). Later also a character in a television series; Jessamyn West, *Cress Delahanty* (1953).

2. "Chinese girl," in *The Good Earth* by Pearl Buck (1931); "A German boy," in *All Quiet on the Western Front* by Erich Maria Remarque (1929); "A Zulu father," in *Cry the Beloved Country* by Alan Paton (1948).

3. Benedict Freedman and Nancy Freedman, *Mrs. Mike* (1947).

4. Henry Gregor Felsen, *Hot Rod* (1950).

5. "The ruler of the Queen's navee," a line from an aria sung by the pompous Sir Joseph Porter, K.C.B., First Lord of the Admiralty, in Gilbert and Sullivan's light opera *Pinafore*.

6. Dr. Benjamin Spock, pediatrician and social activist renowned for his book of many editions, *Baby and Child Care*, first published in 1946.

7. Anna Curry, who later became director of the Pratt Library.

8. David Eli Lilienthal, widely respected U.S. statesman and chair of the Atomic Energy Commission 1946–1950.

Chapter III

1. The offer was made by Harold Hamill, former assistant director at the Pratt Library, then head of Kansas City Public Library.

2. The article was "Adult Books for Teen-agers," *Library Journal* 75 (15 October 1950):1765–73.

3. The article was "Wisdom Crying in the Streets," *Library Journal* 68 (1 May 1943):347–49.

4. Kathleen Norris, popular and prolific romance novelist in the 1940s, wife of writer Frank Norris, and author of *Hearbroken Melody, Mother, The Sea Gull, Sisters*, and others; Zane Grey, popular and prolific writer of westerns.

5. Wendell Wilkie, *One World* (1942) (U.S. presidential candidate in the election of 1944).

Chapter IV

1. Obviously, Edwards uses the adjective "gay" in this sentence not to indicate homosexuality but in the sense of "cheerful, carefree."

2. Dwight Lyman Moody (1837–1899), popular and influential evangelist, and Ira D. Sankey (1840–1908), evangelist, organist and singer, who traveled and performed with Moody.

Chapter V

1. Betty Smith, *A Tree Grows in Brooklyn* (1943); Pearl Buck, *The Good Earth* (1931); John Hersey, *Hiroshima* (1946); Erich Maria Remarque, *All Quiet on the Western Front* (1929); Claude Brown, *Manchild in the Promised Land* (1965).
2. Somerset Maugham, *Of Human Bondage* (1915); Emily Bronte, *Wuthering Heights* (1847); Nicholas Monsarrat, *The Cruel Sea* (1951); Irving Stone, *Love Is Eternal* (1954); Mildred Walker, *Winter Wheat* (1944); Margaret Mitchell, *Gone with the Wind* (1936); Gwen Terasaki, *Bridge to the Sun* (1957); Agnes Keith, *Three Came Home* (1947).
3. Clifton Fadiman, literary critic and popularizer of reading and well-known radio and television master-of-ceremonies in the 1950s. Author of *The Lifetime Reading Plan* (1960).
4. "Ouida" was the pseudonym of Louise de la Ramee (1839–1908), and author of *A Dog of Flanders* (1863); also *Moths, In a Winter City, Chandos, Bebee*, and others.
5. Jesse Stuart, author of *The Beatinest Boy* (1953), *The Good Spirit of Laurel Ridge* (1953), *Red Mule* (1955), and others.
6. Although the term *Communistic* here is meant jocularly, the year 1957, when this was written, was the height of the anti-communist sentiment stirred up by Senator Joseph McCarthy's investigations.

Chapter VI

1. From "Excelsior!", a poem by Henry Wadsworth Longfellow (1842), in which a young man persists in climbing a mountain, only to be found frozen to death at the pinnacle, a banner with the strange device, "Excelsior!" clutched in his hand.
2. John Erskine (1879–1951), scholar, teacher, and musician, taught at Columbia University from 1909 to 1937, initiated Great Books courses for undergraduates, co-edited *The Cambridge History of American Literature* and authored *The Private Life of Helen of Troy*.
3. Mary Lee Bundy, *Metropolitan Public Library Users: A Report of a Survey of Adult Library Use in the Maryland-Baltimore-Washington Metropolitan Area* (School of Library and Information Services, University of Maryland, 1968).
4. Morris Raphael Cohen, professor of philosophy emeritus at University of Chicago in 1938.
5. Lawrence Mervil Tibbett (1896–1960), popular American operatic baritone who sang on stage, radio, and in the movies.
6. "The medium is the message" is a much-quoted statement by Marshall McLuhan meaning that "the form of a message determines the way in which

that message will be perceived, and, additionally, that the means of communication have a greater influence on people than the information it carries." (*Dictionary of Cultural Literacy*, 128)

7. VISTA (Volunteers in Service to America) was a domestic Peace Corps-style federal agency during the War on Poverty in the 1960s.

8. The list of 1963 bestsellers by *Publishers Weekly* included *Happiness Is a Warm Puppy* and *Security Is a Thumb and a Blanket*, both by Charles Schulz; *Profiles in Courage* by John F. Kennedy; *O Ye Jigs and Juleps!* by Virginia Carey Hudson; and *I Owe Russia $1200* by Bob Hope.

9. Everett R. Perry, vice-president of the American Library Association, 1930.

10. Agnes Keith, author of *Three Came Home* (1947), *Land Below the Wind* (1939), *Beloved Exiles* (1972), and *Bare Feet in the Palace* (1955).

11. Leo Rosten, *The Education of Hyman Kaplan* (1937); Clarence Day, *Life with Father* (1935).

12. Lowell A. Martin, *Students and the Pratt Library: Challenge and Opportunity*, Deiches Fund Studies of Public Library Service, no. 1 (Baltimore: Enoch Pratt Free Library, 1963).

13. "Lamb's character," in "On Eating Roast Pig," a much-anthologized essay by Charles Lamb (1775–1834) that makes the point that it is not necessary to burn down the whole house to have roast pork.

14. George Orwell, *1984* (1950); William Golding, *Lord of the Flies* (1959); John H. Griffin, *Black like Me* (1961).

Chapter VII

1. In 1971 the ALA Placement Center reported 2.17 applicants for each job opening; by 1974 there were nearly 5 (Margaret Myers, "The Job Market for Librarians," *Library Trends*, Spring 1986, 646).

2. W. H. Webb, "Will the Resources Head Wag the Imperative Tail?" Carnegie Commission on Higher Education Report, *College and Research Libraries* 33(July 1972):269–70.

Chapter VIII

1. The incidents mentioned here were written about in *A Tree Grows in Brooklyn* by Betty Smith; *The Sound and the Fury* by William Faulkner; *The Human Comedy* by William Saroyan; and *Black Boy* by Richard Wright.

Index